INSIDERS' GUIDE®

OFF THE BEATEN PATH® SERIES

Off the Beaten Path®

EIGHTH EDITION

maryland and delaware

A GUIDE TO UNIQUE PLACES

JUDY COLBERT

INSIDERS' GUIDE®

GUILFORD, CONNECTICUT
AN IMPRINT OF THE GLOBE PEQUOT PRESS

The prices, rates, and hours listed in this guidebook
were confirmed at press time. We recommend,
however, that you call establishments to obtain
current information before traveling.

To buy books in quantity for corporate use
or incentives, call **(800) 962–0973**
or e-mail **premiums@GlobePequot.com.**

INSIDERS' GUIDE®

Text design by Linda R. Loiewski
Maps by Equator Graphics © Morris Book Publishing, LLC
Art on page 172 by M. A. Dubé; all other art by Carole Drong, rendered from
photographs by Judy Colbert
Spot photography throughout © Glow Images\Alamy

ISSN 1538-5485
ISBN 978-0-7627-4418-3

Manufactured in the United States of America
Eighth Edition/First Printing

Dedicated to Ben, Rockzana, and Sabrina

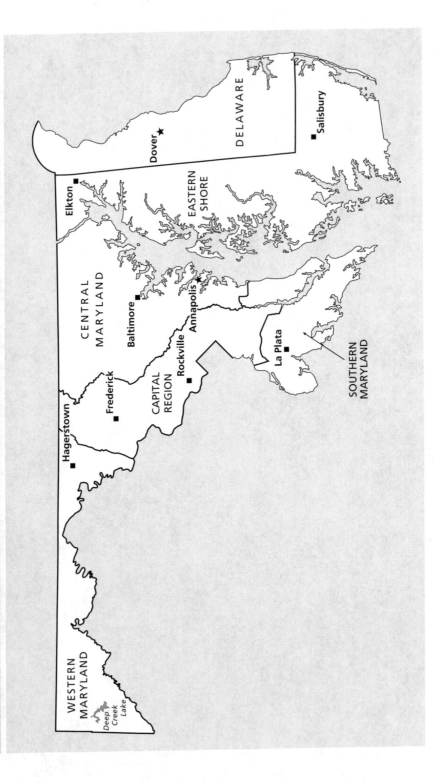

MARYLAND AND DELAWARE

Contents

Introduction

Welcome to *Maryland and Delaware Off the Beaten Path,* eighth edition, where you'll find some of the best food, the most unusual attractions, the friendliest people, the most incredible history, the most wonderful scenery and natural resources, and the best way to spend a few hours off the interstate.

Maryland is often called America in Miniature because the state goes from the seashore (the Atlantic Ocean and the Chesapeake Bay) on the east to the mountains (the Appalachians) on the west. The mountains are not high compared to the Rockies (Backbone Mountain in Garrett County is the tallest, at 3,360 feet), but they provide fair downhill and excellent cross-country skiing. The seashore is among the finest in the East. In one day you can go from one to the other and theoretically ski in the morning and the afternoon; snow skiing one direction, water skiing the other. About the only clime we don't have here is desert, yet there are sand quarries.

Not everything in Maryland, however, is miniature. The National Aquarium in Baltimore is one of the world's largest. The collection at the Walter's Art Museum, also in Baltimore, is world renowned. Maryland also has one of the nation's largest hydroelectric generating stations at Conowingo (Cecil County), the largest colony of African black-footed penguins in the United States (Baltimore City Zoo), one of the largest and finest public libraries in the United States at the Enoch Pratt Free Library (Baltimore City), and the largest wooden dome in the country built without nails (Annapolis). Well, the list continues, but you get the idea.

Maryland is also called the Free State (road signs say KEEP THE FREE STATE LITTER FREE), and if you ask residents, they'd probably cite the freedom of worship advocated by the state's founders. Others might point to Maryland's alliance with the northern states during "the war" and its intolerance of slavery (at least in some parts of the state). These historical facts are true, but the nickname dates from 1917, when the state opposed Prohibition on the grounds that it was a states' rights issue.

And a third nickname is the Old Line State, which honors Maryland's regular line troops who served courageously in the Revolutionary War.

In the summer of 2000, Maryland introduced its Scenic Byways program, celebrating the "roads less traveled." From the mountains to the seashore, thirty-one byways have been designated, encompassing 1,797 miles. The average length of a byway is 60 miles and takes seventy minutes to drive, but lots of side trips are possible. The shortest is 5 miles, along the Historic National

Seaport route, and the longest is 170 miles along the Historic National Road route. As part of this program, 800 new SCENIC BYWAYS signs were erected, a state map was created, and a free 192-page book titled *Maryland Scenic Byways* was published. For information, contact the state highway administration communications office at (410) 545–0303 or (800) 323–6742. The Chesapeake Country Byway, the only National Scenic Byway in Maryland and one of only seventy-five in the country, runs from Stevensville (through Chestertown) to Chesapeake City, with legs to Rock Hall and the Eastern Neck National Wildlife Refuge.

trivia

The state's official fossil, the four-ribbed snail, is an extinct invertebrate that ranged in size from microscopic to 3 or 4 inches in diameter. Fossils can be found at the Cliffs of Calvert, in the Choptank and St. Mary's areas.

There are two historic trails that let you explore some of the highlights of the Civil War and the War of 1812. The **Civil War Trail** includes carefully mapped driving tours that explore the Antietam campaign, John Wilkes Booth's escape from Ford's Theatre after assassinating President Abraham Lincoln, and Baltimore. The **Star Spangled Banner Trail & The War of 1812** is a 100-mile scenic and historic trail that follows the route taken by the British Marines as they invaded the Chesapeake Bay area in 1814.

trivia

The Maryland flag was adopted in 1904. The red and white section is the coat of arms of the Crossland family, the first Lord Baltimore's relatives on his mother's side. The black and gold design is the coat of arms for the Calvert family, Lord Baltimore's relatives on his father's side.

Maryland is also involved with the Gateways Network, coordinated by the National Park Service in partnership with the Chesapeake Bay program. A Gateway is an entrance to the byways and water trails in the National Park Service program. Among the first Chesapeake Bay Gateways in Maryland, Washington, D.C., Virginia, Pennsylvania, and New York, are twelve Gateway sites, one Gateway hub, two regional information centers, seven water trails, and one land trail. And, that's just the beginning. Pick a Maryland Gateway and you may visit the Barge House Museum (Annapolis), the Blackwater National Wildlife Refuge (Cambridge), Jefferson Patterson Park and Museum (St. Leonard), and the Monocacy River Water Trail. For additional information, stop by www.baygateways.net.

As with other places around the country, the demand for telephone numbers has increased exponentially in the past few years. Maryland has four area codes divided in an overlay pattern. Generally, 301 and 240 codes are for the western, suburban Maryland (around Washington, D.C.), and southern Maryland counties. Similarly, 410 and 443 are for Annapolis, Baltimore, and Eastern Shore areas. All local calls require the entire ten-digit number (area code and phone number). Only long-distance calls require the number 1 before the ten-digit number.

In addition to showcasing Maryland's attractions, this book also explores Delaware, which has been called Small Wonder for its diminutive size and its natural beauty. Only 96 miles in length, the state is bordered by the Atlantic Ocean and Delaware Bay on the east and Maryland to the west and south. Delaware proudly boasts the fact that there is no sales tax. That's why you'll find so many outlet stores and other good shopping venues, from small shops to sprawling malls, throughout the state.

The area code for Delaware is 302, and you needn't dial it for local calls within Delaware.

I hope you enjoy reading and using this book as much as I enjoy discovering *Maryland and Delaware Off the Beaten Path*.

Maryland Resources

MARYLAND TOURISM

- **Maryland Office of Tourism,** 217 East Redwood Street, Baltimore 21202; (410) 767–3400, (866) 639–3526; www.mdisfun.org.
- **Allegany County Convention and Visitors Bureau, Western Maryland Station Center,** 13 Canal Street, Suite 306, Cumberland 21502; (301) 777–5132, (800) 425–2067; www.mdmountainside.com.
- **Annapolis and Anne Arundel County Visitors Bureau,** 26 West Street, Annapolis 21401; (410) 280–0445 ext. 19, (410) 974–8188; www.visit-annapolis.org.
- **Baltimore Area Convention and Visitors Association,** 100 Light Street, Baltimore 21202; (877) 225–8466; www.baltimore.org.
- **Baltimore County Convention and Visitors Bureau,** P.O. Box 5426, Lutherville 21094; (410) 296–4886, (877) STAY–N–DO; www.visitbacomd.com.
- **Calvert County Department of Economic Development and Tourism,** 205 Main Street, Courthouse, Prince Frederick 20678; (301) 855–1880 (D.C.), (410) 535–4583, (800) 331–9771; www.ca.cal.md.us/visitors.
- **Caroline County Economic Development Corporation,** 16 North Second Street, Denton 21629; (410) 479–0655; www.tourcaroline.com.

- **Carroll County Visitor Center,** 210 East Main Street, Westminster 21157; (410) 848–1388, (800) 272–1933; www.carrollcountytourism.org.
- **Cecil County Tourism,** 1 Seahawk Drive, Suite 114, North East 21901; (410) 996–6290, (800) CECIL–95; www.seececil.org.
- **Charles County Tourism,** 200 Baltimore Street, La Plata 20646; (301) 645–0558, (800) 766–3386; www.explorecharlescomd.com.
- **Dorchester County Tourism,** 2 Rose Hill Place, Cambridge 21613; (410) 228–1000, (800) 522–TOUR; www.tourdorchester.org.
- **Tourism Council of Frederick County Inc.**, 19 East Church Street, Frederick 21701; (301) 228–2888, (800) 999–3613; www.visitfrederick.org.
- **Garrett County Chamber of Commerce,** 15 Visitors Center Drive, McHenry 21541; (301) 387–4386 ext. 13, (800) 800–5557; www.garrett chamber.com, www.deepcreeklakeinfo.com.
- **Hagerstown/Washington County Convention and Visitors Bureau,** Elizabeth Hager Center, 16 Public Square, Hagerstown 21740; (301) 791–3246 ext.15; (888) 257–2600; www.marylandmemories.org.
- **Harford County Tourism Council Inc.,** 220 South Main Street, Bel Air 21014; (410) 272–2325, (800) 597–2649; www.harfordmd.com.
- **Howard County Tourism,** P.O. Box 9, 8267 Main Street, Ellicott City 21043; (410) 313–1900, (800) 288–TRIP; www.visithowardcounty.com.

Jousting in Maryland

The state sport is jousting, the oldest equestrian sport in the world, with men and women competing. Like other sports and competitions, jousting originated as a test of a man's occupational skills. In Maryland, the challenge in jousting is not to toss a man off his horse, but to spear a series of metal rings while riding on a horse.

The 80-yard course has three arches from which rings are suspended; in each round, the size of the rings decreases. These are not huge rings to begin with: The largest ring is 1¾ inches in diameter and the smallest is ¼ inch.

There are numerous jousting tournaments throughout the year. The schedule usually starts in April and continues through to the Maryland State Championship and the Nationals in October. Events may take place in Hagerstown, Frederick, St. Mary's City, Easton, Annapolis, Denton, Trappe, Port Republic, Lily Pons, Clear Spring, Chestertown, and Havre de Grace. Each tournament has its pageantry and fun, its food, and its partying. Usually there is an admission charge, which often is used to benefit a charitable organization. Call the Maryland Jousting Tournament Association at (410) 820–7751 for a schedule of events.

- **Kent County Office of Tourism,** 400 High Street, Second Floor, Chestertown 21620; (410) 778–0416; www.kentcounty.com.
- **Conference and Visitors Bureau of Montgomery County,** 111 Rockville Pike, Suite 800, Rockville 20850; (240) 777–2060, (877) 789–6904; www.visitmontgomery.com.
- **Ocean City Office of Tourism/CVB,** 4001 Coastal Highway, Ocean City 21842; (410) 723–8600, (800) OC–OCEAN; www.ococean.com.
- **Prince George's County Conference and Visitors Bureau Inc.,** 9200 Basil Court, Suite 101, Largo 20774; (301) 925–8300, (888) 925–8300; www.visitprincegeorges.com.
- **Queen Anne's County Department of Business and Tourism,** 425 Piney Narrows Road, Chester 21619; (410) 604–2100, (888) 400–RSVP; www.discoverqueenannes.com.
- **St. Mary's County Division of Travel and Tourism,** P.O. Box 653, Governmental Center, 23115 Leonard Hall Drive, Leonardtown 20650; (301) 475–4200, (800) 327–9023; www.stmarysmd.com/tourism.
- **Somerset County Tourism,** 11440 Ocean Highway, Princess Anne 21853; (410) 651–2968, (800) 521–9189; www.visitsomerset.com.
- **Talbot County Office of Tourism,** 11 South Harrison Street, Easton 21601; (410) 770–8000; www.tourtalbot.org.
- **Wicomico County Convention and Visitors Bureau,** 8480 Ocean Highway, Delmar 21875; (410) 548–4914, (800) 332–TOUR; www.wicomico tourism.org.
- **Worcester County Tourism,** 104 West Market Street, Snow Hill 21863; (410) 632–3110, (800) 852–0335; www.visitworcester.org.

OTHER WEB SITES AND INFORMATION

- **Maryland Department of Natural Resources;** www.dnr.state.md.us
- **Farmers Markets;** www.mda.state.md.us/mdproducts/farmers_market_dir.php
- **Maryland Fall Foliage Hotline;** (800) LEAVES–1

MARYLAND WELCOME CENTERS

The Welcome Centers offer maps, local traffic conditions (major road construction), brochures about the area and the rest of the state, and assistance in planning your trip.

All Welcome Centers are open daily from 9:00 A.M. to 5:00 P.M. except Thanksgiving, Christmas, New Year's Day, and Easter. The eateries at the Chesapeake House are open for extended hours, with the Burger King open twenty-four hours a day.

- **Youghiogheny Overlook Welcome Center,** Interstate 68 East, mile marker 6 (east of West Virginia state line), P.O. Box 297, Friendsville 21531; (301) 746–5979.
- **Interstate 70 West Welcome Center,** I–70 West, mile marker 39 (just east of the Washington County–Frederick County line), General Delivery, Myersville 21773; (301) 293–4161.
- **Interstate 70 East Welcome Center,** I–70 East, mile marker 39 (just east of the Washington County–Frederick County line), P.O. Box 419, Myersville 21773; (301) 293–2526.
- **Sideling Hill Exhibit Center,** 3000 Sideling Hill, 6 miles west of Hancock, Hancock 21750; (301) 678–5442.
- **U.S. Highway 15 Welcome Center,** US 15, 1 mile south of Pennsylvania, P.O. Box 695, Emmitsburg 21727; (301) 447–2553.
- **Interstate 95 South Welcome Center,** I–95 South, mile marker 37 (just south of State Route 32), P.O. Box 288, Savage 20763; (301) 490–2444.
- **Interstate 95 North Welcome Center,** I–95 North, mile marker 37 (just south of Route 32), P.O. Box 1058, Savage 20763; (301) 490–1333.
- **Chesapeake House Welcome Center,** I–95 North/South, mile marker 97 (includes fast-food restaurants, gift shop, and country market), P.O. Box 785, Perryville 21903; (410) 287–2313.
- **State House Visitor Center,** State Circle, Annapolis 21401; (410) 974–3400.
- **Crain Memorial Welcome Center,** U.S. Highway 301 North, 12480 Crain Highway (just north of the Governor Nice Memorial Bridge), Newburg 20664; (301) 259–2500.
- **U.S. Highway 13 Welcome Center,** US 13 North, 144 Ocean Highway (just north of the Virginia state line), Pocomoke City 21851; (410) 957–2484.
- **Bay Country Welcome Center,** US 301 North/South, 1000 Welcome Center Drive, Centreville 21617; (410) 758–6803.
- **BWI Airport Welcome Center,** BWI Airport, Third Floor, Terminal Building, Baltimore 21240; (410) 691–2878.

BICYCLING INFORMATION

Bicyclists are prohibited from riding bicycles on Maryland Transportation Authority toll facilities, including bridges, tunnels, and approach roads. Understanding that this can be an oops in your travel plans, the Authority offers the following services as a courtesy to bikers:

Authority personnel will transport bikes and bikers across the Thomas J. Hatem (U.S. Highway 40, Susquehanna River) and Harry W. Nice (US 301, Potomac River) Bridges for the normal toll fee when time, personnel, and equipment permit. Call (410) 575–6650 for the Hatem Bridge, and (301) 259–4444 for the Nice Bridge, Monday through Friday 8:00 A.M. to 4:30 P.M. Try to give them at least an hour's notice.

MAJOR MARYLAND NEWSPAPERS

- The *Capital,* 2000 Capital Drive, Annapolis 21401; (410) 268–5000 (editorial), (410) 268–4800 (circulation), (301) 261–2200 (Washington, D.C.); www.capitalonline.com.
- *Washington Post,* 1150 Fifteenth Street, Washington, D.C. 20071; (202) 334–6000 (editorial), (202) 334–6100 (circulation); www.washington post.com.
- *Baltimore Sun,* 501 North Calvert Street, Baltimore 21278; (410) 332–6000; www.sunspot.com.
- The *Star Democrat,* 29088 Airpark Drive, Easton 21601; (410) 820–6505; www.stardem.com.

PUBLIC TRANSPORTATION

- **Amtrak,** (800) USA–RAIL; www.amtrak.com.
- **Baltimore Washington International Airport (BWI),** (410) 519–0000, (301) 261–1000, (800) 435–9294; www.bwiairport.com.
- **Washington Metropolitan Area Transit Authority (WMATA),** (202) 637–7000; www.wmata.com.

FAST FACTS ABOUT THE OLD LINE STATE

- **Area (land):** 10,455 square miles (27,077 square kilometers), forty-second in size
- **Capital:** Annapolis
- **Largest city:** Baltimore
- **Number of counties:** twenty-three, plus Baltimore City
- **Highest elevation:** Backbone Mountain, 3,360 feet (1,024 meters)
- **Lowest elevation:** sea level, along the Atlantic Ocean
- **Greatest distance from north to south:** 124 miles (199 kilometers)
- **Greatest distance from east to west:** 238 miles (383 kilometers)
- **Coastline:** 31 miles (50 kilometers) of Atlantic Ocean coastline, 3,190 miles (5,134 kilometers) of Chesapeake Bay coastline
- **Population:** 5,600,388 (2005 estimate), nineteenth among the states
- **Population density:** 573 persons per square mile

- **Population distribution**: 86 percent urban, 14 percent rural
- **Median family income:** $89, 608 (family of four)
- **Statehood:** April 28, 1788 (seventh state)
- **Nickname:** the Old Line State, the Free State, America in Miniature
- **State flower:** black-eyed Susan
- **State tree:** white oak
- **State motto:** *Fatti maschii, parole feminine* (Manly deeds, womanly words)
- **State bird:** Baltimore oriole
- **State fossil shell:** *Ecphora quadricostata*
- **State cat:** calico
- **State horse:** Thoroughbred
- **State dog:** Chesapeake Bay retriever
- **State reptile:** diamondback terrapin *(Malaclemys terrapin)*
- **State fish:** striped bass (rockfish, *Morone saxatilis)*
- **State crustacean:** Maryland blue crab *(Callinectes sapidus)*
- **State insect:** Baltimore checkerspot butterfly *(Euphydryas phaeion)*
- **State dinosaur:** *Astrodon johnstoni*
- **State boat:** skipjack
- **State song:** "Maryland, My Maryland"
- **State sport:** jousting
- **State folk dance:** square dancing
- **State theaters:** Center Stage, Baltimore; Olney Theater Center, Olney (summer theater)
- **State drink**: milk

FAST FACTS ABOUT THE CHESAPEAKE BAY

- At 200 miles long by 25 miles wide at some points, covering about 4,400 square miles, the Chesapeake Bay is five times as large as the state of Maryland. It is the largest estuary in the United States.
- The bay holds about 19 trillion gallons of water.
- The average depth of the bay is just 21 feet, but at Bloody Point, near Kent Island on the upper Eastern shore, the water is 174 feet deep.
- More than 3,000 species of plants and animals, including 295 types of fish, live in the bay. It is the biggest producer of blue crabs in the country.
- Forty-eight rivers and one hundred small tributaries flow into the bay, with the Susquehanna River contributing about 50 percent of the bay's fresh water.
- The population of the Chesapeake Bay watershed, which stretches over six states, is 15.5 million.

- Historians debate whether Viking explorer Thorfinn Karlsfennias (in the eleventh century), Italian sailor Giovanni da Verrazano (in 1524), or Spanish explorer Pedro Menendez de Aviles (in 1566) was the first European in the bay.
- The name Chesapeake is derived from the Native American word *Tschiswapeki*. Earlier names included "Great Waters," "Mother of Waters," and "Great Shellfish Bay."
- The biggest problem endangering the bay is pollution, in the form of nitrogen and phosphorus.
- Thomas Point Shoal Lighthouse, built in 1875, is the most photographed lighthouse on the Chesapeake.

CLIMATE OVERVIEW

Maryland enjoys, if that's the word, hot and humid summers (temperatures are sometimes in the 90s) and cold and snowy winters. An average of 16 inches of snow falls each year in the Baltimore–Washington, D.C., corridor. In 1997–1998, there was only 0.1 inch of snow, while a few years earlier there were 70 inches of the white stuff (if this is Friday it must be snowing, or if it's snowing, it must be Friday).

Keep in mind, of course, that there's more likely to be snow in the mountainous western part of the state (Garrett County gets an average of 120 inches), while the Eastern Shore is almost snowless. Summer temperatures will usually be ten to twenty degrees cooler in the mountains than at the beach.

Actually, the weather can be quite pleasant most of the year, and the state has at least its share of seasons, with beautiful spring blossoms, showy summers, fall foliage, and winter wonderlands. The Chesapeake Bay is large enough to create its own weather systems.

FAMOUS SONS AND DAUGHTERS OF MARYLAND

- Karen Allen, movie actress (1955–)
- George Armistead, Lt. Col. Defended Fort McHenry (1780–1818)
- Benjamin Banneker, astronomer, essayist, surveyor, and mathematician (1731–1806)
- Henry Blair, inventor (1807–1860)
- Eubie Blake, musician (1883–1983)
- John Wilkes Booth, actor and assassin of Abraham Lincoln (1838–1864)
- James M. Cain, author (1892–1977)
- Charles Carroll, American Revolutionary War leader and signer of the Declaration of Independence (1737–1832)
- John Carroll, clergyman (1735–1815)

- Samuel Chase, jurist, lawyer, and signer of the Declaration of Independence (1743–1811)
- Bosley Crowther, movie critic (1905–1981)
- Stephen Decatur, naval hero (1779–1820)
- John Dickinson, patriot and lawyer (1732–1808)
- Frederick Douglass, statesman and abolitionist (1818–1895)
- Olivia Floyd, Confederate agent and messenger (1825–1906)
- Jimmie Foxx, baseball player (1907–1967)
- Francis "Frank" Francois, politician (1934–)
- Mary Katherine Goddard, first woman postmaster (1738–1816)
- Robert "Lefty" Grove, baseball player (1900–1975)
- Alan Frank Guttmacher, physician (1898–1974)
- Dashiell Hammett, author (1894–1961)
- John Hanson, politician and farmer (1715–1783)
- Frances Ellen Watkins Harper, author, orator, social reformer, and suffragist (1825–1911)
- Matthew Henson, first explorer to reach the North Pole (1866–1955)
- Alger Hiss, public official (1904–1966)
- Johns Hopkins, merchant, banker, philanthropist, and founder of hospital bearing his name (1715–1783)
- William "Judy" Johnson, baseball player (1899–1989)
- Al Kaline, baseball player (1934–)
- Francis Scott Key, poet and attorney (1779–1843)
- Barry Levinson, film producer (1942–)
- Thurgood Marshall, Supreme Court justice (1908–1993)
- Barbara Ann Mikulski, United States Senator (1936–)
- Dr. Samuel A. Mudd, physician charged and pardoned in Lincoln assassination plot (1833–1883)
- Charles Wilson Peale, portraitist (1741–1827)
- Mary Pickersgill, maker of the "Star Spangled Banner" (1776–1857)
- Emily Post, journalist and etiquette expert (1872–1960)
- George Herman "Babe" Ruth, baseball player (1895–1948)
- Paul S. Sarbanes, United States Senator (retired) (1933–)
- Elizabeth Bayley Seton, first American-born saint of the Roman Catholic church (1774–1821)
- R. Sargent Shriver Jr., diplomat and director of the Peace Corps (1915–)
- Wallis Warfield Simpson, Duchess of Windsor (1896–1986)
- Upton Sinclair, writer and social critic (1878–1968)
- Gen. William Smallwood, American Revolutionary War hero and Maryland governor (1732–1792)

- Thomas Stone, one of four Maryland signers of the Declaration of Independence (1743–1787)
- Helen Taussig, pediatric cardiologist (1898–1986)
- Harriet Tubman, abolitionist and organizer of the Underground Railroad (1820?–1913)
- Leon Uris, author (1924–2003)
- John Waters, film producer (1946–)

Delaware Resources

DELAWARE TOURISM

- **Delaware Tourism Office,** 99 Kings Highway, Dover 19901; (302) 739–4271, (866) 2–VISIT–DE; www.visitdelaware.com.
- **Bethany-Fenwick Chamber of Commerce,** Delaware Route 1, Bethany Beach 19930; (302) 539–2100, (800) 962–7873; www.bethany-fenwick.org.
- **Brandywine Valley Tourist Information Center,** Route 1, Longwood Gardens, Pennsylvania 19348; (610) 286–6145, (800) 228–9933.
- **Dagsboro Area Chamber of Commerce,** P.O. Box 380, Dagsboro 19939; (302) 732–3637.
- **Delaware Memorial Bridge Information Center,** Interstate 295 at the Delaware Memorial Bridge, P.O. Box 71, New Castle 19720; (302) 571–6340.
- **Delaware State Chamber of Commerce Visitor Center at Bridgeville,** Route 13, Box 69, Bridgeville 19933; (302) 337–8877.
- **Delaware State Visitor Center,** 406 Federal Street, Dover 19901; (302) 739–4266; www.destatemuseum.org.
- **Greater Delmar Chamber of Commerce,** P.O. Box 416, Delmar 19940; (302) 846–3336; www.delmar.de.us.
- **Greater Georgetown Chamber of Commerce,** 140 Layton Avenue, Georgetown 19947; (302) 856–1544; www.georgetownde.com.
- **Kent County Convention and Visitors Bureau,** 9 East Loockerman Street, Suite 203, Dover 19901; (302) 734–1736, (800) 233–KENT; www.visitdover.com.

trivia

According to the Graduate College of Marine Studies at the University of Delaware, there are as many as sixty-two species of shark roaming the eastern waters of North America, including the Delaware and Maryland coasts. Typical mid-Atlantic sharks include the common hammerhead shark, the Atlantic mako shark, the sand shark, the smooth dogfish shark, the spiny dogfish shark, and the sandbar shark.

- **Laurel Chamber of Commerce,** 444 North Poplar Street, Laurel 19956; (302) 875–9319; www.laurelchamber.com.
- **Lewes Chamber of Commerce and Visitors Bureau,** 120 Kings Highway, Lewes 19958; (302) 645–8073; www.leweschamber.com.
- **Greater Milford Chamber of Commerce,** 11 South DuPont Highway, Milford 19963; (302) 422–3344; www.milfordchamber.com.
- **Greater Millsboro Chamber of Commerce,** Village Green Complex, 317 Main Street, Millsboro 19966; (302) 934–6777.
- **Historic New Castle Visitors Bureau,** 42 the Strand, New Castle 19720; (302) 322–8411, (800) 758–1550; www.visitnewcastle.com.
- **Chamber of Commerce of Milton,** 424 Mulberry Street, Milton 19968; (302) 684–1101; www.historicmilton.com.
- **Rehoboth Beach–Dewey Beach Chamber of Commerce,** 501 Rehoboth Avenue, Rehoboth Beach 19971; (302) 227–2233, (800) 441–1329; www.beach-fun.com.
- **Greater Seaford Chamber of Commerce,** 1200 West Stein Highway, Second Floor, Box 26, Seaford 19973; (302) 629–9690; www.seaford chamber .com.
- **Selbyville Chamber of Commerce, Hoosier and Railroad Avenue,** Selbyville 19975; (302) 436–5526.
- **Smyrna Visitor Center,** 5500 North DuPont Highway, Smyrna 19977; (302) 653–8910.
- **Sussex County Convention and Tourism Commission,** P.O. Box 240, Georgetown 19947; (302) 856–1818, (800) 357–1818; www.southern delaware.com.
- **Greater Wilmington Convention and Visitors Bureau,** 100 West Tenth Street, Suite 20, Wilmington 19801; (302) 652–4088, (800) 489–6664; www.wilmcvb.org.

MAJOR DELAWARE NEWSPAPERS

- *Newark Post,* 168 Elkton Road, Newark 19713; (302) 737–0724; www .mondotimes.com.
- *News-Journal,* 950 West Basin Road, New Castle 19720; (302) 324–2700.
- *Philadelphia Inquirer,* 440 North Broad, Wilmington 19801; (302) 654–6033; www.philly.com/mld/philly.

PUBLIC TRANSPORTATION

- **Philadelphia International Airport;** (215) 492–3000; www.phl.org.
- **Amtrak,** (800) USA–RAIL; www.amtrak.com.

- **Salisbury/Ocean City/Wicomico Regional Airport,** (410) 548–4827; www.airnav.com/airport/ksby.

FAST FACTS ABOUT THE FIRST STATE

- **Area (land):** Delaware ranks forty-ninth in the nation, with a total area of 1,982 square miles (5,133 square kilometers)
- **Capital:** Dover
- **Largest city:** Wilmington
- **Number of counties:** three
- **Highest elevation:** 447.85 feet (136.5 meters) above sea level, in New Castle County
- **Lowest elevation:** sea level, along the Atlantic Ocean
- **Greatest distance from north to south:** 96 miles (154.46 kilometers)
- **Greatest distance from east to west:** 35 miles (56.3 kilometers)
- **Coastline:** almost 300 miles (482.7 kilometers)
- **Population:** 843,524 (2005 estimate), forty-fifth among the states
- **Population density:** 401 persons per square mile
- **Population distribution:** 73 percent urban, 27 percent rural
- **Statehood:** December 7, 1787 (first state)
- **Nicknames:** the First State, Small Wonder, Blue Hen State
- **State flower:** peach blossom
- **State tree:** American holly
- **State motto:** Liberty and Independence
- **State bird:** blue hen chicken
- **State song:** "Our Delaware"
- **State bug:** ladybug
- **State fish:** weakfish (aka sea trout, gray trout, yellow mouth, yellowfin trout, and tiderunner)
- **State beverage:** milk
- **State mineral:** sillimanite
- **State colors:** Colonial blue and buff
- **State marine animal:** horseshoe crab
- **State fossil:** belemnite
- **State butterfly:** tiger swallowtail
- **State soil:** Greenwich loam
- **State herb:** sweet goldenrod
- **State star:** Delaware diamond (*Ursa major*)
- **State microinvertebrate:** stonefly

CLIMATE OVERVIEW

Delaware's climate is moderate year-round. Average monthly temperatures range from 75.8 to 32.0 degrees. The average temperature in the summer months is 74.3 degrees. About 57 percent of the days are sunny. Annual precipitation is approximately 45 inches. Temperatures along the Atlantic Coast are about 10 degrees warmer in winter and 10 degrees cooler in summer than the rest of the state. The average growing season varies from 170 to 200 days.

FAMOUS SONS AND DAUGHTERS OF DELAWARE

- Richard Allen, religious leader (1760–1831)
- Valerie Bertinelli, actress (1960–)
- Joseph Biden, U.S. Senator (1942–)
- Robert Montgomery Bird, author (1806–1854)
- Emily Perkins Bissell, social reformer (1861–1948)
- Annie Jump Cannon, astronomer (1863–1941)
- John Clayton, U.S. Senator (1796–1856)
- E. I. DuPont, inventor (1771–1834)
- Pierre DuPont, industrialist (1870–1954)
- Dallas Green, baseball player and manager (1934–)
- Henry Jay Heimlich, physician and developer of Heimlich maneuver (1920–)
- Absalom Jones, first black priest of the Protestant Episcopal Church (1746–1818)
- John P. Marquand, novelist (1893–1960)
- John Bassett Moore, attorney (1860–1947)
- Ryan Phillippe, actor (1974–)
- Howard Pyle, illustrator (1853–1911)
- Jay Saunders Redding, teacher (1906–1988)
- Judge Reinhold, actor (1965–)
- Caesar Rodney, politician (1728–1784)
- Christopher Short, baseball player (1937–1991)
- Elisabeth Shue, actress (1963–)
- Edward Robinson Squibb, founder of Squibb Pharmaceuticals (1819–1900)
- Estelle Taylor, actress (1894–1958)

Western Maryland

Western Maryland's three counties—Garrett, Allegany, and Washington—are a combination of farmlands, rugged mountains, sedate streams, and white-water rivers.

The products of farms and iron furnaces needed to be transported to customers between Wheeling, West Virginia, and the East Coast. So through this territory came the National Pike, which now is Alternate Route 40. It was the first road across the country funded by the federal government. This was long before President Eisenhower dictated there would be a national system of interstate highways. Along the road are many of the original mile markers, white metal (although they look like stone) obelisks that stand about 3 feet high.

Recently, there has been a huge push to attract tourism to this area. Completed projects include the $54 million Rocky Gap Lodge and Golf Resort that opened a few years ago and a new adventure sports complex near Wisp (the state's only major ski resort). Visitors can enjoy a golf course in the summer and skiing at Wisp in the winter. Also completed were an amphitheater next to the Rocky Gap resort, a couple of museums, and a $15 million C&O Canal refurbishment.

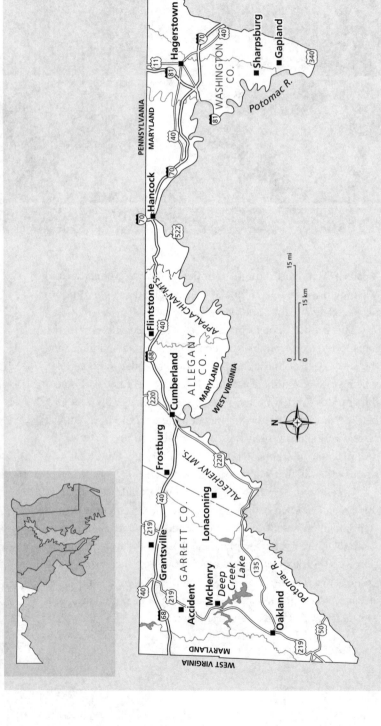

WESTERN MARYLAND

Garrett County

Perhaps Garrett County is best known for ***Deep Creek Lake,*** the largest lake in Maryland (all Maryland lakes were made by humans). In 1925 a dam 1,300 feet long and 62 feet high was constructed to provide hydroelectric power, and the lake resulted. Deep and Cherry Creeks, seven stream runs, and two glades feed it. In 1999 Maryland bought the lake for $7.8 million to ensure the area remains available as a recreation site. Deep Creek Lake State Park, 898 State Park Road, Oakland, is open from sunrise to sunset. Contact (301) 387–4111 or www.dnr .state.md.us/publiclands/western/deepcreeklake.html.

Railroads were once an efficient means of transportation in this area (the county was named for John Work Garrett, president of the B&O Railroad). Today Interstates 81, 68, and 70 provide the lifelines connecting this part of the state with the rest of the country. The geographic features that isolated Western Maryland for so many years also made it attractive to vacationers; residents from Washington, D.C., and Baltimore traditionally have come here to escape the summer heat. Now, it's a four-season resort area, with lots of condos climbing up the hillsides. Here you will find traces of Amish and Scottish culture, of hardy stock and friendly people. You will note some wealth, both in property and in cultural heritage. As yet, you will not find hundreds of thousands of tourists, but the numbers are increasing steadily. You will find hospitality, tranquillity, perseverance, a dedication to remembering the "old ways," and beautiful mountain scenery.

trivia

The Garrett County Chamber of Commerce, knowing how to promote its county's treasures, offers a *Fly Fishing in Western Maryland* brochure, which includes information about the rivers, streams, and Deep Creek Lake, as well as what lures to use and when. Call (800) 800–5557 or (301) 334–1948.

JUDY'S FAVORITE ATTRACTIONS IN WESTERN MARYLAND

Antietam Battlefield	Sideling Hill Exhibit area
Boonesborough Museum of History	Washington County Museum of Fine Arts
LaVale Toll Gate House	Western Maryland Scenic Railroad

Home Sweet Home

Just 13 feet from the shores of Deep Creek Lake is the **Lake Pointe Inn,** a bed-and-breakfast inn. It is the oldest house on the lake, dating from the late 1800s. 174 Lake Pointe Drive, McHenry; (301) 387–0111, (800) 523–LAKE; www.deepcreekinns.com.

As you drive around the lake, you can look for the homes that were featured in the Travel Channel's program, *Vacation Home Search.* That could be when you realize that the old summer cottages are being expanded or even torn down for larger homes. Or, stop by Bear Elegance Salon, (866) 388–BEAR or (301) 387–0600, and talk with Kathleen Seaman, the owner and senior stylist, who styled Cat Greenleaf, the host of the show.

Rafters on the ***Upper Youghiogheny River*** (or Upper Yough, pronounced "yock") fight their way over Gap and Bastard Falls and through rapids with names like Charlie's Choice, Rocky III, Cheeseburger, and Meat Cleaver. In the 9-mile ride there are twenty Class IV and V rapids (the top of the scale being class VI) and a downhill drop of 100 to 120 feet per mile. These rapids can provide some tough but exhilarating times; an experienced guide is a necessity.

When the White Water Canoe/Kayak World Championships were held in the United States for the first time in 1989, they were held on nearby Savage River, another popular rafting place. Then, in 1992 the river was the site of the canoe and kayak team Olympic trials.

A 1,600-foot recirculating white-water course is the newest addition to the ***Adventure Sports Center Complex,*** located on Marsh Mountain in McHenry. Years into the planning and designing stages (and more than $12 million in investments), the course is based on the design of in-river courses with an irregular alignment, eddies, rock outcroppings, all on top of a mountain. The course conditions can be modified with a "Wave Shaper," which adjusts features, allowing it to be converted from a white-water river with continuous action needed for slalom to a river with big drops, waves, and pools that are fun for free-style kayaking and rafting. This flexibility means it will be great for those who want to try these sports and those who defy them. A streamside amphitheater seating 600 allows spectators a front-row seat from a dry perspective.

trivia

The town of McHenry was settled about 1805 by Col. James McHenry, aide to Gen. George Washington, signer of the Declaration of Independence, and the man for whom the Baltimore fort was named.

Other activities at the center include rock climbing, hiking, mountain biking, and snow shoeing. Plans have been announced for the construction of an International Whitewater Hall of Fame and Museum where the first six inductees were announced and honored on October 14, 2005. Two of them are from Maryland. One of those named is Davey Hearn (www.daveyhearn.com), a two-time World Champion gold medalist in single canoe, a six-time team gold medalist, and an eight-time silver medalist. The committee says "He has been a dominating force in canoe slalom, producing paddling techniques and boat design innovations over a twenty-six year competitive career and is a holder of the Top Ten Sportsman of the Year award by the United States Olympic Committee." A Life Time Achievement Award was given to Bill Endicott "in recognition and honor of his outstanding and substantial contributions to white-water sports and related activities nationally and internationally." Until construction is completed, you can see the "Wall of Fame" at the Deep Creek Lake–Garrett County Visitors Center. Adventure Sports Center, 685 Mosser Road; (301) 387–3250; www.adventuresportscenter.com.

trivia

Garrett County has the state's highest mountain (Backbone, at 3,360 feet), the longest waterfall (Muddy Creek Falls, at 52 feet), and the largest lake (Deep Creek, with a length of 12 miles and a 65-mile shoreline).

Other recreational pastimes in Garrett County include water sports, skiing (downhill and cross-country), hiking, camping, golfing, horseback riding, hunting, dog sledding, snowboarding, and mountain biking. The mountains in this area receive about 120 inches of snow a year, more than Anchorage, Alaska, which makes for good downhill skiing at Wisp (Deep Creek Lake) and extraordinary cross-country skiing.

Within the more than 90,000 acres of public land, Garrett County has cleared and marked trails in New Germany State Park, 6 miles of maintained trails around Herrington Lake, and an additional 6 miles of primitive trails. Deep Creek and Swallow Falls State Parks have marked hiking trails that are suitable for cross-country skiing. Ski rentals are available at Herrington Manor State Park (301–334–9180; www.dnr.state.md.us/publiclands/western/herringtonmanor.html) and New Germany State Park (301–895–5453; www.dnr.state.md.us/publiclands/western/newgermany.html).

The ***Wisp Ski Resort*** in McHenry is the only downhill ski facility in the state. In 2006 they opened its North Camp, offering ten more trails and two quad chairlifts. Bear Claw Snow Tubing Park at Wisp has trails for snow tubing, with a lift to pull you and tube back up the mountain so you don't have

TOP ANNUAL EVENTS IN WESTERN MARYLAND

FEBRUARY

State Police Deep Creek Dunk,
Deep Creek,
(410) 789–6677,
(800) 541–6677,
www.somd.org

MARCH

Turning Sap into Syrup,
Swallow Falls State Park,
(301) 224–9180,
(301) 387–6938,
www.dnr.state.md.us

APRIL

**Maryland House and
Garden Pilgrimage,**
Statewide,
(410) 821–6933,
www.mhgp.org

MAY

**National Pike Festival and
Wagon Train,**
various locations,
(301) 791–3246,
www.nationalpikefestival.org

Sharpsburg's Memorial Day Parade,
Town Square,
(301) 432–8410

JUNE

George's Creek Days,
Lonaconing,
(301) 463–2189

Grantsville Days,
Grantsville,
(301) 895–5387,
(301) 387–4386,
www.grantsvilledays.com

Heritage Days,
Cumberland,
(301) 722–0037,
www.heritagedaysfestival.com

McHenry Highland Festival,
Garrett County Fairgrounds, McHenry,
(301) 387–3093,
www.highlandfest.info

Western Maryland Blues Fest,
Hagerstown,
(301) 739–8577, ext.116,
www.blues-fest.org

to waste time and energy trekking and schlepping back up the hill. Another winter activity is the annual Beachin' Weekend, in March, with music, swimsuit slalom, and games.

Because Deep Creek Lake and the Wisp Resort are about two hours from Pittsburgh and three hours from Washington, D.C., and Baltimore, this has become a favorite getaway destination for those who don't care to deal with airports when they think vacation. Wisp is known for its four-season appeal, so think golf, the Sewickley Spa, fly fishing, summer skiing (on their 130-by-20-foot artificial slope ski slide), skate park (20,000-square-foot paved and wood facility), paintball, downhill mountain biking, disc golf, chairlift rides (great for fall foliage viewing), bonfires, nature program, horseback riding, day camps,

JULY

Maryland Symphony Orchestra
Independence Celebration,
Sharpsburg,
(301) 797–4000,
www.mdsymphony.com

Rocky Gap Country Music
Bluegrass Festival,
Allegany College,
(888) ROCKYGAP

Summer Festival and Quilt Show,
Grantsville,
(301) 895–3332,
www.spruceforest.org

AUGUST

Augustoberfest,
Downtown Hagerstown,
(301) 739–8577, ext. 183

Garrett County Agriculture Fair,
Garrett County Fairground,
(301) 334–4715, ext. 321

SEPTEMBER

Apple Butter Boil,
Oakland,
(301) 334–9180

Sharpsburg Heritage Days,
Sharpsburg,
(301) 432–6856,
www.sharpsburghistoricalsociety.org

OCTOBER

Alsatia Mummers' Parade,
Hagerstown,
(301) 739–2044

Autumn Glory Festival,
Garrett County,
(301) 387–4386

Greater Gortner Airport Fly-in,
Oakland,
(301) 334–3541

DECEMBER

Christmas Model Train Open House,
Allegany Fairgrounds, (301) 777–5905

and other individual and family activities (296 Marsh Hill Road; 301–387–4911; www.wispresort.com or www.skiwisp.com).

As you drive into McHenry on Route 219, just past the visitors center on your right, you'll see a striking log building that is the home of the *Katahdin Cedar Log Homes,* headquartered in Oakfield, Maine. During office hours, there's a business center in there for sending faxes and packages, photocopying, and other office needs, as well as providing information about their homes, of course.

Rather than let it sit empty when the offices are closed, the 5,500 square foot lodge is available for parties and special events (wedding receptions, business retreats, reunions) for groups of up to forty-nine people. There's a demo kitchen, executive meeting room, cozy nooks, a fieldstone embraced double-sided fireplace in the great room, lots of deck space for an outdoor reception; and downstairs has a home theater area (a/v room), and a game room with Foosball, pool, and game tables. You can request Catering by the Champions (Don and Brenda Champion), or hire your own.

Because Garrett County is still dry, Judy Day, who helps arrange all the events, says the Sunday Sports Club is a unique feature. Three screens, a 10-foot, a 50-inch, and a 32-inch, will have different sports, from football, NASCAR, hockey, to baseball, depending on the season. The $50 admission charge lets you watch a game, run some errands, come back for another game. Bring your own beer or wine or purchase it through McHenry Beverage Shoppe.

A four-bedroom lodge, also by Katahdin, is less than 3 miles away, with a huge kitchen, great room, and a pond, so you can schedule a corporate retreat or friends-and-family getaway. The lodge rents for $400 a night or $2,500 a week.

If you're thinking you've heard the name Katahdin before and you're a fan of the ABC television show *Extreme Makeover: Home Edition,* then you are thinking right. Dozens of Katahdin employees came from across the country to build that amazing home.

For more information about the Cabin Run Lodge Conference Center & Event Venue at 35 Towne Centre Way, McHenry, call (301) 387–3263 or visit www.cabinrunlodge.com.

Just behind the lodge is **Featherstone,** "cool stuff for your home," where Stan Mayer helps you select the perfect lighting fixture, ceiling fan, designer plumbing fixtures, and custom kitchen appliances. There's also hardwood flooring, veneer, stone and decking products, and custom kitchen appliances. It's the place to find that absolutely must-have or quirky accessory that puts the final touch to your decor; 37 Towne Centre Way; (301) 387–4188; www.featherstonemd.com.

Reportedly Western Maryland has the only town in the country named **Accident,** about 10 miles north of Deep Creek on U.S. Highway 219. The story is that King George II gave George Deakins a land grant for 600 acres in Western Maryland in 1751. Deakins sent two engineers on separate missions to find his paradise. By accident each selected the same plot, starting at the same tall oak tree. Deakins called this plot "The Accident Tract," and the name endures; locals wouldn't have it any other

> ## trivia
>
> The *Our Fathers House Log Church* near Altamont is among the last log churches in the eastern United States still in use. Reportedly, the church was constructed for $50. (301) 334–1948.

way. Most noted by visitors are the Accident Garage, the Accident Fire Department, and the Accident Professional Building.

The **Drane House,** built by James Drane in the late eighteenth century, just east of Accident, is one of the few original frontier plantation homes remaining in this area. A key to Accident's past, the one-and-a-half-story log and frame house has been restored and is open for free tours upon request. The Drane House is on Accident-Bittinger Road, Accident. Call the Accident Town Hall, Monday, Wednesday, and Friday, at (301) 746–6346.

Vacationers have been seeking respite in Garrett County for hundreds of years, and traces of that history can be found throughout the county. The Shawnee Indians summered here. People from the sun-baked, humid cities of Washington and Baltimore came here to enjoy the cool mountain climate as early as 1851. That is when the Baltimore and Ohio Railroad ran its line to Oakland, which would become the county seat. The train no longer stops in Garrett County, but the Oakland station, an outstanding and picturesque Queen Anne structure built in 1884, remains.

Oakland is the county seat, so you're most likely to find a variety of interests addressed here.

The **Oakland Post Office mural** at 22 South Second Street, Oakland, was created by Robert Gates in 1942; it portrays a buckwheat harvest. Gates also did the mural in the Bethesda Post Office, which depicts the Montgomery County Farm Woman's Cooperative Market.

There is such an interesting blend of history here, from Native American to Civil War, and such an interest in genealogy, that you might want to spend a few hours at the **Garrett County Historical Museum,** with its exhibits portraying the history of the county's residents. There's a large genealogy library here too.

There is no admission fee to the museum (contributions are accepted, though), which is located at 107 South Second Street, Oakland. Generally, it's open from 11:00 A.M. to 4:00 P.M. Monday through Saturday in the summer and Thursday through Saturday in the winter. Call (301) 334–3226; www.deepcreektimes.com/gchs.html.

Tropical Christmas Trees

In 1989 Frank "Doc" Custer (now retired) sent 3,200 of his white pine and balsam fir Christmas trees to the Bahamas. This was the first time that a Maryland grower had exported trees outside the United States. Custer planted his first tree in 1956, and his Mountain Top Tree Farm, outside Oakland, is one of the largest tree farms in the state. As you drive around the county and spot perfect trees for your next holiday season, remember some of them may be going to Nassau to brighten up the holidays for someone who misses snow and cold weather. Mountain Top Tree Farm is located at 145 Pine View Drive, Oakland; (301) 334–5979; www.realchristmastrees.org.

About 10 miles out of Oakland off Cranesville Road is the Nature Conservancy's **Cranesville Sub-Arctic Swamp,** covering more than 500 acres (plus more in West Virginia). This natural phenomenon is a remnant of a boreal forest that produces growth normally found in arctic regions. So, you geologists, biologists, and nature lovers can see many rare species of flora and fauna. Although the ice sheet or glaciers of the last Ice Age (15,000 years ago) didn't reach this far south, they did lower the temperatures here, making this area a suitable habitat only for northern or colder clime plants and animals. They stayed this far south, even though the colder weather retreated north, because of a natural phenomenon known as a frost pocket, in which the surrounding hills trap cold air and moisture.

Among the plants you'll find here are the tamarack or larch (*Larix laricina*) and the tiny, round-leaved sundew (*Drosera rotundifolia*), an insectivorous plant. Additionally, this is the only significant site in Maryland where you can see creeping snowberry (*Gaultheria hispidula*). There are nineteen different plant communities, from shrubby wetlands to hardwood forest, in Cranesville.

One of the animals you might see is the northern water shrew (*Sorex palusyris punculatus*), and among the state-rare breeding birds are the golden-crowned kinglet, alder fly-catcher, Nashville warbler, and saw-whet owl.

In 1965 Cranesville Swamp became one of the first National Natural Landmarks to be designated by the National Park Service. It's open to the public for photography, nature study, birding, and walking, with four color-coded marked trails (with interpretive signs) through the woods to a 500-foot boardwalk. The trails start from either the drive into the swamp or from the parking lot, and all trails lead to the boardwalk. Please stay on the trails and the boardwalk so you don't take a chance of harming the plants.

Pets, even on a leash, are not allowed, nor is smoking or all-terrain vehicles. Remove nothing except your trash. Camping and fires are not allowed either.

Do wear sensible shoes, sunblock, insect repellent, and socks pulled up over your pants' cuffs to protect against chiggers, mosquitoes, ticks, poison ivy, and poison sumac. Bring field glasses and a good field guide to help you enjoy your visit.

Understand that the roads into the swamp are not paved. So, although the swamp can be gorgeous under a snow cover, you may need a four-wheel-drive vehicle to get there. Although open to the public during daylight hours, the conservancy likes you to call ahead of time to tell them you'll be wandering along their boardwalks. The number is (301) 656–8673.

Deep Creek Lake Discovery Center, run by the Department of Natural Resources as an interpretive environmental center, is the fun place to take the children so they can touch fossils, put their hands in a black bear paw print (compare that to the plaster of Paris hand mold they made in kindergarten), see underwater ecology through a microscope, and participate in such programs as hiking and boating safety. Within the 6,000-square-foot building are a classroom, an a/v-equipped conference area for educational programs, and a gift shop with environmental and educational toys, souvenirs, field guides, and books. The Discovery Center is open daily from 10:00 A.M. to 5:00 P.M. in the summer, and on weekends the rest of the year; 898 State Park Road, Swanton; (301) 387–7067; www.dnr.state.md.us/publiclands/western/discovery.html.

Garrett County is home to numerous artists and there is joy in visiting each and every one of them. For those who don't have that kind of time, stop by the ***Shoppe at Heritage Square,*** the 1884 B&O Railroad Station in Oakland, to buy items made in the county. The store carries apparel, soaps, stained glass, and pottery from local craftspeople. The farmers provide salsa and pepper jellies and honey. Trains, books, and puzzles, dolls, and dollhouse furniture will delight the child in all of us. Yes, the antiques that are used to display all these items are for sale. The Shoppe is open daily from 9:00 A.M. to 5:00 P.M., with extended Friday night hours in the summer; (301) 334–1243.

Garrett County has drawn even more artistic talent with the relocation of Mark and Laura Stutzman, who operate Eloqui illustration studio. You've seen

Bubble, Bubble, No Toil or Trouble

Yes, there is a connection between the name Deer Park and Deer Park bottled water that's part of the Perrier Group of America (distributed from New York to Florida and ranked number two in the mid-Atlantic market). The water comes from a spring that's 3,000 feet above sea level, in the midst of hundreds of acres of woodlands. The water is moved directly from the source through gravity-fed pipes to the bottling plant.

Calling All Yoders

There are more than 200 Yoders listed in the phone book in Maryland (and that doesn't include Yoders who have married and changed their names). A Yoder House has been constructed at Spruce Forest, made of "Yoder Stones." In other words, it will be built with stones collected from the foundations of Old Yoder homesteads in the area and perhaps other stones of Yoder importance. A genealogy display will trace the family from 1340 to today. For more information about this nonprofit organization, write to Yoder House Project, 177 Casselman Road, Grantsville 21536; www.yodernewsletter.org.

Mark's work on numerous McDonald's packages *(Batman, Jurassic Park),* but he's best known for designing the Elvis Presley postage stamp for the "Legends in American Music" series. Look for activities sponsored by the Garrett Lakes Arts Festival, and you'll probably find both Mark and Laura in attendance. Thier studio is at 100 G Street, Oakland; (301) 334–4086; www.eloqui.com.

I bought my first piece of **Simon Pearce** glass from his original workshop in Quechee, Vermont, perhaps two decades ago. So, it was a real thrill when I learned he'd opened a workshop and store in Maryland in January 1999, occupying 190,000 square feet of space in the old Bausch & Lomb factory. His style is pretty enough to put in a museum and comfortable enough to use. Hold a goblet in your hand and you may think it was made just for you. You may find glassware, pottery, flatware, candles, desk accessories, lampshades, table linens, and wooden serving pieces.

About twenty glassblowers work in teams of two, and you can watch them perform their magic daily from 9:00 A.M. to 5:00 P.M., although after 3:00 P.M. there's usually only one or two teams. They may be working on anything from Stratton stemware to lamps. Simon Pearce, 265 Glass Drive, Mt. Lake Park; (301) 334–5277; www.SimonPearce.com.

Solomon Sterner opened the **Casselman Inn,** Main Street, Grantsville, in 1824 to take in travelers from the National Pike. As is usual with restaurants, inns, and hotels along the pike, this one is on the north side, or the side that westbound travelers would be on. The two-story Federal-style brick house (with bricks made on the property) has nine guest rooms, each individually decorated with antiques. A newer forty-room motel has handcrafted furniture created by members of the community. Stop by for dinner or visit the bakery downstairs where you can savor the smells while you watch breads, cakes, and pies being made. The restaurant is open from 7:00 A.M. to 8:00 P.M. (or until 10:00 P.M. during the summer) Monday through Saturday. The phone number is (301) 895–5055. The phone number for the restaurant is (301) 895–5266; www.thecasselman.com.

When the nearby *Casselman Bridge* on Alternate Route 40 East in Cassel-man River Bridge State Park was built in 1813, it was the largest single-span stone-arch bridge in America. Gracefully curving 50 feet above the river, it was constructed so that the Chesapeake and Ohio Canal could travel beneath its span. The canal never came this far, but the bridge carried traffic for 125 years. It is now closed to motorized traffic, but the Casselman River Bridge State Park, Route 40 East, Grantsville, has a picnic area and a scenic spot to enjoy for a few minutes or a few hours. Yes, it is on the National Register of Historic Places. For information, call (301) 895–5453; or visit www.dnr.state.md.us/publiclands/west ern/casselman.html.

Just east of Casselman Bridge is *Penn Alps,* home to numerous crafters who work in log cabins that have been brought here from the surrounding country-side. The *Spruce Forest Artisan Village* features a number of artisans in log cabins and rustic structures set among towering spruce trees. You may find a vil-lage blacksmith, a weaver, a basket maker, a stained glass worker, a teddy bear artist, or a potter. They make items you don't usually see in your average sou-venir stand. The shops in the village are open May through October, Monday through Saturday 10:00 A.M. to 5:00 P.M. Four artisans are on the premises by chance and by appointment from November through April. The village is at 177 Casselman Road, Grantsville; call (301) 895–3332; the Web site is www .spruceforest.org.

About a mile east of Grantsville, still on the National Pike, is the *Fuller-Baker Log House.* The privately owned house is representative of those con-structed on the Allegheny frontier, except that it is large enough to have been a tavern. It is believed to be the only remaining log tavern on the National Pike between Cumberland and Wheeling. Maryland's first governor, Thomas John-son, owned the property when the house was built in 1815, but it is named for two other longtime residents. The first was Henry Fuller, who came to the area in 1837 to work as a stonemason. The Bakers were also early settlers and owned the house at a later date. The house in now on the National Register of Historic Places.

About 20 miles east of Oakland is the *Baltimore and Ohio Viaduct* at Bloomington. It was opened in 1851 to connect the port of Baltimore with industrial Wheeling and the Ohio Valley. A Confederate raiding party schemed to demolish the viaduct but was driven away by Union troops before the bridge could be blasted. Blasting holes drilled by Capt. John H. McNeill and his McNeill's Rangers are still visible on the bridge. Today the three-span (each 56 feet across and 28 feet high) stone-and-concrete bridge carries the railroad across the North Branch of the Potomac River. The Baltimore and Ohio Viaduct is on Route 135, just west of the Garrett and Allegany county line.

For additional information, contact Garrett County Chamber of Commerce, 15 Visitors Center Drive, McHenry 21541; (301) 387–4FUN; www.garrettchamber .com

Allegany County

Outdoor enthusiasts enjoy Allegany County and Cumberland, the county seat. Within the county borders are Rocky Gap and Dan's Mountain State Parks, Green Ridge State Forest, and the C&O Canal National Historical Park, where people can hunt, boat, fish, camp, bike, hike, and explore history.

Culture lovers need not despair that this is just sports and fun, though, for *American Style* magazine has named Cumberland the twenty-first best small city for art lovers. They cite "this former railroad center . . . is a textbook example of arts revitalization." An Arts and Entertainment district, so designated as one of twelve in Maryland, and coordinated locally by the Allegany Arts Council, has attracted numerous artists to the area, which in turn attract other businesses to the area. The magazine says the Savilla Gallery (52 Baltimore Street; 301–777–2787) is a "don't miss" site, "showing the work of national, regional, and local artists," and 60 North Centre Gallery (60 North Centre Street; 301–722–7666; www.ncentregallery.com) is described as "highlighting western Maryland art." Look for a free self-guided "Saturday Arts Walk" through the Arts and Entertainment District, rotating exhibits of local artwork at the Rocky Gap Lodge and Resort, and the annual Mountain Maryland Artists' Studio Tour.

When looking for performing arts, check the Frostburg State University Cultural Events Series that may feature the Maryland Symphony Orchestra, a Shakespeare production, a noted vocalist, bluegrass workshops and performances, and much more.

The ***Allegany Arts Council,*** located on the downtown Cumberland Mall, has twenty-four arts organizations actively involved in choral singing, theater, cinema, photography, crafts, instrumental music, and visual arts. A gallery exhibits works that are for sale. It's open from 10:00 A.M. to 4:00 P.M. Tuesday through Friday, and from 11:00 A.M. to 4:00 P.M. on Saturday, or by appointment. It is located at 52 Baltimore Street. Contact (301) 777–2787 or www .alleganyartscouncil.org.

Cumberland is considered the ***mibster capital*** of the country. For some reason the marble players of this town far surpass the players from other towns. A recent world champion was a twelve-year-old from Cumberland. If it has been a while since you played, or if you have never tried your hand at it, visit

Constitution Park. In addition to the Little League baseball field, picnic groves, swimming pool, wading pool, two playgrounds, railroad caboose, 1937 fire truck, army tank, horseshoe pits, and courts for basketball, tennis, shuffleboard, volleyball, and badminton, there are two game areas with three marble rings each. Games and tournaments are held regularly at the park; six national marble champions have played and practiced here on their way to victory.

Constitution Park is off Williams Street in the southeast area of Cumberland. From Maryland Avenue turn left on Williams Street to reach the park entrance. Call (301) 722–2000.

A brochure is available to help you walk through the **Victorian Historic District of Cumberland,** beginning at the east bank of Will's Creek and extending to the western property line of 630 Washington Street. The brochure highlights the architectural details and historical importance of about three dozen buildings. One of these is the History House Museum, which has eighteen rooms available for touring and features Victorian furniture, antiques, and displays pertaining to Allegany County's history. For more information about the historic district, call (301) 777–5905.

There is also a brochure available on the Fort Cumberland Walking Trail, which highlights the site of the 1755 fort with plaques on its history. The trail passes by George Washington's headquarters, a cabin that he used when he served at the fort as an aide to Gen. Edward Braddock during the French and Indian War. Another brochure, this one entitled *Walking Tour of Historic Downtown Cumberland,* highlights the architectural gems in the Downtown Pedestrian Mall area.

The **Western Maryland Station Center,** which was in service from 1913 until 1976, now houses the Allegany County Convention and Visitors Bureau, the Western Maryland Scenic Railroad, the Canal Place Authority, and the new C&O Canal National Historical Park Visitor Center. The center has an interpretive display in the station, where photographs, models, and artifacts are exhibited. Call (301) 724–3655 or (800) 989–9394; or log on to www.canalplace.org.

In La Vale, just west of Cumberland, you will find the only remaining tollhouse (circa 1836) in Maryland.

The **La Vale Toll Gate House** shows life as it was when the National Road (Route 40) came this way. There's a neat sign showing the tolls for various animals, pedestrians, and wagons. This is the only remaining tollgate on the National Road in Maryland. The furnishings are fascinating as well; be sure to ask about the "courting candle."

The House is at 14302 National Highway, La Vale, and is open 1:30 to 4:30 P.M. Saturday and Sunday May through October, and by appointment. Call (301) 729–3047 or (301) 729–1681 for more information.

Pedestrian Crossing

The 317-foot, one-lane, wooden-plank bridge crossing the North Branch of the Potomac River, linking Green Spring, West Virginia, with Oldtown, Maryland (about 15 miles southeast of Cumberland), was one of the last privately owned toll bridges. The bridge, constructed in 1937, was closed in 1995 because of "the deteriorated structural condition" of the Maryland-side abutment and evidence of pier decay, according to Allegany County Public Works officials. Without the 50-cent toll bridge, those who want to travel between the two areas face an additional 40-mile commute. The bridge remains open to pedestrians; www.yodernewsletter.org.

In June 2002 the U.S. Department of Transportation named the National Road, America's first federally funded highway, an "All-American Road." This means that the road conceived by George Washington and funded during Thomas Jefferson's presidency will have a higher priority when seeking federal funds from the Federal Highway Administration. Work is underway to develop a Web site trip planner, construct wayside pull-offs, and install interpretive exhibits at the pull-offs and state welcome centers.

Maryland lays claim to 170 miles of the highway that also runs through Pennsylvania, West Virginia, Ohio, Indiana, and Illinois. For more information about All-American Roads and National Scenic Byways, visit the FHA Web site at www.byways.org.

Paralleling the Potomac River to Cumberland was the Chesapeake and Ohio Canal. The canal was part of George Washington's dream of a water system that would unite the Atlantic with the Ohio River. The canal is now a National Historical Park. The 184½-mile towpath is used year-round by nearly four million hikers, cyclists, paddlers, anglers, picnickers, and nature enthusiasts who enjoy seeing the restored aqueducts and canal locks and communing with nature. Canal Place, a $45 million plan that will once again fill the canal with water, provide barge rides, restaurants, shops, a museum, and more, is ongoing.

trivia

If you'd like to see the historical marker for the 3,360-foot highest point in the state on Backbone Mountain, take U.S. Highway 50 east of Redhouse and you'll be at the crest of the Alleghenies.

In the meantime the staff at Canal Place coordinate activities and events, including the C&O CanalFest/Railfest, keeping the story of the canal alive. For more information, contact the Canal Place Preservation and Development Authority, Western Maryland Railway Station, 13 Canal Street, Room 301, Cumberland 21502. Call (301) 724–3655 or (800) 989–9394 (Maryland only); TTY/TDD: (800) 735–2258. The Web site is www.canalplace.org.

The *C&O Canal National Historical Park Visitor Center* features exhibits relating to the history of the canal in Cumberland. Entering the exhibit center through a likeness of the famous Paw Paw Tunnel, you'll discover displays about boatbuilding, the importance of the coal industry to the canal operations, and Cumberland as a transportation center. Cumberland, known as the gateway to the West and home of the "Narrows," was the beginning point of the National Road and a major railroading center in addition to serving as the western terminus of the C&O Canal. The visitor center, 13 Canal Street, Room 304, Cumberland, is open daily from 9:00 A.M. to 5:00 P.M. Call (301) 722–8226.

The *Transportation and Industrial Museum,* 13 Canal Street, Cumberland, is open Tuesday through Sunday from 10:00 A.M. to noon and 2:00 to 4:00 P.M. The telephone number is (301) 777–5905.

The romance of early twentieth-century steam railroading is with us once more on the *Western Maryland Scenic Railroad,* where passengers take a 16-mile ride combining mountaintop scenery and rich transportation history. The Western Maryland features a locomotive built in 1916 by the Baldwin Locomotive Works for the Lake Superior & Ishpeming Railroad, based in Michigan. It is a Consolidation 2-8-0 used from 1916 to 1956 for switching and freight hauling in Michigan's Upper Peninsula. It was on display at the Illinois Railroad Museum from 1971 until it was purchased by the WMSR in 1992.

As the train steams its way up the 2.8 percent grade on the westward trip from Cumberland to Frostburg, it travels along old Western Maryland Railway and Cumberland and Pennsylvania Railway rights-of-way. Riders view many memorable sights, including the famous Cumberland Narrows (a natural 1,000-foot breach in Will's Mountain known as the "Gateway to the West"), an iron truss bridge, Bone Cave, and Helmstetter's Horseshoe Curve.

Other interesting sights along the way include the 1,000-foot Brush Mountain Tunnel, the Allegheny Front, Victorian architecture, the C&O Canal, Buck's Horse Farm, and the frontier town of Mt. Savage (where America's first iron rails were produced). At the Frostburg terminus you can get a close-up view of the engineer and fireman in blue-and-white overalls and the locomotive turntable, which reverses the engine for the return journey.

At the other end, in Frostburg, is the Old Depot Center complex, which now features a restaurant and the *Thrasher Carriage Collection.* This collection offers more than fifty examples of early nineteenth- and twentieth-century horse-drawn vehicles. Built by the finest manufacturers, the vehicles include a Vanderbilt family sleigh and the formal coach used by Theodore Roosevelt at his inauguration. The museum is open 11:00 A.M. to 3:00 P.M. Tuesday through Sunday May through September, daily during October, and weekends only in November and December. Call (301) 689–3380; www.thrashercarriage museum.com.

The rail trip takes about three hours, including a ninety-minute layover in Frostburg. A special dining car has been dedicated as the Gov. William Donald Schaefer Special for the governor who was credited with inspiring state, local, and private development of the scenic railroad.

The train runs on a seasonal schedule, so call for days and times. There's an expanded schedule in October for fall foliage viewing. Ticket prices for the year 2004 were $20.00 and up for adults, $18.00 and up for seniors age sixty and older, and $10.00 and up for children age twelve and younger.

Charter trips and special events such as dinner trips or trips featuring murder mysteries, dinner theater, or dancing are scheduled periodically. Private parties for weddings, birthdays, business meetings, school outings, and other events also may be booked. Write to Western Maryland Scenic Railroad, Western Maryland Station, 13 Canal Street, Cumberland 21502, or call (800) TRAIN–50 or (301) 759–4400. Visit the WMSR on the Internet at www.wmsr.com.

The **Mt. Savage Museum & Historical Park** is an 1800s ironworks house built to house laborers. It's also where Cardinal Edward Mooney was born. Mooney (1882–1958) was the archbishop of Detroit from 1937 until 1946, when he was named a cardinal. There's no admission fee to the museum, located at the Mt. Savage Historical Park, and the hours vary, so call first: (301) 264–4175.

Just as the railroad and the canal played an important part in the area's development, the National Pike has a claim to fame. You can drive to the top of either side of the **Cumberland Narrows** for an unparalleled view, on a clear day, of Cumberland and the surrounding countryside. To reach the eastern wall of the Narrows, take Will's Mountain Road off Piedmont Avenue to the parking lot of Artmor Plastics, park, and walk about 2 blocks. To reach the western wall, take exit 41, the Sacred Heart Hospital exit, off I–68. Go through the traffic light and up the hill to Bishop Walsh Road, where you will turn right to the high school. Drive to the back of the school, where the road ends, and walk through the woods, past the water tower, to the edge—about a five-minute walk. This is not a prepared path and it is not wheelchair accessible. The park is open from dawn to dusk. Call (301) 777–5132.

Whatever diversion you prefer, you're almost certain to find it in and around the 3,000-plus acres of **Rocky Gap State Park.** There are rugged mountains, the 243-acre Lake Habeen (fed by Rocky Gap Run after it tears through a mile-long gorge lined with steep cliffs), camping (30 of the 278 sites have electric hookups), boating (no gas-powered boats), and fishing (panfish, catfish, brown and rainbow trout, large and smallmouth bass—but you need a valid Maryland anglers license if you're sixteen or older). There's also hiking (you can see the gorge from the overlook on the quarter-mile-long Canyon Overlook Trail). For the serious hiker, try the 5-mile Evitts Homesite Trail that has a 1,000-foot climb in 2.5 miles, a nature center (including an on-site aviary), and so much more.

You can take your choice of accommodations, from your own tent or camper to a cabin or chalet or you can stay at the gorgeous Rocky Gap Lodge and Golf Resort. The eighteen-hole course features a Jack Nicklaus signature design carved out of the mountain. But don't despair, only the front nine has challenging elevation changes; the back nine has expansive, gently rolling fairways. Well, maybe you should worry; even Nicklaus hasn't broken par on this course. Hmm. Each golf cart has a ProLink GPS (Global Positioning System) that's supposed to make the rounds faster and lower the scores. Maybe you should bring bread crumbs along, too.

The lakeside lodge has 220 rooms, meeting space, dining, a sandy beach by the lake, spa services, and a fire pit for roasting those s'mores under the stars.

What more could a person want?

Rocky Gap State Park, 12500 Pleasant Valley Road, Flintstone; (301) 777–2139 (park headquarters), (301) 777–2138 (camper contact, seasonal phone line Memorial Day–Labor Day), (888) 432–CAMP (2267), or www.dnr.state.md.us/publiclands/western/rockygap.html for reservations.

The ***Lonaconing Iron Furnace*** was erected about 1836 by the George's Creek Coal and Iron Company and produced iron for the next twenty years. When the furnace was constructed, it was unique in several respects. It was 50 feet high and 50 feet square at the base—a daring departure from contemporary furnaces, which were 30 feet high and 30 feet square. Moreover, it was the first furnace built in this country that successfully used coke fuel at a time when all furnaces were using the less-efficient charcoal.

The furnace was built against a hillside because it was fed from the top. The site was chosen because the necessary iron ore, coal, wood, clay, limestone, sandstone, and water were readily available, although transporta-

Lonaconing Iron Furnace

tion to the marketplace was not convenient. Castings made here included stoves, farming implements, and dowels for the C&O Canal lock walls.

Today the furnace is the backdrop for a pleasant town park in Lonaconing, where you can stop to lunch at the picnic tables or enjoy the play equipment. A sign notes the location of the former Central School, and a bronze plaque honors Robert Moses "Lefty" Grove, a native son who was elected into the Baseball Hall of Fame in 1947. Lauded as the greatest left-handed pitcher of all time, he played for the Philadelphia Athletics from 1925 to 1933 and the Boston Braves from 1934 to 1941.

The furnace is located on Route 36, 35 East Main Street, Lonaconing; (301) 463–2289. The park is open daily from sunrise to sunset.

For additional information write to the Allegany County Convention and Visitors Bureau, Western Maryland Station Center, 13 Canal Street, Cumberland 21502, call (301) 777–5138, or visit www.mdmountainside.com.

Washington County

Washington County—the first county to be named after George Washington—was founded on September 6, 1776, just months after our country itself was born. In a Civil War battle fought at Sharpsburg, along Antietam Creek, more than 23,000 casualties were suffered.

Since 1989 an annual remembrance of the **Battle of Antietam** has been held the first Saturday in December. It is signified by 23,110 luminarias, one every 15 feet along a 5-mile route, throughout the fields, and around monuments. Nearly one thousand volunteers systematically set up the luminarias throughout the day and candles are lit starting at 3:00 P.M. About 2,500 cars drive through the illumination each year, from 6:00 P.M. until midnight. The event is free, but donations are appreciated. Cars may enter the event from Maryland Route 34. This is a group effort of the National Park Service, local government agencies, and volunteers.

The idea for the candles came from the Rest Haven Cemetery, which had previously placed a luminaria at every grave site. Borrowing the idea, Hagerstown residents lit luminarias every night for the two weeks prior to Christmas. One night it was the north side of town, another it was the south side, and so it continued throughout the area. Band members of the high schools sold 81,000 lights in the neighborhoods.

In recent years the National Park Service has faced numerous budget cuts, reducing preservation and rehabilitation funding for Antietam and other parks. With more than three hundred War Department plaques, ninety-six monuments, and five hundred cannons on the battlefield, the price of upkeep is steep. The nonprofit Western Maryland Interpretive Association operates the Antietam Partner Program with several ways for individuals and groups to donate funds to the battlefield, including Adopt-A-Monument, Build-A-Fence, and Plant-A-Tree. Funds donated to these programs go directly to Antietam, unlike the entry fee to the park; www.Antietampartner.com.

For more information about Antietam, write to P.O. Box 158, Sharpsburg 21782, call (301) 432–5124, or visit www .nps.gov/anti. The Antietam National Battlefield at Sharpsburg is open daily from 8:30 A.M. to 5:00 P.M. except on major holidays, with extended summer hours. The tour road is open sunrise to sunset.

Washington County parks rate with the best and include the **C&O Canal National Historical Park,** the Appalachian Trail (37 miles), Fort Frederick State Park, Washington Monument State Park, Pen Mar County Park, at least eight other county parks, and Hagerstown City Park.

Tiny Boonesboro has a huge connection to history that you can find in Doug Bast's (pronounced Bost) **Boonesborough Museum of History.** His diverse collection started when he was a child and saved the lead bullets and other items he'd pick up from local farm grounds and battlefields. Look for Confederate landmines, weapons, glassware, china, and more; the list goes on and on for what seems like forever. You can see the reconstruction of a cabinetmaker's shop and a nineteenth-century general store. The museum is open Sunday from 1:00 to 5:00 P.M., May through September and by appointment. 113 North Main Street; (301) 432–6969.

For lodgings with a real twist, you'll want to visit the Tree House Camp at **Maple Tree Campground** near Gathland State Park. The unusual feature of this campground is that you sleep in a tree house. Did you always want one when you were a kid, but you lived in the city, or the only adults around had sixteen thumbs? This is not quite as rustic as you might remember, but it is as close as most of us will ever get. Your tree house—on stilts about 7 feet off the ground—has a couple of bunks (bring a sleeping bag), a woodstove, a table with benches, and a filled wood bin. A communal bathhouse is nearby, you have twenty-six acres of woods to roam through and explore, and you're not far from the Appalachian Trail. You may bring your tent for "regular" camping.

When Phyllis Sorocko started this campground after retirement, she dreaded the idea of tearing up the land and trees for campsites and dumpsites

trivia

The **Washington Monument,**
in the state park of the same name,
was the first monument built and
finished honoring George Washington (as opposed to the first
architectural monument dedicated
in Washington's memory—that's in
Baltimore). Built of local stone by
the citizens of Boonsboro in 1827,
it offers a great view of the valley
below after a short climb. The
Appalachian Trail runs through
the park. (301) 791–4767;
www.dnr.state.md.us.

and was thrilled with this compromise. Pets, on leash at all times, are welcome. Reservations are recommended. There are nine tree houses and four tree cottages. The charge is $36.00 a night for the first four people in a tree house, and $50.00 a night for the first four people in a cottage. Each additional person is $10.00. Field tent sites are $8.00 per person per night, and wooden tent sites are $10.00 a night. The campground is located on 20716 Townsend Road, Gapland. Call (301) 432–5585 or visit www .thetreehousecamp.com.

I love science and hands-on museums like the **Discovery Station** in Hagerstown. It's located in the historic Nicodemus Bank building, across from the county courthouse. The original bank housed the Federal Depository during the Civil War, and the main vault with leaded glass was installed in 1913.

The three floors cover science, technology, and history. The second floor houses the Hagerstown Aviation Museum (included in the admission price). Also, catch the railroad exhibits that cover the important role Hagerstown played in transportation history.

Museum personnel say you should allow at least ninety minutes. And, perhaps best of all, the Treasure Gift Shoppe has gifts, toys, aircraft models, astronaut ice cream (Neapolitan is my favorite), games, books, greeting cards, and so much more, so you can take reminders of the interactive attractions home with you. You can stop by the gift shop without paying museum admission. There is also an Explorer Cafe.

The Discovery Station is open Tuesday through Saturday from 10:00 A.M. to 4:00 P.M., and on Sunday from 2:00 to 5:00 P.M. It is closed on Monday, Thanksgiving, Christmas, New Year's Day, Easter, and on Mother's, Father's, and Independence Days. It is also closed on Sunday during July and August. Admission is $7.00 for adults, $6.00 for children two through seventeen, and $5.00 for seniors (fifty-five and over) and military. The Discovery Station at Hagerstown is at 101 West Washington Street; (301) 790–0076; www.discovery station.org.

The **Washington County Museum of Fine Arts,** which celebrated its seventy-fifth anniversary in 2006, in Hagerstown is an outstanding museum overlooking the fifty-acre City Park Lake (home to numerous waterfowl). It was the idea and gift of Mr. and Mrs. William Henry Singer Jr., who had collected many possessions during their European travels and were looking for a beautiful place to house them. The cornerstone was laid on July 15, 1930, by Mrs. Singer's grandniece, Anna Spencer Brugh.

The museum was built of homewood brick with Indiana limestone trim. Two wings were added in 1949: the Memorial Gallery, in honor of Mr. Singer, who died in 1943, and the Concert Gallery, in honor of Mrs. Singer's love of music. Mrs. Singer was eighty-six when she died in Laren, Holland, in 1962.

Among the museum's collection are the works of Mr. Singer, who was a Postimpressionist painter of note. Many of his landscapes show the fishing villages, fjords, and snow-covered mountains of Norway, where the Singers lived. Also in the collection are old masters, twentieth-century sculpture and painting, and a variety of decorative arts from around the world. The emphasis, though, is on American art.

In addition to tours, the museum offers art classes (weaving, clay, acrylics, quilting, and more), lectures, films, and music recitals. A bimonthly calendar is available.

If you can't afford to own or donate works to the museum, you can still feel as though you own something. You can "adopt" a painting by contributing funds toward a conservator's fee to clean or restore a particular painting in the museum's collection. Frederick Childe Hassam's "White House, Gloucester" (1895) was the first adopted painting in the program that started in October 2004. The house had become yellow and it took Baltimore conservator Sian Jones thirteen hours to restore the work. Tax-deductible adoptions range from a few hundred dollars to $8,000, depending on the piece. You will receive recognition for your part in the work's conservation in the museum's newsletter and on a special object label near the adopted painting.

The museum, located on City Park Lake, is open Tuesday through Friday from 9:00 A.M. to 5:00 P.M., Saturday from 9:00 A.M. to 4:00 P.M.; and Sunday from 1:00 to 5:00 P.M. There is no admission fee, but a donation is requested. Call (301) 739–5727, (301) 739–5764 (TDD), or visit www.wcmfa.org.

Three *Hagerstown Post Office murals* represent different aspects of the railway transportation of mail. The paintings were done by Frank Long of Berea, Kentucky, in 1938 as part of the Section of Fine Arts program—placing appropriate art in federal buildings. The first painting depicts mailbags being loaded onto a train. A central panel depicts a railway post office in operation, with postal clerks sorting letters on a train. The third panel, over the lockboxes, shows figures on the station platform watching an approaching train that will pick up the mail. Frank Long also painted post office murals in Louisville and Berea, Kentucky; Crawfordsville, Indiana; and Drumright, Oklahoma.

trivia

The **Beaver Creek School** is a century-old one-room schoolhouse and museum, with a hat shop, music shop, dressmakers' parlor, and toolshed, that's open on Sunday from 2:00 to 5:00 P.M. June through September; 9702 Beaver Creek Church Road, Hagerstown; (301) 797–8782.

Hagerstown, the county seat of Washington County, is also the home of the *Hagers-Town Town and Country Almanack,* which has been printed since 1797. The weather forecasts generate the most interest, and people swear by them. In fact, a folk tale has it that the book called for snow on July 4, 1874, and that it did snow on that date. Research indicates that the almanac did not predict snow, and the minimum temperature for that day was said to have been in the high sixties—not too conducive to snow.

Airplane and airport food doesn't exactly enjoy a stellar reputation, but you're sure to change your mind when you stop at ***Nick's Airport Inn*** on U.S. Highway 11 at the airport. In fact, many people fly their private planes here just to enjoy the tasty offerings from the Giannaris family. Fresh seafood is brought in from Baltimore and the prices are more than reasonable. Even the crab cakes are worthwhile. Nick's is open Monday through Friday from 11:00 A.M. to 2:00 P.M., Monday through Thursday 5:00 to 10:00 P.M., and Friday and Saturday 5:00 to 10:30 P.M. They're closed on Sunday. 18615 Terminal Drive, Hagerstown; (301) 733–8560; www .nicksairportinn.com.

The ***Wilson Country Store*** is a classic country store with a post office, loose "penny" candy, yard goods, and much more. You'll also see a one-room schoolhouse. The store is on Old Route 40, and it is open Monday through Saturday from 7:30 A.M. to 2:00 P.M. and Sunday from 9:00 A.M. to 5:00 P.M. The general store is at 14921 Rufus-Wilson Road, Clear Spring. Call (301) 582–4718 or (888) 348–2012.

On your way to Wilson Village from Hagerstown, you may stop by the ***Historic Wilson Bridge*** Picnic Area. It's located along Route 40 West, adjacent to Historic Wilson Bridge, which is the oldest, longest, and most graceful of the twenty-three stone-arch bridges in the county. The five-arch span was built in 1819 as an early extension of the National Road to the Ohio Valley. Pennsylvanian Silas Harry erected the structure at a cost of $12,000. Its style represented a triumph for the justices of the Levy Court (until 1829, the body similar to a Board of County Commissioners), who insisted on an all-stone structure in the face of army engineers' arguments that a wooden bridge laid over stone piers would suffice.

The bridge is located about 200 feet north of the west end of the "new" bridge that crosses Conococheague Creek, 5 miles west of Hagerstown on Route

Wilson Country Store

40. This one-acre site offers picnic tables, parking, and canoe access to the Conococheague.

Of particular interest to sports fans is the **Hagerstown Suns** baseball team of the South Atlantic League, an affiliate of the Washington Nationals. This Class-A team draws about 150,000 fans a year. In previous years, loyalists have seen the likes of Jeff Ballard, Jim Palmer, Bill Ripken, and Craig Worthington, all of whom have gone on to be well known in the baseball world. Palmer was elected to the Baseball Hall of Fame in 1989, his first year of eligibility. For information call the Municipal Stadium at (301) 791–6266; www .hagerstownsuns.com.

Seven miles west of Hancock, near the border between Allegany and Washington Counties, is **Sideling Hill.** Interstate 68 diverts traffic off a steep, tricky road that twists to a roundhouse curve at the top of Sideling Hill. The 4½-mile section of the road took twenty-eight months to complete and cost about $21 million. Workers blasted an incredible, breathtaking 360-foot-deep cut in the mountain, which revealed millions of years of geological history. A four-story, wheelchair-accessible interpretive center, which is approachable from both sides of the highway, allows you to see all those layers and folds of multihued rocks that have been exposed by the cut and

trivia

Boonesboro is known for its Civil War museum, but those who really know it know to visit in August and September, when Boonesboro cantaloupes ripen. You can buy them from a roadside stand, particularly on Saturday and Sunday, but it's best to plan an outing and pick your own. Then you'll really enjoy the thin-skinned "Heart of Gold" variety with all its natural sweetness.

trivia

On October 14, 1790, Col. Elie Williams and Gen. George Washington met at the springhouse in Williamsport (in Washington County) to discuss the possibility of the town being the new capital of the United States. The idea was dismissed because the Potomac River was not navigable by large ships.

explains their history. From my perspective, the most curious thing about the area is that the rock layers are in a syncline, which would make me think it would be a valley, not a mountain, but the newer sedimentary layers are on top so a syncline it is. This is one of the best rock exposures in the northeast.

If you can make only one side trip in Maryland, only a momentary detour, this is the one to make. A late-fall visit just may bring a surprise of a southern migration of ladybugs. In 1994 and 1995, there were so many millions of these critters that they obscured the windows and just about any other surface on which they could land. The numbers have decreased in the past year or two, but you'll still find an amazing number of ladybugs on their annual trek.

The interpretive center, at 3000 Sideling Hill, Hancock, is open from 9:00 A.M. to 5:00 P.M. daily, except New Year's Day, Easter, Thanksgiving, and Christmas. For information about Sideling Hill, call the center at (301) 842–2155; www.mgs.md.gov/esic/features/sidel.html.

The Washington County Convention and Visitors Bureau office has a number of interesting brochures, and operates a visitor center in downtown Hagerstown. Those traveling with children, or those who are young at heart, will like visiting Crystal Grottoes caverns or the Discovery Station.

For additional tourism information write to the Washington County C&VB, 16 Public Square, Hagerstown 21740; (301) 791–3246 or (888) 257–2600.

Places to Eat in Western Maryland

BOONESBORO

Old South Mountain Inn,
6132 Old National Pike,
(301) 432–6155,
(301) 371–5400,
www.oldsouthmountaininn
.com

CUMBERLAND

The Inn at Walnut Bottom,
120 Greene Street,
(301) 777–0003,
(800) 286–9718,
www.iwbinfo.com

GRANTSVILLE

Penn Alps Restaurant,
125 Casselman Road,
(301) 895–5985

HAGERSTOWN

Broad Axe,
28 West Franklin Street,
(301) 733–8454,
www.thebroadaxe.com

Cancun Cantina West,
901 Dual Highway,
(301) 797–4422,
(888) 797–4422,
www.cancuncantinawest
.com

Gourmet Goat/GG's,
41 North Potomac,
(301) 790–3454,
www.thegourmetgoat.sams
biz.com

Michelle's Restaurant,
10 East Washington Street,
(301) 733–6608,
www.michellesofhagers
town.com

Roccoco,
20 West Washington Street,
(301) 790–3331,
www.roccoco.com

Schmankerl Stube,
58 South Potomac Street,
(301) 797–3354,
www.schmankerlstube.com

HANCOCK

Lockhouse Restaurant,
11 East Main Street,
(301) 678–6991,
www.hancockmd.com/lock
house.html

**Weaver's Restaurant &
Bakery,**
77 West Main Street,
(301) 678–6346,
www.weaversrestaurant.com

OAKLAND

Four Seasons,
20160 Garrett Highway,
(301) 387–5503,
(888) 590–7283,
www.willothewisp.com

Places to Stay in Western Maryland

ACCIDENT

**Bear Creek Crossing Bed
and Breakfast,**
29380 Garrett Highway,
(301) 746–8623,
www.bearcreekcrossing
bedandbreakfast.com

CASCADE

**Cascade Inn Historic Bed
& Breakfast,**
14700 Eyler Avenue,
(301) 241–4161,
(800) 362–9526,
www.thecascadeinn.com

CUMBERLAND

Inn at Walnut Bottom,
120 Greene Street,
(301) 777–0003,
(800) 286–9718,
www.iwbinfo.com

FROSTBURG

Frostburg Inn,
147 East Main Street,
(301) 689–3831,
www.frostburginn.com

GRANTSVILLE

**Casselman Valley Farm
Bed and Breakfast,**
215 Maple Grove Road,
(301) 895–3419,
www.bbonline.com/md/
casselman

HAGERSTOWN

**Clarion Hotel and
Conference Center at
Antietam Creek,**
901 Dual Highway,
(301) 733–5100,
www.clarionantietam.com

Country Inn & Suites,
17612 Valley Mall Road,
(301) 582–5003,
(800) 456–4000,
www.countryinns.com/hagers
townmd

Four Points by Sheraton,
1910 Dual Highway,
(301) 790–3010,
www.fourpointshagerstown
.com

**Hampton Inn—
Hagerstown/Maugansville,**
18300 Peak Circle,
(240) 420–1970,
www.hamptoninn.com

**Holiday Inn Express Hotel
& Suites,**
241 Railway Lane,
(301) 745–5644,
(888) 551–0222,
www.hagerstownexpress
.com

Inn on Potomac,
400 North Potomac Street,
(301) 739–5679,
(800) 761–8313,
www.innonpotomac.com

**Wingrove Manor Bed &
Breakfast,**
635 Oak Hill Avenue,
(301) 733–6328,
www.wingrovemanor.com

KEEDYSVILLE

Antietam Overlook Farm,
4812 Porterstown Road,
(301) 432–4200,
(800) 878–4241,
www.antietamoverlook.com

MCHENRY

Wisp Mountain Resort,
290 Marsh Hill Road,
(301) 387–5581,
(800) 462–9477,
www.wisp-resort.com

SAVAGE

**Commodore Joshua
Barney House,**
7912 Savage Guilford Road,
(800) 475–7912,
www.joshuabarneyhouse
.com

SHARPSBURG

**Historic Jacob Rohrbach
Inn,**
138 West Main Street,
(301) 432–5079,
(877) 839–4242,
www.jacob-rohrbach-
inn.com

Inn at Antietam,
220 East Main Street,
(877) 835–6011,
www.innatantietam.com

OTHER ATTRACTIONS WORTH SEEING IN WESTERN MARYLAND

**Boonesborough Museum
of History,**
Boonsboro,
(301) 432–6969

Crystal Grottoes Caverns,
Boonsboro,
(301) 432–6336

Fort Frederick State Park,
Big Pool,
(301) 842–2155,
www.dnr.state.md.us/publiclands/
western/fortfrederick.html

**Frostburg State University
Planetarium,**
Frostburg,
(301) 687–4270,
www.frostburg.edu/dept/
engn/planet/planet.html

Jonathan Hager House and Museum,
Hagerstown,
(302) 739–8393,
www.hagerhouse.org

Hagerstown Roundhouse Museum,
Hagerstown,
(301) 739–4665,
www.roundhouse.org

Muddy Creek Falls,
Swallow Falls State Park,
(301) 334–9180

Swallow Falls State Park,
Oakland,
(301) 334–9180,
www.dnr.state.md.us/publiclands/
western/swallowfalls.html

**Washington County Rural Heritage
Museum,**
Sharpsburg,
(240) 313–2839,
www.ruralheritagemuseum.org

Wisp Ski and Golf Resort,
McHenry,
(301) 387–4911 or
(800) 462–9477,
www.wispresort.com

Central Maryland

Perhaps nowhere in the state is there more diversity than in the area referred to as central Maryland. In the rolling foothills and picturesque landscapes of this region are horse farms and vineyards, the commercial center of Baltimore City, huge stone farmhouses and old mills, busy waterways surrounding the Chesapeake Bay and its tributaries, some of the oldest towns in the country, and modern, vibrant cities. This core of five counties and two major cities encompasses it all.

Sixteen million vehicles use the ***William Preston Lane Jr. Bridge*** (Chesapeake Bay Bridge) every year. Only 50,000 people walk across it, though, on Chesapeake Bay Bridge Walk Day. Once Maryland was a leading contender in the number of "kissing" or covered bridges; now there are only a few. See also Frederick and Prince George's Counties in the Capital Washington section for more bridges.

Countless people stop by Annapolis to see its waterfront, Ego Alley (where the expensive boats parade), and the United States Naval Academy. They watch the sailboats in the harbor—even in the winter, when there is a Frostbite series of sailboat races—or the Naval Academy's noon meal formation, when the brigade of midshipmen assembles in front of Bancroft Hall for

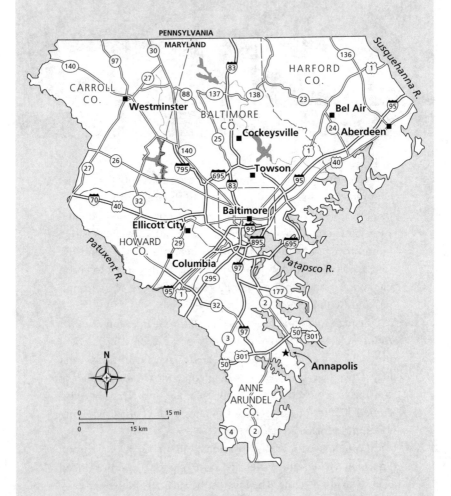

inspection. I chatted with Robert F. Sumrall, who re-creates scale models of the ships that have plied the bay.

Whenever anyone talks about Chesapeake Bay, blue crabs and oysters are sure to be discussed. I include an old inn that is relatively new, and a scenic waterside eatery for sightseeing while you dine.

Trying to pick a starting point is tough, for several interstates lead into and out of this area of five counties and Baltimore City, including Interstate 95 going north to Philadelphia and New York and south to Washington, D.C.; Interstate 83 going north into Pennsylvania; Interstate 70 going into the western part of the state; and Interstate 97 heading south and then east into Annapolis.

Anne Arundel County

Perhaps the best place to start is at BWI, *Baltimore-Washington International Thurgood Marshall Airport,* where millions of people pass through either going to or coming home from some place or picking up a passenger. It may be a scandalous thought, but you might actually want to arrive early or even stay a few minutes, for BWI has become a destination in itself. There's a beautiful observation gallery with information about flying and pieces of airplanes on display. The $6.4 million gallery has cutaway airplane sections (great to view if you or someone in your party has never flown or seen the workings of a plane), an interactive weather station (so you can see what a cold front is and how it affects weather, or check for the temperature in your destination city), and a 147-foot-wide observation window to watch airplanes refueling, taxiing, taking off, and landing. Plunk yourself in front of a computer screen, punch in your flight number, and the screen displays just where the plane is, how high and how fast it's flying, and when it's expected to land. Should you be an aviation history buff (or even just one or the other), then the story of Maryland aviation should satisfy your curiosity. A children's play area is in the lower of the two levels and is open twenty-four hours a day. The upper level with the gift shop, cafe, and interactive displays is open from 9:00 A.M. to 9:00 P.M. There is no admission charge.

JUDY'S FAVORITE ATTRACTIONS IN CENTRAL MARYLAND

Elioak Farm	Oriole Park at Camden Yards tour
Havre de Grace Decoy Museum	U.S. Naval Academy

About fifty shops fill about 56,000 square feet of retail space throughout the airport. Some of the boutiques are a 24-Hour Flower, Discover DC (as in Washington, D.C.), Celebrate Maryland, Hudson News, the Body Shop, and more than two dozen eateries. BWI was one of the first major East Coast airports to establish a Web site for services, general information, and regional tourism information, which offers links to airline and other travel-service Web sites. The Web site, which has a terminal location map and travel tips, is www.bwiairport.com.

A shuttle bus connects the airport to the nearby Amtrak station, and limousine (van and bus) service provides door-to-door transportation to and from the airport. The airport has seen (and is still seeing) a lot of construction in the past few years. New parking structures, terminal expansion, etc., and, of course, increased security means you can't sit in your car in the driveway while awaiting inbound passengers. There is a cell phone area where you can wait until your passenger calls. However, I get around potential auto inspections, backups, and other problems by dropping my car off at **Park 'N Go** airport parking, 790 Camp Meade Road, Linthicum. I catch the shuttle to the airport, then return on it when passenger and luggage are ready to leave. I park there regularly because they'll start a dead battery, change a flat tire, and pick me up and drop me off at my car instead of at a possibly very distant bus stop. Call (410) 850–5300; www.parkngo.net.

BWI is home to the largest USO, for as many as a quarter-million military personnel and family members can use the facility annually. Why so many? Because about three-fourths of the U.S. military personnel being sent to Europe or the Middle East travel through BWI. The $1.1 million, 5,000-square-foot USO International Gateway Center has a nursery, television lounge, sleeping room, computer room, and free coffee. The lounge is located in the lower level, near baggage claim number ten, and it's open from 9:00 A.M. to 10:00 P.M. daily.

Figuratively flying in and out of BWI almost as frequently as planes and passengers has been the **stained-glass crab sculpture.** After spending four years in a warehouse, the crab, now named *Calinectes douglassi,* was returned to the airport in December 2001 and situated between Concourses C and D. Jackie and John Douglass of Shady Side, Maryland, created this 400-pound crab in 1986. It's gorgeous and almost delectable enough to eat. It certainly makes one want to go out and steam up a bushel of those savory crustaceans. For various reasons it was displayed; it wasn't; it was; etc. The crab is made of white glass from West Germany and multicolored Blenko glass from West Virginia— about 5,000 pieces of glass in all. It's 5 feet high, 10 feet wide, and 7 feet deep.

In 1996 the crab was stored during the airport's expansion. Anne Arundel County executive Janet S. Owens, reelected in 1998, said she wanted it back again. But it needed a pedestal and a $17,500 glass enclosure to prevent harm being done to it. It also needed about $5,000 in repairs to fix stress fractures sustained during the move and storage. Now we're talking about more money than the cost of the original sculpture. Maybe they could suspend it from the ceiling instead of floor-mounting it. Anyway, if you see it upon your arrival/departure at BWI, you'll know what it is.

About 3 miles from the airport is an incredible restaurant, one that receives my vote for the best crab cake in the entire state of Maryland! Others must agree because the *G&M* restaurant goes through about 500 pounds of crab meat a day! These crab cakes are about 8 ounces of backfin crab meat with almost no filler. That's large enough to take home half of it for another meal, yet you can order a crab cake platter, which has just about everything from soup to nuts, including two crab cakes. I've even taken a

buy'tilit'stimetofly

Just 2 miles from the BWI runway, off the Baltimore-Washington Parkway at Route 100, is Arundel Mills, home to about 200 outlet, off-price, and retail stores, movie theaters (twenty-four screens), a bowling alley, restaurants, and more in what the Mills Corporation calls Shoppertainment. Not exactly off the beaten path, but at least you have an explanation for all that traffic you see on your way to and from the airport. 7000 Arundel Mills Circle, Hanover; (410) 540–5100; www.arundelmillsmall.com.

cooler full of them to Los Angeles to satisfy those ex-East Coast pats living on the Left Coast. G&M has three eating areas, one with tablecloths, one in the bar where smoking is allowed, and one in the carryout area. A crab cake sandwich with a side of fries and coleslaw or potato salad is a little more than $11 as of this writing, and they now offer a shipping service. G&M is open from 11:00 A.M. to 11:00 P.M. Monday through Saturday and until 10:30 P.M. on Sunday. 804 North Hammonds Ferry Road, Linthicum; (410) 636–1777; www.gandm restaurant.com.

When airport construction was started on May 4, 1947, the airport site was known as Friendship, and many old homes and farms on the 3,200-acre tract were demolished. Only Rezin Howard Hammond's home was left standing, where it remains today at the edge of the airport. Originally known as Cedar Farm because of the cedar trees on the property, it was built in 1820 from bricks made of clay dug on the farm. It is now the ***Benson-Hammond House*** and is used by the Anne Arundel County Historical Society, whose purpose is to encourage appreciation among the general public of "the smaller centers of culture where so much of our heritage lies hidden." Within the house are a collection of dolls, a display of tokens known as "picker checks" (made of aluminum, fiberboard, and brass stamped into various shapes and used as

America's First Radar

Among the items receiving grants from the Maryland Commission for Celebration 2000 for historic preservation is America's first radar, SCR-270. The SCR (Signal Corps Radar) 270 is considered to be the first operational radar in the United States; it was manufactured in Baltimore between 1941 and 1943. It allowed scientists to bounce the first radio signals off the moon. The only extant reconstructed SCR-270 radar is at the Historical Electronics Museum in Linthicum, and the $10,000 award will go toward restoring the historically significant artifact.

currency by farmers, each of whom had his own set of checks with his initials), and a miniature replica of Angel's Store in Pasadena. The museum is open for tours on special occasions and Thursday through Saturday from 11:00 A.M. to 3:00 P.M. from spring through December. The suggested donation is $2.00 a person. The Browse and Buy Shoppe is also located at the house; it is open for the same Thursday hours and other times as volunteers are available.

Call the Benson-Hammond House, Aviation Boulevard and Andover Road, Linthicum, at (410) 768–9518 for tours and additional information.

A second Browse and Buy Shoppe is located at Jones Station, at the corner of Old Annapolis and Jones Station Roads. This late-nineteenth-century building was one of the "step-down transformer" power stations for one of the two railroads serving Annapolis. Hours at the Browse and Buy Shoppe are Tuesday through Saturday, 10:00 A.M. to 3:00 P.M.; call (410) 544–3370.

Should you be wandering this way on a Sunday afternoon and you'd like to wander about as far off the beaten path as you're likely to get in Anne Arundel County, head east on State Route 100 to *Hancock's Resolution* near the end of Bayside Beach Road and the community of Bayside Beach. Formerly a farm that encompassed more than 400 acres, this circa 1785 farmhouse and outbuildings have been restored to their nineteenth-century appearance. Because the house never had indoor plumbing or electricity, restoration was a fairly simple matter and the work was completed within a year. John Henry "Harry" Hancock was the last Hancock to live in the house and was almost ninety when he died in 1962. His main concession to his advancing years was an oil heater when he could no longer chop wood for the fireplace. There's no definitive answer regarding the meaning of "Resolution," but the assumption is there had been some family disagreements about the property ownership and when it was finally resolved, the name was given.

Included in the $250,000 restoration of the ironstone (a local sandstone) farmhouse and property are plantings of typical crops including heirloom yel-

low cucumbers (little round vegetables), heirloom beans, Thomas Jefferson's red hibiscus, yellow tomatoes,
flax, hops, the coralberry, strawberries,
and the Anne Arundel County melon.
Fruit orchards also may be planted.

Harry Hancock left no heirs, so
the Annapolis Foundation acquired the
property, and the county signed a
twenty-five-year lease in 1989. James
Morrison, president of the Friends of
Hancock's Resolution, became interested in the restoration project in the
late 1990s, and it has been through his
efforts and the work of many other
volunteers that you will be able to take
a peek at life long ago. That's proba-

bly Morrison greeting you in his Sunday-go-to-meeting clothing when you visit.

Hancock's Resolution is open on Sunday from 1:00 to 4:00 P.M. April
through October. Take Route 100 east to a left at Magothy Bridge Road. Turn
right at Fort Smallwood Road, and then right on Bayside Beach Road for about
2½ miles. The address is Bayside Beach Road, Pasadena. For more information,
call (410) 222–7317 or (410) 255–4048; www.historichancocksresolution.org.

Annapolis

Take Route 100 west to I–97 south, tool into historic Annapolis, and prepare
yourself for a treat. Annapolis is full of authentic colonial architecture; Colonial
Williamsburg in Virginia had to re-create what is already here. Annapolis is
called a "museum without walls" because of the dozens of eighteenth-century
buildings in the city, but Annapolitans are quick to point out that it is a living
museum, not an artificial one. Annapolis is Old-World charm, the United States
Naval Academy, sailboats and powerboats by the hundreds (212,435 boats were
registered in Maryland in 1999), antiques shops, taverns, and, most of all, narrow, winding, hilly, and brick-paved streets that invite walking and exploring.

Onyx, a mixed lab/chow who has been dubbed the "Honorary Mayor of
Annapolis," greets you as you enter **ARTFX**. As far as I'm concerned, ARTFX
is the most "dangerous" place (for my living space and wallet) in Annapolis,
but an essential shopping spot whenever I'm looking for a beautiful, handcrafted gift. Erik and Megan Evans opened the space in August 2001 so they

Distinctively Annapolis

Since 2000 the National Trust for Historic Preservation has designated a dozen distinctive communities through the country that offer authentic experiences. If you ever feel you could be in any town in any state, then head for one of the distinctive places. Look for interesting architecture, a sense of place and character, a dynamic downtown area, and a strong commitment to historic preservation and revitalization.

Annapolis personifies that description and then some. It was selected as a distinctive destination in 2005 because of the fifteen hundred restored historic buildings that provide the largest concentration of eighteenth-century architecture in the county. The Trust noted its water-based historical existence, the U.S. Naval Academy, and its year-round emphasis on arts and entertainment, and the fact that it is active and alive and more than a museum. It was selected from eighty nominations from forty-four states.

could sell Megan's hand-built pottery that combines white low-fire earthenware and stoneware. All of her glazes are food safe and the pottery is dishwasher, oven, and microwave safe. You may have seen her work in *American Style* magazine and on the HGTV *That's Clever* show.

About seventy noted and upcoming artists are featured, most of whom are local to the Annapolis, Baltimore, and Washington, D.C., area, covering a variety of media and prices that range from a few to many dollars. You will see pottery, jewelry, glass, sculpture, soy and beeswax candles, wood-turnings, etched leaves, jewelry boxes, photography, paintings, and wheel-thrown crab pottery. "First Sunday Arts" features demonstrations and a reception in the evening on the first Sunday of the month to introduce a featured artist. ARTFX is open Tuesday through Saturday from 11:00 A.M. to 6:00 P.M., and Sunday from 1:00 to 6:00 P.M., closed Monday. It is at 45 West Street; (410) 990–4540 or (877) 857–4540; www.artfxgallery.org.

The *Banneker-Douglass Museum* is installed in a handsome Victorian-Gothic structure that was the Mount Moriah African Methodist Episcopal Church, the first African Methodist Episcopal Church of Annapolis, serving the community from 1874 until 1971. A storm damaged the building in 1897, so it was rebuilt with its present Gothic-Revival facade, including the splendid stained-glass rose window. The building is listed with the National Register of Historic Places, as a National Historic District, and in the National Register of Historic Districts.

The museum is named for Benjamin Banneker (mathematician, scientist, astronomer, and surveyor) and Frederick Douglass (writer, journalist, civil libertarian, abolitionist, and U.S. minister and consul general to Haiti), both of whom were born and lived in Maryland. Banneker was appointed to serve on a commission that surveyed and laid out the capital. He had such a phenomenal memory that he produced, in detail, Pierre L'Enfant's plans for the District of Columbia when L'Enfant left—with the plans—before the job was finished. There are rotating displays within the Hall of National Greatness, the Gallery of Black Maritime History, the Herbert M. Frisby Hall (Frisby was a Baltimore science educator, war correspondent for African-American newspapers, and explorer who made twenty-one trips to the Arctic region and was the second black explorer to reach the North Pole), and the reference library. The museum features African-American arts and crafts, lectures, and films, all to encourage a better understanding of the contributions of African-Americans to Maryland and the United States. Today's legacy is represented by such prominent African-American artists as Josephine Gross, Gerald Hawkes, Laurence Hurst, and Hughie Lee-Smith, whose works adorn the walls of the gallery. The museum received a multimillion dollar expansion and reopened in February 2006. A new permanent exhibit, "Deep Roots, Rising Waters," explores the history of African-Americans in Maryland from the 1630s to the Civil Rights Movement.

The Banneker-Douglass Museum is located at 84 Franklin Street, Annapolis. Hours are Tuesday through Friday 10:00 A.M. to 3:00 P.M., and Saturday noon to 4:00 P.M. There is no admission charge. Call (410) 216–6180; www.marylandhistoricaltrust.bdm.

trivia

Each of these four signers of the Declaration of Independence, Charles Carroll, Samuel Chase, William Paca, and Thomas Stone, had homes in Annapolis. Three of the homes are still open to the public. William Paca's house and gardens is on the National Historic Landmark list and is a huge Georgian mansion at 186 Prince George Street; (410) 990–4538 or (800) 603–2040. Charles Carroll, the only Catholic to sign the Declaration, was one of the wealthiest men in Colonial America. His home, with eighteenth-century terraced gardens, is a restoration in progress, and overlooks Spa Creek; 107 Duke of Gloucester; (410) 269–1737; http://charlescarrollhouse.com. Samuel Chase built the Chase Lloyd House in 1769 at 22 Maryland Avenue; (410) 263–2723.

trivia

Thanks to the $65.9 million in tourism tax revenue, Anne Arundel County taxpayers pay about $335 less in additional taxes, according to a study released in November 2006. Expressed another way, the county school system receives nearly $300 per student. Tourism accounts for 12 percent of the county's employment.

JANUARY

Maryland State Police Polar Bear Plunge,
Sandy Point State Park,
(410) 789–6677,
www.somd.org

FEBRUARY

Irish Evening of Music and Poetry,
Columbia,
(410) 772–4568,
www.hocopolitso.org

MARCH

Antique Bottle Show and Sale,
Essex Campus,
(410) 531–9459,
www.baltimorebottleclub.org

Baltimore Area Woodcarving Show,
Catonsville,
(410) 887–0900

Downtown Bel Air Chocolate Festival,
Bel Air,
(410) 638–1023,
www.downtownbelair.com

Greater Baltimore–Washington Marble Show,
Perry Hall,
(410) 887–5187

Maple Sugarin' Festival,
Westminster,
(410) 848–9040

Maryland Day,
Annapolis,
(410) 990–4539,
www.annapolis.org

St. Patrick's Parade,
Baltimore,
(410) 837–0685

APRIL

Decoy, Wildlife Art, and Sportsman Festival,
Havre de Grace,
(410) 939–3739
www.decoymuseum.com

My Lady's Manor Steeplechase Races,
Monkton,
(410) 557–9466,
www.ladewgardens.com

Patuxent Cleanup,
various towns,
(301) 349–8200, ext. 6,
www.cleanpatuxent.org

Skipjack *Martha Lewis* Bull and Oyster Roast,
(410) 939–4078,
www.skipjackmarthalewis.org

MAY

Baltimore City's Rite of Spring,
Baltimore,
(410) 323–0022,
www.flowermart.org

Chesapeake Bay Bridge Walk,
Annapolis,
(877) BAYSPAN,
www.mdta.state.md.us

Columbia Triathlon,
Ellicott City,
(410) 964–1246,
www.tricolumbia.org

Decoy and Wildlife Art Festival,
Havre de Grace,
(410) 939–3739
www.decoymuseum.com

Delaware Valley Quilt Show,
North East,
(302) 368–8626,
www.dca.net//ladybugsquilt

Flower and Jazz Festival,
Westminster,
(410) 848–9393

Flower and Plant Market,
Union Mills,
(410) 848–2288,
www.carr.org/tourism/index.htm

German-American Festival,
Jessup,
(301) 577–6488,
www.geocities.com/agas_dc

Ladew Plant Sale,
Monkton,
(410) 557–9466

Lithuanian Festival,
Catonsville,
(410) 646–0261

Preakness Race,
Baltimore,
(410) 542–9400

JUNE

Charles Village Garden Walk,
Baltimore,
(410) 243–5033,
www.charlesvillage.net

Columbia Festival of the Arts,
Columbia,
(410) 715–3044,
www.columbiafestival.com

HonFest,
Baltimore,
(410) 243–1230

Latinofest,
Patterson Park, Baltimore,
(410) 783–5404,
www.latinofest.org

Maryland Rose Show,
Baltimore,
(410) 367–2217

Strawberry Festival,
Sykesville,
(410) 386–3880,
http://ccgov.carr.org/farm

JULY

**Baltimore Symphony Orchestra
Fourth of July Celebration,**
Hunt Valley,
(410) 783–8000

Carroll County 4-H and FFA Fair,
Westminster,
(410) 848–3247,
www.carrollcountyfair.com

Catonsville's July Fourth Celebration,
Catonsville,
(410) 744–7042

Cecil County Fair,
Fair Hill,
(410) 392–3440,
www.cecilcountyfair.org

Harborplace's Birthday Celebration,
Baltimore,
(800) HARBOR–1

Harford County Fair,
Bel Air,
(410) 838–8663,
www.farmfair.org

AUGUST

Annapolis Rotary Crab Feast,
Navy–Marine Corps Memorial Stadium,
Annapolis,
(410) 263–2448

(continued on next page)

Baltimore Pow Wow,
Patterson Park, Baltimore,
(410) 675–3535,
www.baic.org

Dutch Picnic Festival,
Westminster,
(410) 847–0344,
www.trinitywired.org

Hart's Annual Peach Festival,
North East,
(410) 287–2650

Havre de Grace Art Show,
Havre de Grace,
(410) 939–9342

Havre de Grace Seafood Festival,
Havre de Grace,
(410) 939–1525

Howard County Fair,
West Friendship,
(410) 442–1022,
www.howardcountyfair.com

Iron Girl Columbia Women's Triathlon,
Ellicott City,
(410) 964–1246,
www.tricolumbia.org

Maryland Renaissance Festival,
Annapolis,
(410) 266–7304,
(410) 573–1508,
www.rennfest.com

Maryland Renaissance Festival,
Crownsville,
(410) 266–7304,
www.rennfest.com

Maryland State Fair,
Timonium,
(410) 252–0200,
www.marylandstatefair.com

Old-Fashioned Corn Roast Festival,
Union Mills,
(410) 848–2288,
http://tourism.carr.org/unionmil.htm

Peach Festival,
Westminster,
(410) 848–7748

SEPTEMBER

Anne Arundel County Fair,
Crownsville,
(410) 923–3400

Baltimore Book Festival,
Baltimore City,
(410) 752–8632,
www.promotionandarts.com

Baltimore Crab and Beer Festival,
Fells Point,
(800) 830–3976,
www.mdcrabfest.com

Catonsville Arts and Crafts Festival,
Catonsville,
(410) 719–9609,
www.catonsville.org

Duck Fair,
Havre de Grace,
(410) 939–3739,
www.decoymuseum.com

Howard County Farm Heritage Days,
West Friendship,
(410) 631–2569,
www.farmheritage.org

Living American Flag Program,
Fort McHenry,
Baltimore,
(410) 563–3524,
www.flagday.org

Maryland Seafood Festival,
Sandy Point State Park,
Annapolis,
(410) 266–3113,
www.mdseafoodfestival.com

Maryland Wine Festival,
Westminster,
(410) 386–3880,
(800) 654–4645,
http://ccgov.carr.org/farm

New Market Days,
New Market,
(301) 865–5544,
www.nmdays.com

Smallwood Festival,
Westminster,
(410) 848–8254,
www.deerparklionsclub.org

OCTOBER

**Great Chesapeake Bay
Schooner Race,**
Baltimore,
(757) 393–2224,
www.southernbranch.com/schoonerrace

Scottish Highland Games,
Crownsville,
(410) 849–2849,
www.aasfi.org

United States Powerboat Show,
Annapolis,
(410) 268–8828,
www.usboat.com

United States Sailboat Show,
Annapolis,
(410) 268–8828,
www.usboat.com

NOVEMBER

Lights on the Bay,
Annapolis,
(410) 260–3161

DECEMBER

Eastport Yacht Club Lights Parade,
Annapolis,
(410) 263–0415,
www.eastportyc.org

First Night Annapolis,
Annapolis,
(410) 268–8553,
www.firstnightannapolis.org

Maryland Wine Festival,
(800) 654–4645,
www.carrollcountyfarmmuseum.org

Dem Bones, Dem Bones

In July 1989 some fifteen small, brittle bones, carefully wrapped in yellowed paper, were gently placed in a golden urn and laid to rest in a shady cemetery plot near St. Mary's Church in Annapolis. In mid-1987 the Reverend John Murray of St. Mary's had found these remains of St. Justin, who was beheaded at the age of twenty-six in the second century A.D. According to Murray, it is not unusual for churches in Europe to have special tombs containing the relics of saints or martyrs, but few churches in the United States can claim such items because the country is so young. St. Justin's remains arrived in Baltimore in 1873 so the Reverend Joseph Wissel could protect them while Italy was in the middle of a political upheaval. The Reverend Wissel and those who followed him displayed them prominently, but during the 1960s the church was renovated and the remains were placed in a box in a church safe. Call (410) 263–2396 for additional information.

There are many interesting things to see at the **U.S. Naval Academy.** Start with a visit to the **Armel-Leftwich Visitor Center** (just inside and to the right of Gate 1 off King George Street), where you'll see a movie (*To Lead and To Serve*) and displays about life as a midshipman. You can then explore on your own or take a seventy-minute guided tour. The hours of operation vary according to the day and the season, but the noon tour departs at 11:45 to see the Noon Meal Formation, weather permitting. The center is open from 9:00 A.M. to 5:00 P.M. March through November, and 9:00 A.M. to 4:00 P.M. the rest of the year. It is closed Thanksgiving, Christmas, and New Year's Day. Call (410) 263–6933 or log on to www.usnavyonline.com for more information. *NOTE:* Unless you have Department of Defense identification, you must park off the Academy grounds (handicapped tags excepted). All visitors sixteen and older must have a photo ID. Check the security requirements at www.USNA.edu.

A short walk from the visitor center, along the seawall, is the foremast of the USS *Maine,* still misshapen from the mysterious explosion in Havana Harbor on February 15, 1898. The mast was recovered on October 6, 1910, and erected along the Academy Seawall at Trident Point on May 5, 1913.

At the site of the Noon Meal Formation is the Tecumseh Statue (in front of Bancroft Hall), a bronze replica of the wooden figurehead that graced the USS *Delaware.* It is frequently decorated by midshipmen as a symbol of victory and passed exams. Bancroft Hall Dormitory, 52 King George Street, houses the *entire* 4,000-member brigade and (depending on who you consult) is either *the* largest dormitory in the world, or only one of the largest. Take a peek around the building, check out one of the model rooms, and delight in the murals and artworks that decorate the public areas.

One of the most fascinating exhibits in Annapolis is the display of model ships at the ***U.S. Naval Academy Museum*** on the ground floor of Preble Hall, housed in the Class of 1951 Gallery. My mind is totally boggled every time I visit this exhibit. In the collection are ship models from about the time the pilgrims landed in America to just after the War of 1812. The big (100-gun) ships took one person from four to six years to build, plus another year for the rigging. More likely than one person doing all the work, there would have been a master model maker supervising a crew of workers or apprentices, thus speeding up the process. You'll also want to see Bone Ships, which were crafted by prisoners of war on frigates from meat bones. They are intricate and accurate portrayals of the fighting ships of the times.

The main floor of the museum houses your typical 30,000-item collection of naval history, including class rings of all the graduating classes of the academy, silverware from naval vessels, flags, uniforms, medals, weapons, navigational instruments, documents, and the stories of several naval heros, including John Paul Jones. The Naval Academy Museum provides a valuable and convenient reference source for studying naval history. Proceeds of the museum's massive fund-raising drive will be used to modernize the exhibits and the exhibit area.

The museum, in Preble Hall, 118 Maryland Avenue, is open Monday through Saturday from 9:00 A.M. to 5:00 P.M., and Sunday from 11:00 A.M. to 5:00 P.M. It is closed on Thanksgiving, Christmas, and New Year's Day. There is no admission charge. Call (410) 293–2108 or log onto www.usna.edu/museum for details.

The Governor as Head of the Church

Yeah, forget about this separation of church and state thing. According to old Maryland law, the governor is the head of the Episcopal Church in Maryland. This was also true when Marvin Mandel, of Jewish background, was elected to the state's highest position (1969–1979). Mandel says he received a letter from St. Anne's (the church at Church Circle) very early in his gubernatorial days asking for a contribution—as head of the church, of course. He agreed, with the request that he be allowed to present the sermon at an upcoming church service. The church agreed. The last time I talked to Mandel, he no longer remembered how much he donated or what the topic of his sermon was.

For almost two years the church (the third on this site) was invaded by plumbers, woodworkers, and other crafters working on a multimillion-dollar renovation. Expansion wasn't possible because of its historic background and a number of unmarked graves on the property. Among the treasures in the church is a Tiffany window (south wall) depicting Anne instructing Mary at her knee. 199 Duke of Gloucester Street; (410) 267–9333; www.stannes-annapolis.org.

Maynard-Burgess House

In May 2000 the Maryland Commission for Celebration 2000 awarded several "Save Maryland's Treasures" grants for historic preservation. One of the properties that received such a grant, to the tune of $22,500, is the Maynard-Burgess House in the historic district of Annapolis. This was the home of two successive African-American families from 1847 to 1900, and the structure shows the lives of free blacks in the 1800s. The funds will go toward the rehabilitation of the interior of the Maynard-Burgess House as a museum.

Also on the ground floor is the *U.S. Naval Institute and Bookstore* for books and other naval-related items. The institute has 100,000 members and advances scientific and literary knowledge of the sea services. It publishes *Proceedings* and *Naval History* magazines, has published more than 400 books, and has a collection of more than 450,000 historic photographs. The store, at 118 Maryland Avenue, is open Monday through Saturday from 9:00 A.M. to 5:00 P.M., and Sunday from 11:00 A.M. to 5:00 P.M. (410) 295–3754 or (800) 233–8764.

The basement of the *Naval Academy chapel* is one of those "gee, I didn't know that" spots that I love to take visitors to, because that's where the crypt of Revolutionary War hero John Paul Jones is located. A little history and some personal effects complete this final resting place.

A new oak organ console, a gift of the Naval Academy graduating class of 1951, now rings out in the chapel. With five manual keyboards, a pedal board, 520 draw knots, fifty-three coupler tabs, 171 thumb pistons, and forty-seven foot controls, it took the R.A. Colby Inc. Company of Johnson City more than one thousand hours to build. It's said to be the largest organ of its type and unique because of its detail. Oh, and the price tag ran between $700,000 and $800,000.

Three Coins in the Fountain

No, it's not the famed Roman Trevi Fountain, just a decorative three-tiered bronze item on the Government House lawn. Hilda May Snoops, a longtime companion of former governor William Donald Schaefer, commissioned it in 1990. Showing crabs, oysters, corn, terrapins, and tobacco leaves, the fountain was turned off by Parris Glendening (Schaefer's successor) as a water-conservation effort even though it's a recirculating operation. Once Glendening was out of office, the fountain was turned on again.

Upstairs the chapel is pretty awesome as well, with Tiffany studio–designed stained-glass windows behind the altar and elsewhere. Built on the highest point of ground at the academy (or "in the Yard"), the chapel cornerstone was laid in 1904 by Admiral Dewey. When you see television coverage of newly married couples leaving a chapel under raised swords, this is the chapel they're exiting. Call the United States Naval Academy Grounds at (410) 263–6933 or log on to www.usna.edu/chaplains for more information.

The skipjack is the symbol of the Chesapeake Bay waterman. These boats were developed in the 1890s, and they are the last surviving commercial sailing fleet in the United States. The oyster-dredging boats have become an endangered species, as their number has dwindled from roughly 1,500 a century ago to about eighty on the water in 1958. There are only three dozen in working condition now.

Annapolis is called America's Sailing Capital for a reason—people are always sailing. Yes, even during the winter. The ***Frostbite Sailing Series*** is for those who don't mind donning tons of cold-weather gear as long as the wind can fill a sail. About seventy sailboats gather at the mouth of the Severn River near the Naval Academy seawall every Sunday afternoon (there is a break for the holidays) and compete from 1:00 P.M. until sunset. Regulations require a minimum number of sailors and no spinnakers. If you'd like to participate, stop by the Annapolis Yacht Club, 2 Compromise Street, about noon, to join the fun; (410) 263–9279 or (410) 269–0779; www.annapolisyc.com.

Ship of State

Some people are just luckier than others, and Robert F. Sumrall has to be among the luckiest of the lucky, for his occupation is playing with model ships. Sumrall was the curator charged with repairing and maintaining the U.S. Naval Academy's fleet of 225 little ships, some of them more than 300 years old (he retired in August 2006). Sumrall built his first model when he was six and went on to be a naval architect, author, historian, model builder, and one of the most highly regarded authorities on ship models and model construction. Sumrall has built models of significant and famous Maryland ships, including the *Dolphin,* the *Pride of Baltimore,* the *J.T. Leonard* (a unique oyster dredger), and the skipjack *Minnie V.* Most of the work Sumrall did for the academy museum was in the realm of repair, maintenance, and restoration. He also has done an interpretive model of the *Arizona* wreck for the National Park Service memorial at Pearl Harbor, and he is doing another of the Japanese flagship *Akagi*. Private collections in Coronado, Virginia Beach, and New York, and a gallery in Old Town Alexandria hold his battleship *Wisconsin* and several destroyers.

Long Live the King

The Maryland Inn, located on Church Circle, was constructed by Thomas Hyde in 1772 and has operated continuously as an inn since the late eighteenth century. This triangular piece of land, called the "drummer's lot," was where the town drummer, or crier, told of the day's news in the early eighteenth century. The inn was the first in Annapolis, and hidden off a back wall in the basement is a bricked entrance to a tunnel that goes to the State House. The city's second Starbucks now occupies the space. The Maryland Inn is at 16 Church Circle, Annapolis. Call (410) 263–2641 or (800) 847–8882; www.historicinnsofannapolis.com.

The National Sailing Hall of Fame and Museum opened during the 2006 Volvo Ocean Race in May 2006 and resides in a temporary setting at the pier end of City Dock. Dedicated to preserving the history of sport sailing and its impact on our culture, it honors those who have made outstanding contributions to the sport and hopes to inspire and encourage junior sailing development. The exhibit is open daily from 10:00 A.M. to 5:00 P.M.; (410) 295–3022 or (877) 295–3022; www.nationalsailinghalloffame.org.

While at Annapolis Dock, stop by to see the ***Alex Haley statue,*** dedicated in December 1999. The life-size statue stands near the spot where the author's ancestor Kunte Kinte was brought ashore from a slave ship. Ed Dwight, a former astronaut, was the sculptor. You may also have seen his *Jazz: An American Art Form* series of seventy bronzes depicting famous jazz musicians; he is also responsible for creating the Black Patriots Memorial in Washington, D.C.

Another statue, this one of former Maryland state comptroller ***Louis L. Goldstein,*** was installed between the Goldstein Treasury Building and the Income Tax Building in Annapolis in mid-2000. Goldstein died in 1998 at the age of eighty-five after six decades of public service and was well-known for his "God bless y'all real good." Sculptor Jay Hall Carpenter, chosen from nearly two dozen artists who submitted proposals, is best known for his twenty-two years at the Washington National Cathedral. Carpenter never met Goldstein, but he studied photographs and videos to capture the comptroller's movements, expressions, and gestures.

The ***Kunta Kinte–Alex Haley Memorial*** site at the City Dock now has a 100-foot Story Wall, an 18-foot Compass Rose, and an Alex Haley sculpture commemorating the 1767 arrival of Kunta Kinte on the slave ship, *Lord Ligonier.* Haley recaptured this moment and others in his Pulitzer Prize–winning book, *Roots,* which was then made into the Emmy Award–winning television

Aris T. Allen

As you drive around Annapolis, you may notice Aris T. Allen (1910–1991) Boulevard (State Route 665). Allen was president of his class at Howard University while in medical school there, becoming a physician and flight surgeon during the Korean conflict in the early 1950s. He served in the Maryland House of Delegates and then the state Senate, and was the first African-American chair of the state Republican party. As a delegate to the Republican National Convention he served as the secretary of the convention, the person who calls the roll of states for voting. He also ran for lieutenant governor with former U.S. Senator J. Glenn Beall Jr. You can find a statue of Allen near the intersection of Forest Drive, Chinquapin Round Road, and Aris T. Allen Boulevard in Annapolis.

series of the same name. The Story Wall has text from Haley's book. Call (410) 841–6920; www.kuntakinte.com.

Perhaps it's fitting that the **Annapolis Maritime Museum,** in Eastport, succumbed to Hurricane Isabel in September 2003. It took two years of hard work to restore the Barge House. There's an exhibit about the **Thomas Point Shoal Lighthouse** with a documentary entitled *Legacy of the Light.* An Eastport Walking Tour, in person or online, is available that describes the historical importance of this area. The museum is at 723 Second Street; (410) 295–0104; www.annapolismaritimemuseum.org.

Maritime Republic of Eastport

Across Spa Creek from downtown Annapolis is Eastport, originally home to the close-knit community of construction workers who built the Naval Academy. Lately it has become much more gentrified, but as of a singular moment in January 1998, the cohesion became palpable again. For that's when the Annapolis town fathers closed the Spa Creek bridge for three weeks for much needed repairs. That didn't totally isolate the residents of Eastport; they could get back and forth through a slightly more circuitous route, but they were concerned that "outsiders" would not take the effort to frequent the local businesses. A group of Eastporters decided it was time to promote their town, so they staged a mock secession from Annapolis and renamed their community the Maritime Republic of Eastport (aka MRE). They created T-shirts and sponsored a half-mile race, and other festivities to make sure people remembered to find their way over there. Imagine their pleasure when business actually increased during the three-week period! Since then, they've been celebrating and reaffirming the anniversary of their secession, continuing the half-mile race (started by a cannon and rifle shots), a parade, a dog show, and more.

Besides quaint shops, sailing, and friendly people, Annapolis is steeped in history and **History Quest** serves as an orientation center with a film and exhibits so you can follow the city's history from the 1700s to current times. The facility opened in April 2006 and lets you explore the city known as the museum without walls before you start your explorations. Located near the City Dock, at 99 Main Street, it's open daily from 9:00 A.M. to 7:00 P.M.; (410) 267–6656; www.annapolis.org/history_center.html.

Annapolis has always been a vital area for commerce and trade, particularly when it comes to importing and exporting goods. But it played one of its most unusual commercial roles in 1862, when it became the major depot in the East for holding exchanged prisoners of war. Prisoners were held here until their back pay (earned during their incarceration) could be given to them. At first they were camped at St. John's College, but the eight small, wooden barracks were inadequate for groups as large as 6,000 men at one time. Two hundred fifty acres of farmland outside Annapolis were rented from Charles S. and Ann Rebecca Welch for $125 per month, and barracks and other buildings were constructed there. The forty-four barracks and all other buildings were sold at auction some time after 1865, when all the prisoners had been released. All that remains of this mustering place for Union prisoners, called Camp Parole, is the name of the town, **Parole,** on the western side of Annapolis.

Whether by land or sea, when you're near Annapolis you may as well take a drive or sea cruise over to **Cantler's,** noted for Jimmie Cantler, hospitality, crabs all year, and delicious food since the 1970s. The crab-cake and soft-shell crab sandwiches are superb. Cantler's is located at 458 Forest Beach Road, Annapolis. Call (410) 757–1311 for directions or log onto www.cantlers.com.

An unofficial declaration of spring's arrival is the annual **Chesapeake Bay Bridge Walk Day,** held on the first Sunday in May. The walk was first held in 1975 after a Towson, Maryland, scout leader who noticed that one span was closed for construction suggested one span could be closed for a daylong walk. An estimated 50,000 pedestrians, as well as people in wheelchairs and on crutches, cross the eastbound lanes of the bridge, and the only automobiles and trucks permitted are official vehicles and media trucks. Jogging, running, skateboarding, biking, and pets (except Seeing Eye dogs) are prohibited; an early morning race has been established for those who want to speed across the bridge instead of spending about ninety minutes walking and investigating various expansion joints, girder construction, architectural design, and engineering and assembly facets. Pedestrians normally are not allowed on the 4⅓-mile structure connecting the Annapolis area to the large spit of land known as the Eastern Shore. Blue waters lap innocuously about 185 feet below the twin spans of the bridge, also known as the William Preston Lane Jr. Memorial

Bridge. Parking lots in Annapolis, at Anne Arundel Community College, and also on the Eastern Shore start filling up at 8:00 A.M. Buses start taking walkers to the east side at 9:00 A.M. There is no charge for parking, but there is a $1.00 charge for the bus. Call (410) 228–8405 or (877) BAYSPAN, or visit www.mdta .state.md.us for information.

Capt. Salem Avery was a waterman of the 1860s, and to the delight of the members of the Shady Side Rural Heritage Society, his home on the banks of the West River became available to them to use as a museum. The **Captain Salem Avery House** opened its doors in 1989 as a museum to "protect, document, and illustrate the history and traditions" of Shady Side. The society members are particularly pleased that they were able to obtain some of the original Avery furniture from the owners of the house. They're also pleased as punch (or should that be grog?) that the museum was named to the National Register of Historic Places in December 2005. The Captain Salem Avery House is located at 1418 East West Shady Side Road, Shady Side. The house is open by appointment and on Sunday from 1:00 to 4:00 P.M., March through December. There is no admission fee. Call (410) 867–4486 for additional information. The Web site is www.averyhouse.org.

Check out the **Smithsonian Environmental Research Center** in Edgewater for a slew of family-oriented activities, from toddler to 50 uppers and 60 uppers and beyond. An outreach program started in 2006 offers hands-on experiments, projects for home-schoolers, lunchtime speakers' series, and more at the three-thousand-acre science center. SERC is open Monday through Saturday from 9:00 A.M. to 4:30 P.M.; 647 Contees Wharf Road, Edgewater; (440) 482–2200; www.serc.si.edu/public_programs.

The new multimillion-dollar **Historic London Town and Gardens Visitor Center** in Edgewater opened in spring 2006. It's an orientation center, an educational facility for interpreting on-site archaeological finds, and a museum. The center, a large part of which is underground, is an excellent example of a re-adaptive use of an old wastewater treatment plant. Take time to wander through the eight-acre woodland garden; (410) 222–1919; www.historiclondon town.org.

For those who love to spoil a good walk by playing golf, and if you'd love to try some of those killer holes where the championship tourneys are played, then make a stop at **Renditions Golf Course,** in Davidsonville. This is a course with hole designs taken from other courses. So, holes 6, 7, and 8 are modeled after Augusta National holes 11, 12, and 13. Hole 13 is the number 17 from TPC at Sawgrass. And, number 16 is number 16 from Shinnecock Hills.

Rates, including greens fee, cart fee, and unlimited range use prior to your round, range from $49 after 3:00 P.M. on weekdays to $89 on weekends and holidays (plus 10 percent tax). If you haven't brought your clubs with you, you can rent Callaway Steelhead clubs for $35 per set. When you're finished (or before you start), there's a 10,000-square-foot clubhouse, restaurant and bar, golf shop (with large photographs of Bobby Jones, Gene Sarazen, Ben Hogan, Jack Nicklaus, and Tiger Woods, each holding one of golf's grand trophies), and much more.

Renditions is located at 1380 West Central Avenue (State Route 214), Davidsonville. Call (888) 451–4144 or (410) 798–9798 for more information and tee times. Or visit its Web site at www.renditionsgolf.com.

For additional information about Anne Arundel County, write to the Annapolis and Anne Arundel County Conference and Visitors Bureau, 26 West Street, Annapolis 21401. Call (410) 280–0445 or log on to www.visit-annapolis.org.

Baltimore City

Now, zip on back to I–97 and head north to Baltimore. It's a slight left zig (off a right-hand ramp) to the beltway (Interstate 695) to the west, and then a hop north onto the Baltimore–Washington Parkway (which becomes Russell Street), and there you are.

As you enter, on your left you'll see the Lee Electrical building, at 600 West Hamburg Street, near Camden Yards, and on it a **_Wyland whale painting,_** which former mayor Kurt L. Schmoke dedicated in 1993. The mural is of extinct Atlantic gray whales, and it's 260 feet long by 20 feet high. Wyland was born in 1956 in Detroit, and it's said he created his first painting, of dinosaurs, at the age of four. He first saw a whale a decade later, and began painting whales and dolphins in 1972. Wyland painted his first whale mural in 1981 in Laguna Beach, California.

Almost across the street is the **_M&T Bank Stadium,_** home of the Ravens football team, and not far away is **_Oriole Park at Camden Yards,_** where the Baltimore Orioles baseball team nests for home games. The O's management has tried to solve the problem of scalped tickets by having a scalp-free zone where people who have tickets to sell meet with people who want to buy tickets, with the stipulation that the sellers can't charge more than face value. The scalp-free zone is wonderful, and other teams should adopt this practice.

Make a reservation to take the approximately ninety-minute walking tour of the stadium. They're given Monday through Saturday at 11:00 A.M., 1:00 and 2:00 P.M., and Sunday at 12:30, 1:00, 2:00, and 3:00 P.M., except when there's a day game or other day event scheduled. As you take the tour, you'll hear that the warehouse, which houses the Orioles offices, souvenir shop, reception areas, and Camden Club, is the longest brick building east of the Mississippi (it's 1,016 feet long by 51 feet wide). The tour guide may also tell you that the warehouse is longer than the Empire State Building is tall. The validity of that statement depends on whether you count antennas. At the very least, this is a long building. Should your guide not tell you, ask about the unbreakable windows and how many home-run balls have hit the building on the fly (to give you a clue, none in regulation play). As

trivia

The Ravens stadium, home to the NFL Baltimore Ravens, made its theatrical debut in 2000 as Nextel Stadium, the home field of the Washington Sentinels, in the movie *The Replacements.* Those who've seen the film are sure to recognize the distinctive purple seating.

you walk around the stadium, you'll see the townhomes or row houses across the street that were part of an urban revitalization project. It's said they went for $1.00 a piece and were overpriced. The stipulation, of course, was the buyer had to renovate and was obligated to a residency requirement. The tour takes you to a party room, a sky suite, the press room, some of the 25 miles (length depending on your tour guide) of beer pipe for draft brews (so they don't have to schlep kegs around the stadium, clean up, have refrigeration for the kegs at each refreshment stand, and so on). The tour, as of 2006, costs $7.00 and is well worth it. Located at 333 Camden Street, Baltimore; (410) 547–6234; www.theorioles.com.

For years the old Camden Yard station (at the north end of the warehouse) stood as a silent reminder of Baltimore's railroad history. Now it's open and welcomes you. On the ground floor you'll find the ***Sports Legends at Camden Yards.*** There are more than 10,000 artifacts covering the Orioles, the Baltimore Colts and Johnny Unitas, the Negro Leagues in Baltimore, Maryland college sports, the Baltimore Ravens, and the Maryland Athletic Hall of Fame. The Museum is open daily from 10:00 A.M. to 6:00 P.M. (7:30 on baseball game days) from April through October, and Tuesday through Sunday from 10:00 A.M. to 5:00 P.M. from November through March. The admission fee is $10.00 for adults, $8.00 for seniors, and $6.50 for children. A combination ticket to the Sports Legends and Babe Ruth Birthplace is $14.00 for adults, $11.00 for seniors, and $9.00 for children; 301 West Camden Street; (410) 727–1539; www.sportslegendsatcamdenyards.com.

Upstairs in the old station is ***Geppi's Entertainment Museum.*** Dedicated to the art of illustration, comic books, and Americana, it is sure to be one of those places that make you think (or say), "I had one of those." Or, maybe bring back memories of "It's Howdy Doody Time." Now, singing this ditty at home might bring looks of disbelief, but at GEM, you can show those scoffers what or who Howdy Doody was, and throw in Betty Boop, Captain America, Captain Video, and other relics that have contributed so much to our pop culture. Steve

Geppi, born in the Little Italy section of Baltimore, became the world's largest distributor of English-language comic books, all from his love of comic books as a child. He turned another childhood love, baseball, into reality when he became part of the local ownership of the Baltimore Orioles in 1993. It's on the second floor of the Camden Station, above Sports Legends at Camden Yards. GEM is open daily from 10:00 A.M. to 6:00 P.M. (call for evening hours) from April through October, and Tuesday through Sunday from 10:00 A.M. to 5:00 P.M. November through March. Admission is $10.00 for adults, $9.00 for seniors, and $7.00 for students; 301 West Camden Street; (410) 625–7060; www.geppismuseum.com.

According to *American Style* magazine Baltimore is the eleventh best big city art spot, citing the Baltimore Museum of Art, American Visionary Art Museum (www.avam.org), Walters Art Museum (www.thewalters.com), Contemporary Museum (www.contemporary.org), Craig Flinner Gallery (www .flinnergallery.com), and the C. Grimaldis Gallery (www.cgrimaldisgallery .com). Adding to that appeal is the policy change in 2005 that eliminated an admission fee charged for the BMA and the Walters.

Besides the delectable art attractions at BMA, there's a 200-seat theater (where Rob Hatch screened the winning entries in the 2006 48-Hour Film Project competition) and *Gertrude's,* with cuisine by noted cookbook author and TV show host John Shields. Along with outdoor dining, there's a $10 menu on Tuesday evenings. Check the children's menu and remember BMA members receive a 10 percent discount off a minimum $5.00 purchase. The museum is closed Monday and Tuesday; 10 Art Museum Drive; (410) 573–1700; www.artbma.org.

A spectacular way to start your Baltimore visit is at the *Top of the World observation deck and museum.* On a clear day you will see an eye-opening, five-sided panoramic view of the city, its harbor, and beyond from the twenty-seventh floor of the tallest pentagonal building west of Houston, designed by I. M. Pei. Exhibits, films, and audiovisual material will familiarize you with Bal-

Fifteen Minutes of Warhol

The Baltimore Museum of Art has the second largest collection of Andy Warhol's work on permanent display, located in the $10 million wing that opened in 1994. Included in the display are several pieces that had never been on permanent public exhibit, including *Brillo Box, Del Monte Box,* and gold *Jackie.* The New Wing for Modern Art has an unusual design allowing the display of the large Warhol works. Instead of doors in the middle of each exhibit room, the "doors" are located at the corners, normally dead areas in an exhibit space. This also allows visitors a chance to look into the other three connecting galleries. An energy-saving cooling system creates big sheets of ice overnight when energy costs are low, which then are dropped into an underground pool during the day to sustain the seventy-degree temperature desired in the building. The museum is located at 10 Art Museum Drive; (443) 573–1700; www.artbma.org. *NOTE:* As of October 2006 the BMA no longer charges an admission fee.

timore's past, present, and future. The observation deck is open from 10:00 A.M. to 9:00 P.M. daily from Memorial Day through Labor Day, and from 10:00 A.M. to 6:00 P.M. Wednesday through Sunday September through May. Admission is $5.00 for adults, $4.00 for seniors, and $2.00 for children ages three through twelve. The phone number is (410) 837–8439; www.bop.org/topworld/index .html.

Much of Baltimore revolves around the Inner Harbor, where the World Trade Center is. Here you'll find a carousel, the festival marketplace with its eateries and boutiques, paddle- or pedal boats, the Maryland Science Center, the aquarium, and a submarine, the USS *Torsk.* The 311-foot black submarine (with

Charming, Just Charming

Foodies who can't get enough of Duff Goldman, cake baker extraordinaire, owner of **Charm City Cakes,** host of *Ace of Cakes* on the Food Network, and food contest competitor, can bow to the King as they drive by his place. This is not a walk-in storefront bakery, but a place that takes special orders as much as a year in advance. An unexpected drop-in is not welcome, although you might try calling to see if you can stop by to watch Duff and his genius team at work. He might even welcome your scout troop or other group of visitors. Charm City is located at 123 West 27th Street; (410) 235–9229; www.charmcitycakes.com. In the second season of *Ace of Cakes,* Goldman makes a treadmill cake for the twentieth anniversary of SportFit, a fitness center in Bowie (south of Baltimore via I–97 and State Route 3) owned by his father, Morrie Goldman.

trivia

Faidley's Seafood in Baltimore's Lexington Market reportedly shipped 2,800 orders of its famous crab cakes, each handmade by Nancy Faidley Devine, during Christmas week of 2003. Started in 1886 by John W. Faidley Sr. and now operated by descendants Bill and Nancy Devine, Faidley's is at 203 North Paca; (410) 727–4898; http://faidleyscrabcakes.com.

a shark's-tooth grin at one end) sits by the aquarium. Under the command of Bafford E. Lewellen, the sub sank two small Japanese ships on August 14, 1945. The Japanese surrendered the next day, so the *Torsk* sank the last ships of World War II. Each year some 100,000 people tour the *Torsk*, located at Pier 3, East Pratt Street, Baltimore. Call (410) 396–3453 or visit www.uss torsk.org. Admission is $8.00 for adults, $6.00 for seniors, and $4.00 for children six to fourteen years of age.

Almost a State Cookie

Maryland doesn't have a state cookie—yet. But some members of the legislature are hoping to have the apple oatmeal cookie so honored. So far the measure has not succeeded.

Here's the recipe from the Admiral Fell Inn's famous "Milowe" cookie (named for one of the first ghosts at the Inn):

Ingredients:

3 pounds butter
1 quart brown sugar
4½ cups sugar
4 eggs
2 tablespoons vanilla extract

12 cups rolled oats
6 cups flour
3 teaspoons kosher salt
3 tablespoons baking soda
6 cups diced, skinless dried apples

Yields approximately 10 dozen cookies.

Preparation:

Preheat oven to 350 degrees.
In mixer, cream butter until fluffy. Add both kinds of sugar to butter and blend together until light and fluffy. Incorporate eggs. Add vanilla extract and mix well.
In a bowl, stir together oats, flour, salt, and baking soda. Slowly add oat mixture to ingredients in mixer and stir slowly until combined. Add apples and mix slowly until combined. Drop by tablespoon onto baking sheet, leaving at least 2 inches between cookies. Bake about 8 to 10 minutes, or until slightly crispy around the edges.
Let cool on wire racks and store in airtight containers.
Option: sprinkle powdered sugar on cooled cookies.

The Admiral Fell Inn; 888 South Broadway; Historic Fell's Point; Baltimore; (410) 522–7377; www.harbormagic.com.

On That Note

The eponymously named *Roy's Restaurant,* one of Roy Yamaguchi's Hawaiian fusion eateries, is a few blocks from the active Inner Harbor and definitely worth wending your way to Aliceanna Street for. The miso butterfish is spectacular, and the chocolate soufflé is every chocoholic's wish fulfilled.

The menu is only part of the story though, for the restaurant management also serves the community's cultural needs as epitomized with a fund-raiser at the National Aquarium of Baltimore in October 2006. It was in conjunction with the opening of the aquarium's new "Animal Planet Australia: Wild Extreme" exhibit. Attendees heard the debut of Australian composer Peter Sculthorpes' new *Baltimore Songlines,* performed by the internationally acclaimed Verdehr Trio; dined on Roy's Kona lobster mango hand rolls, coconut and yellow curry poached Australian blue prawns, macadamia nut tart, and other delicacies; and saw a preview of the new exhibit. Roy's is located at 720 B Aliceanna Street; (410) 659–0099; www.roysrestaurants.com.

Summer hours are 10:00 A.M. to 8:30 P.M. Shorter hours apply the rest of the year, and the sub is only open Friday through Sunday in the winter.

In July 1999 the **USS Constellation** returned to Baltimore's Inner Harbor. When last in the harbor, her timbers were so rotten that the mast had to be removed, lest it fall through the bottom of the ship to the bottom of the harbor. Originally thought to have been built in 1797 and the sister ship of Boston's USS *Constitution,* after three years of restoration, she's known to be a sloop of war built in 1854, the last Navy ship powered solely by sail. A thirty-six-gun frigate bearing the name *Constellation* was dismantled in 1853. A second ship was built a year later (but in Norfolk, not in Baltimore as the first ship had been). Nearly 12 feet longer than the first, the second *Constellation* is the one that's in the harbor now. It served in the Mediterranean in the mid-eighteenth century, as an antislavery patrol ship, as a supply ship for famine-stricken Ireland, and for a dozen years as a training ship for the U.S. Naval Academy. The Navy still honors the name, with its USS *Constellation* aircraft carrier.

If you saw the ship before its restoration, you may notice that the second gun deck, added to make it look more like the older frigate, has been removed, and her stern is rounded now, instead of squared off.

The *Constellation* is open for tours daily from 10:00 A.M. to 6:00 P.M. May through October and from 10:00 A.M. to 4:00 P.M. the rest of the year. It's closed on major holidays. Admission to the ship is $7.50 for adults, $6.00 for seniors sixty and older, and $3.50 for children six through fourteen. The address is

Architectural Monument with a View

The Washington Monument and Museum in Baltimore, a 178-foot column, was the nation's first architectural monument (distinguishing it from the monument honoring George Washington that's in Boonsboro in western Maryland). Robert Mills, architect of the Washington Monument in Washington, D.C., designed it. You reach the top via a 228-step spiral stairway, where you can get a four-window panoramic view of the city. I'm not sure what the difference is in that definition of "architectural monument" compared to the one in Washington State Park, for they both claim they were the first. The marble, a white, crystalline metalimestone, is Cockeysville marble, from a quarry near Texas, about 1½ miles north of Baltimore. This stone was also used for the first 152 feet of the Washington Monument in Washington, D.C. It's open Tuesday through Sunday from 10:00 A.M. to 4:00 P.M. Admission is $1.00. (410) 396–0929.

Pier 1, Inner Harbor, 301 Pratt Street, Baltimore. Call (410) 539–1797 or (888) 225–8466, or log on to www.constellation.org.

On May 28, 1989, the *Maryland Vietnam Veterans Memorial,* a circular-shaped version of the national Vietnam memorial, was dedicated to the memory of 1,046 Marylanders who were killed or became missing in action in the Vietnam conflict. The names and inscriptions are readable whether one is standing, in a wheelchair, or at a child's-eye level. The veterans' names are etched into granite, along with this inscription:

MARYLANDERS, WHILE IN THIS PLACE, PAUSE TO RECALL OUR NATION'S IDEALS, ITS PROMISE, ITS ABUNDANCE, AND OUR CONTINUING RESPONSIBILITIES TOWARD THE SHARED FULFILLMENT OF OUR ASPIRATIONS. REMEMBER, TOO, THOSE WHOSE EXERTIONS AND SACRIFICES UNDERLIE THESE BLESSINGS. REMEMBER, INDEED, THE LIVING AND THE DEAD.

Funds were raised by Maryland veterans who called themselves "The Last Patrol." They marched across the state during sweltering August heat in 1986,

Let There Be Entertainment!

After a massive $26.8 million renovation, the *Peabody Institute* of the Johns Hopkins University (the nation's oldest music conservatory) has reopened. Set in Baltimore's Mount Vernon Cultural District, the Peabody is host to more than 800 musical and dance performances a year. Its newly refurbished concert space now rivals those of other major American cities. The address is 1 East Mount Vernon Place, Baltimore; (410) 659–8100; www.peabody.jhu.edu.

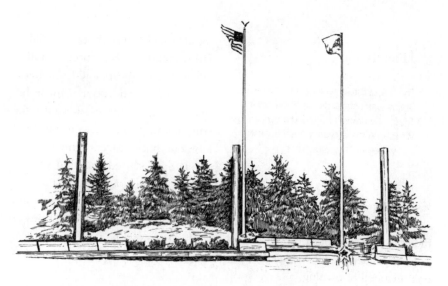

Maryland Vietnam Veterans Memorial

from Oakland in western Maryland to Ocean City in the east, and another 200 miles from Point Lookout to Baltimore the next year. Architect Paul Spreiregan designed the monument that stands beside the Patapsco River in Middle Branch Park, off State Route 2.

The **Book Thing** of Baltimore never sells a single book. It gives them away. Russell Wattenberg is the owner of this store that "puts unwanted books into the hands of those who want them." So, if you've been boating along the Intracoastal Waterway or driving around and you've finished the book you brought with you, stop by the Book Thing and drop off your reading material, then pick up something you haven't read yet. The store is open weekends from 9:00 A.M. to 6:00 P.M. As Wattenberg says, "Buses and hovercraft welcome." So are donations, from money and volunteers to plastic grocery bags and gift certificates to Home Depot, Staples, gas stations, etc. Find the Book Thing at 3001 Vineyard Lane; (410) 662–5631; www.bookthing.org.

Old Baltimore has long been known for its blocks and blocks of row houses, with their brightly scrubbed white-marble steps. Almost as historic, but not nearly as well known, are the **painted screens** for windows and doors that decorate the houses lining the streets of East Baltimore. It is said that William Oktavec painted the first screen on a hot summer day in 1913. Oktavec was a green grocer whose fresh produce was wilting in the heat, so he took it inside and painted groceries on the screens to show his customers what he had available.

When you understand that this area is all cement and brick, with very little greenery, no front yards, and few gardens or trees, you can appreciate the thoughts some had about providing a little colorful decoration. Another advantage of the painted screens is that windows and doors can be left open for the breezes, because the paint allows those who are inside to look out, but outsiders cannot see in.

People started painting on the screens pictures of red-roofed bungalows and ponds with ducks or swans swimming around in them. There are rainbows and religious scenes, but mostly the artwork reflects the memories of the inhabitants' home countries in Europe and scenes of a new life in America. The scenes depicted the single-family, country-cottage homes of the sort everyone dreamed of owning.

For the best screen viewing, start at the former Haussner's Restaurant at 3242 Eastern Avenue, and travel along both sides of Eastern Avenue. The Hatton Senior Center, at the corner of Fait and South Linwood Avenue, has screens in each of its twenty windows. This generally is a seasonal display, with the screens in place between May and October. Six or seven screen painters remain, but they are in their fifties or older. They still work away at it, saying, "Practice makes perfect, and perfect practice makes art."

You can have a screen painted for about $25 and up, even if you do not live in or visit Baltimore. Write the Painted Screen Society of Baltimore, Box 12122, Baltimore 21281; (410) 744–0703. Or you can check out the work of Dee Herget at www.screenpainter.com; (410) 391–1750. Select the subject you want, send her the screening, and she'll create your keepsake.

There are a number of "wow!" looking places in Baltimore, and the ***Reginald F. Lewis Museum of Maryland African American History & Culture*** certainly is among them. Opened in June 2005, the $33,000,000 facility features in-depth collections of artifacts, rare objects, and interactive exhibits covering more than 350 years of African-American history and culture. Lewis was an entrepreneur and philanthropist, and the International Law Center building at Harvard Law School is named after him. Other attractions in the 82,000-square-foot facility include a resource center, a theater, classrooms, a recording/listening oral history studio, museum shop, cafe, and a distance-learning lab. It is the largest museum dedicated to African-American history on the East Coast. With its outside terrace and reception areas, it's also a great place to hold a function. The museum is at 830 East Pratt Street; (443) 263–1800; www.africanamerican culture.org. Admission fees are $8.00 for general, $6.00 for senior citizens and college students (with identification), and free to members and children six and

Lights, Camera, Action!

The NBC television series *Homicide: Life on the Street* was shot primarily in the Fell's Point area of Baltimore, one of the stops on the water-taxi route. You can catch glimpses of buildings used in the series, from the police headquarters to the bar across the street. Barry Levinson, the show's producer, is a Baltimore native who attended Forest Park High School, and he has set many of his movies, including *Diner, Tin Man,* and *Liberty Heights,* in town and in the suburbs of his younger days.

John Waters also is a product of the area and has shot a lot of his films here. *Hairspray* was set here. Divine, the female impersonator who starred in *Pink Flamingos, Mondo Trasho,* and *Polyester* and died on March 7, 1988, grew up at 1824 Edgewood Road in Loch Raven (no, his parents aren't living there anymore). Divine is buried in Prospect Hill Cemetery, York Road, Towson.

Another series, HBO's *The Wire,* is also shot in Baltimore. It is written by David Simon (who wrote the book on which *Homicide* was based). Look for familiar settings around Port Discovery and other locales in the area.

under. The museum is open Tuesday through Saturday, from 10:00 A.M. to 5:00 P.M. and Sunday from noon to 5:00 P.M.

Public transportation around Baltimore City has become pretty convenient in the last few years. The subway system is fine. There's also **Ed Kane's Water Taxi,** which makes seventeen stops around the harbor, going to almost every popular waterfront attraction, including Harborplace, the Maryland Science Center, the National Aquarium in Baltimore, the Baltimore Museum of Industry, Fell's Point, Little Italy, and Canton. Thus, you can park for the day and take the water taxi around to various spots you want to visit, not having to worry about finding parking places, having correct change, or fighting traffic. The blue-and-white water taxis, or water buses, run about every eight to eighteen minutes April through October and about every forty-five minutes the rest of the year. Operating hours vary by the season. Adult fare is $8.00; the fare for children age ten and under accompanied by an adult is $4.00. These prices cover unlimited use on the day of purchase. Call (410) 563–3901 or (800) 658–8947; www.thewatertaxi.com.

trivia

The oldest remaining commercial structure in the Fell's Point area of Baltimore is possibly the last surviving colonial coffeehouse, built between 1770 and 1772. In May 2000 the Maryland Commission for Celebration 2000 awarded $22,500 to help restore the *London Coffee House,* located at 854 South Bond Street.

Another option is the **light-rail system,** taking you from the suburbs to Oriole Park at Camden Yards and back again for less expense and aggravation than driving into the city and parking. It runs from Glen Burnie to Hunt Valley Mall, with stops in downtown Baltimore, including Camden Yards, and there are spurs to BWI Airport and Penn Station. It operates about every fifteen minutes from 6:00 A.M. to 11:00 P.M. Monday through Saturday, and every thirty minutes from 11:00 A.M. to 7:00 P.M. on Sunday. Hours are extended or modified during the baseball season. Free parking is available at designated light-rail stops, and all light-rail trains are wheelchair accessible. The cost is $1.60 per trip, $3.50 for an all-day pass that's good on the subway, the

trivia

A summer Baltimore delicacy that dates back to at least the turn of the last century, a snowball is shaved ice, not crushed ice. It's topped with whatever flavors you want, but the hands-down quintessential topping is marshmallow. Chocolate is always on the top-ten list, but there's still marshmallow on top. There are a number of places where you can buy a snowball, but one of the favorites, with more than fifty flavors, is the **Old Fashioned Ice Cream Shoppe** at 9150–17 Baltimore National Pike, Ellicott City; (410) 480–2856; www.old fashionedicecreamshoppe.com.

bus system, and the light-rail. Call (410) 539–5000; www.mtamaryland.com.

For additional Baltimore information, write the Baltimore Area Convention and Visitor Center, 100 Light Street, 12th Floor, Baltimore 21202, call (410) 659–3700 or (888) BALTIMORE, or log on to www.baltimore.org.

Toby's Dinner Theatre of Columbia helped put Columbia on the map. A lot of talented performers came through its doors, including Ed Norton. Now there's a second Toby's venue, this one in Canton. Among the shows set for the 2007 season are *The Full Monty, Grease, Fiddler on the Roof, Dreamgirls,* and *Holiday Hot Nostalgia.* A huge buffet precedes the show; 5625 O'Donnell Street; (410) 649–1660 or (866) 649–1669; www.tobysdinnertheatre.com.

Should you cross the Francis Scott Key Bridge (instead of taking the tunnels or driving around the west loop of the Baltimore Beltway), look for a large, dark, hexagonal bulk sitting in the water at the southwest end of the bridge. It's **Fort Carroll,** sitting on a three-acre constructed island of brick and stone, a structure built under the supervision of engineer Robert E. Lee before he became superintendent of the United States Military Academy. Although not completed, the fort was officially named for Charles Carroll (1737–1832), the last surviving signer of the Declaration of Independence. A lighthouse was added in 1853.

After years of neglect, the Fort was once again staffed at the approach of the Spanish–American War in 1898 and new construction began; but that wasn't completed either until 1900 and the Spanish–American War was history. The lighthouse was automated in 1920, and in 1921 the Army removed what remained of the military equipment, taking it to Fort Howard. The island has been purchased, leased, and used as a private picnic area over the years, but time and Mother Nature have pretty well destroyed it. Today it's a crumbling structure overrun with trees and vines and is said to be the home to the most diverse colony of bird species within 100 miles. Its future is uncertain. If you'd like to see the fort, rather than trying to see what's happening as you're speeding over the bridge, you can check out photos at www.geocities.com/baltforts/Fort_Carroll.

Baltimore County

Baltimore City is surrounded on the east, north, and northwest by Baltimore County, and the easiest way out of the city (barring rush-hour accidents) is to the north along I–83.

One of the things I like to do is check out ***post office murals.*** No, they're not murals of post offices, but located in them, painted and installed in the late 1930s and early 1940s. Heading north and then a little to the east brings you to Towson and a set of murals at the Towson Post Office that caused a real ruckus.

Nicolai Cikovsky, a Russian-born, naturalized citizen, was an artist who lived in Washington, D.C. In 1939 he gave the postmaster, at the postal official's request, a series of panels depicting "Milestones in American Transportation." The populace took one look and cried foul. They declared the subject of the paintings was trite, derivative, and clichéd. They also were upset by inaccuracies, such as a wagon pulled by horses without reins, smokestack smoke going the wrong direction (ahead of the train), a train looking like a model railroad engine rather than a real locomotive, and a gun holster worn backward. This was the work of a painter who had studied at several distinguished schools in Russia, taught in the United States at the Corcoran Gallery, and sold paintings to the Chicago Art Institute, the Whitney Museum of American Art, and numerous other celebrated galleries across the country. The residents thought the paintings looked like bad "B" movie posters, at best. They wanted murals that reflected the life and history of Towson, and they wanted the artist to visit the area; often artists only went to see the location where their paintings would hang. The upshot is that the errors were corrected, and the murals stayed. They can still be found at 101 West Chesapeake Avenue, Towson—no longer the main post office, but the finance office.

The ***Glenn L. Martin Aviation Museum*** is on a much smaller and intimate scale than the huge aviation museum in the Smithsonian Institution com-

trivia

The lyrics to the "The Star-Spangled Banner," as penned by Francis Scott Key in 1814 after watching the Battle of Baltimore, are on display at the Maryland Historical Society in Baltimore. (410) 685-3750; www.mdhs.org.

plex in Washington, D.C. This collection honors and promotes the contributions to aviation of Martin and his company. Look for industrial models of aircraft and rockets, wind tunnel models, restored and partially restored aircraft, and photos documenting the growth of the company. People of a "certain" age are sure to find wonderful childhood memories among the exhibits.

The museum is open Wednesday through Saturday from 11:00 A.M. to 3:00 P.M. (except holidays). It's located in Hangar 5, Suite 531, Martin State Airport, Middle River; (410) 682–6122; www.marylandaviationmuseum.org. There is no admission charge, but contributions are always welcome.

At Towson State University, in the Fine Arts Center, is the **Asian Arts and Cultural Center** at the Roberts Gallery. The gallery is named in honor of Frank Roberts, who donated a large number of Asian artifacts and artworks to start this collection. Changing and permanent displays of Asian, African, and pre-Columbian works are featured. Concerts, films, lectures, and workshops are sponsored throughout the school year. The Asian Arts Center in the Fine Arts Building is open Monday through Friday 11:00 A.M. to 4:00 P.M. and Saturday from 1:00 P.M. to 4:00 P.M. No admission is charged. Groups are welcome by appointment. Call (410) 704–2807 or visit www.towson.edu/asianarts.

If you saw Clint Eastwood's film *Absolute Power* then your visit to Maryvale will be a déjà vu moment for you; the castle at **Maryvale Preparatory School** was the setting where the dastardly deed was done. The stone manor, set on 150 acres, was constructed in 1917 and modeled after Warwick Castle in England. Its Gothic arched windows, a great hall with European oak-paneled walls, diamond-paneled beveled-glass doors opening onto the terrace, boxwood gardens, stone towers, and incredible staircase are available for rent for your special event. As the school says, it fulfills "every girl's fantasy of the perfect storybook wedding." Maryvale, open by appointment only, is at 11300 Falls Road, Brooklandville (just north of the I–695 and I–83 intersection). Call (410) 252–3528 or visit www.maryvale.com. (See an additional note about the film in the Cecil County section.)

Southerners have known the joys of **Krispy Kreme doughnuts** since 1937. A few years ago, sophisticated New Yorkers became devout fans. Then, on November 3, 1998, KK came to Baltimore, disrupting traffic and not meeting the demand for donuts, even though the 3,000-square-foot store is capable of making 270 dozen doughnuts per hour, or 6,480 dozen doughnuts per day. By far, the company's most famous and best-selling product is the glazed, yeast-raised doughnut known for generations as the "Krispy Kreme Original Glazed." If you've never seen a doughnut being made, then you should definitely pop on over to KK to watch the old-fashioned doughnut machine. When the glowing, red-hot HOT DOUGHNUTS NOW light is on, the doughnuts are literally coming out hot *now,* and that's when you should eat them. Krispy Kreme locations include 8010 Belair Road, Belair (410–663–5255); 6604 Ritchie Highway, Glen Burnie (410–760–9356); 2129 York Road, Timonium (410–308–3576); and 10021 Reisterstown Road, Owings Mills (410–356–2655); www.krispykreme.com.

One of the remaining covered bridges in Maryland connects Harford and Baltimore Counties and crosses over Gunpowder Falls. The *Jericho Covered Bridge* was constructed in 1864 and measures 88 feet, with a 14⅔-foot roadway. Steel beams, steel stringers, steel crosstie rods, and bottom chord were installed later for reinforcement, and today it remains in good condition. To reach the bridge, take State Route 152 from exit 74 off I–95, turn left onto Jerusalem Road, and proceed to Jericho Road; (410) 638–3509.

Ashland Furnace is one of the six relatively easy-to-reach furnaces in Maryland (the others are Catoctin Furnace, Lonaconing Iron Furnace, Antietam, and Principio in Cecil County; and Nassawango in Worcester County). Said to have been named for the Kentucky home of Henry Clay, Ashland's three furnaces, engine room, and casting house were kept functioning from around 1844 to 1893. Originally there were also large storage buildings for raw materials and a village with a school, church, store, and about five dozen houses. The ore was mined in Phoenix, Glencoe, Riderwood, Texas, Oregon Ridge, and other parts of what is now north-central Baltimore County.

West of Ashland Furnace is the *Oregon Ridge Park and Nature Center,* a great place to take a break after hours of driving and seeing regular tourist attractions. Within its 836 acres are a number of marked trails of varying length and difficulty, downhill and cross-country skiing areas, a greenhouse, an archaeological research site, an outdoor stage, and a launching site for hang gliders. Starting in the nature center, you can see how a honeybee hive works, look at local flowers and plants in the greenhouse, or check on such live animals as fish, frogs, mice, salamanders, snakes, and Stubby, the pet opossum, all native to the park.

A huge tree exhibit reveals the various parts of the forest ecosystem, from the worms and moles living among the roots and underbrush to the owls and hawks perching in its highest limbs. The area's history is depicted by artifacts retrieved from archaeological digs in the park. These items were reclaimed from the digs by students in the Baltimore County public school system. Students also constructed a full-scale replica of an 1850s storage shed, set on its original foundation outside the nature center. The nature trails crisscross the park, so a hiker sees the natural interactions of birds, fields, ponds, streams, swamps, wildlife, and woods.

For those who like nature on the cultured side, summer concerts are presented here by the Baltimore Symphony. Oregon Ridge Park and Nature Center, Beaver Dam Road, is reached by the Shawan Road exit 20-B off I–83; go west 1 mile, turn left on Beaver Dam Road, bear right at the fork, and follow the signs to 13555 Beaver Dam Road, Cockeysville. Oregon Ridge Nature Center is open from 9:00 A.M. to 5:00 P.M. Tuesday through Sunday. Call (410) 887–1815 for more information or log on to www.oregonridge.org.

Southwest of Oregon Ridge is Owings Mills, and there you'll discover **Wild Acres Trail,** a mile-long wildlife habitat demonstration trail that was opened in 1989. It's part of the seventy-two-acre Gwynnbrook Wildlife Management Area, and the trail features twenty-three ways gardeners and wildlife watchers can help invite birds, butterflies, and other animals to their property. Trail maps are available for the self-guided tour, and the trail is open from dawn to dusk daily except on Wednesday. No pets are allowed. Included along the trail are a backyard pond and rock garden; a bee, butterfly, and hummingbird garden; nesting structures for birds and squirrels; bird feeders; and a variety of garden plants that produce fruit eaten by all sorts of animals. Other examples are shown for owners of large properties. More than 120 kinds of birds live in or visit the Gwynnbrook area, making bird-watching a marvelous recreational attraction. Photo opportunities are wondrous because of the wildflowers that bloom in the spring and fall. (410) 356–9272.

From Owings Mills, head south to Catonsville, where you'll find **post office murals** done by Avery Johnson in 1942. Johnson painted five scenes of historic note, entitled *Incidents of History of Catonsville.* The murals start with Native Americans, go on to farmers rolling tobacco in hogsheads to market, and then depict the romance of Richard Caton and Mary "Holly" Carroll. Holly, the daughter of Declaration of Independence signer Charles Carroll, was only sixteen when Caton proposed. Her father refused because he said Caton had a reputation for not paying his debts. Caton prevailed, and they were married in 1788. Charles Carroll built a house for them, Castle Thunder, on Frederick Road, where the library is now; then he built a newer home in Green Spring Valley (that home still stands). The last panel shows Caton, Holly, and Charles Carroll with his plans for the town of Catonsville.

Several years ago the post office roof began to leak, and that did not bode well for the plaster walls or the paintings. The late Thomas Cockey, whose family history also goes back to the eighteenth century, decided the murals should be repaired. Federal officials balked at the $35,000 repair bill, but

Cockey (as in the town of Cockeysville, also in Baltimore County) and the Historical Society prevailed. A plaque documenting the story depicted in the panels has been installed by the society.

For additional tourism information contact the Baltimore County Conference and Visitors Bureau, P.O. Box 5426, Towson Town Mall, Lutherville 21094; (410) 296–4886 or (877) 782–9636; www.visitbacomd.com.

Carroll County

West of Baltimore County, out State Route 30 or 140, you're getting into horse country with some beautiful scenery to go along with your history. The county was named for Charles Carroll, an American Revolutionary War leader and Maryland signer of the Declaration of Independence.

Near Westminster, the county seat, is the ***Carroll County Farm Museum.*** This complex has a general store that's reminiscent of the 1800s and sells items handcrafted by Farm Museum artisans, souvenirs, nickel candies, and much more. Among the activities scheduled on the grounds are a Civil War encampment (19th Georgia Regiment), Fall Harvest Days, a fiddlers' convention, a day devoted to antique farm machinery, and a day to celebrate Maryland wines.

General admission is $5.00 for adults, $3.00 for those ages seven to eighteen and sixty and over, and free for those under age seven. Group tours and rates are available. Higher admission prices apply for special events. The museum is open weekends May through October from noon to 5:00 P.M. and Tuesday through Friday in July and August from 10:00 A.M. to 4:00 P.M. It's located at 500 South Center Street, Westminster. Call (800) 654–4645 or log on to www.carrollfarmmuseum.org.

Final Resting Place

In 1992 Frederick Hubbard Gwynne and his wife, Deborah, moved to a farm in rural Maryland. You may remember him as Fred Gwynne, the tall (6'5") and lanky actor who portrayed Herman Munster in TV's *The Munsters* and as Gunther Toody in *Car 54, Where Are You?* He also played the part of Big Daddy in the 1974 Broadway revival of *Cat on a Hot Tin Roof,* among many other distinguished parts. His last films were *Fatal Attraction, Pet Sematary,* and *My Cousin Vinny.* He also wrote several children's books, including *A Little Pigeon Toad, A Chocolate Moose for Dinner, The King Who Rained,* and *Pondlarker.* Gwynne died of pancreatic cancer on July 2, 1993, just days short of his sixty-seventh birthday. He is buried at Sandymount Methodist Church off Old Westminster Pike.

Carroll County's streams, valleys, farms, woodlands, and villages provide an ideal backdrop for exploring off the highway, and the best way to do that is by bicycle. Each route is on a separate map with its own description of the tour. Brochures are available at the visitor center in Westminster.

For example, the Taneytown route, northwest of Westminster, is nearly 14 miles long, beginning at Taneytown Memorial Park. The moderately hilly ride takes you through rustic areas filled with deer and pheasants. The New Windsor tour, west of Westminster, travels for 8 miles through the rolling hills of Wakefield Valley. Attractions include Robert Strawbridge's Home (the birthplace of American Methodism, 2650 Strawbridge Lane, New Windsor) and A Greater Gift Shop at the New Windsor Service Center (500 Main Street, New Windsor).

Shirley's Book and Gift Shop in Taneytown gives you the impression that it's been here since the town began, although it actually opened in 2004. The store hosts various programs, including one in which high school students tutor younger students. Another program invites local authors to talk about their books and autograph copies. The used book section of the store has books priced from $1.00 to $5.00, and you can turn in your old books for store credit. Shirley's is open Wednesday from noon to 5:00 P.M., Thursday from noon to 6:00 P.M., Friday and Saturday from 10:00 A.M. to 6:00 P.M., and Sunday from 10:00 A.M. to 2:00 P.M. It is located at 2 Frederick Street; (410) 756–9235.

According to local legend, you and I are not the only visitors to Carroll County. Several apparitions also frequent the countryside, and you may even meet a friendly one. The first of the ghosts of Carroll County is at the Shellman House on East Main Street in Westminster. A little girl in white, they say, delights at having visitors stop by the visitor center, located at the Historical Society of Carroll County, 210 East Main Street, Westminster; (410) 848–6494; www.hscc .carr.org. Spirits, in addition to the liquid kind, are said to reside at Cockey's Tavern, 216 East Main Street; since the early 1800s this tavern has been the site of political rallies for Andrew Jackson, antitax meetings, fancy balls, and all-night debauchery. At Main and Court Streets, the ghosts of slaves supposedly return to the Carroll County auction block, where slave trading was done in pre–Revolutionary War times. Other specters have been reported at Ascension churchyard, the courthouse, the old Westminster jail, McDaniel College (Levine Hall has a musical ghost), and Avondale—the home of Legh Master, the most celebrated of Carroll's ghosts—on Stone Chapel Road in Wakefield Valley. It is said that Master was a tyrant, a miser, a lecher, and a cad.

Two Confederate ghosts reportedly visit the last remaining building of Irving College on Grafton Street, and during a full moon, an Indian walks along a ridge in the tiny town of Lineboro. For those of you who choose to pursue these nocturnal visitors, talk with the Historical Society.

Additional tourism information is available from the Carroll County Visitor Center, 210 East Main Street, Westminster; (410) 848–1388 or (800) 272–1933; www.carrollcountytourism.org.

Harford County

Head northeast of Baltimore City and east of Baltimore County, and you're probably taking I–95 to or from the Northeast corridor. Take a few minutes off that interstate, known as the Gateway to the Chesapeake Bay, and you'll find that Harford County goes from covered bridge to lighthouse.

Havre de Grace (pronounced as it is spelled, not with a French pronunciation) is the home of the *Concord Point Light.* Constructed in 1827, it is the oldest operating lighthouse on the East Coast. Following its decommissioning in 1975, it was vandalized and then, thank goodness, restored, and it is now in tip-top shape. You can climb the twenty-eight steps plus six steps on a ladder and see an impressive view of the Susquehanna River and Chesapeake Bay from the top of the 39-foot lighthouse. The lighthouse is open on Saturday and Sunday afternoon from 1:00 to 5:00 P.M. May to October, or by appointment. It is located at the foot of Lafayette Street in Havre de Grace. The phone number is (410) 939–9040. From the lighthouse you can walk a half mile via a promenade (boardwalk) along the shore of the Chesapeake Bay to Tydings Park at Lafayette and Concord Streets.

Another interesting attraction is the *Susquehanna Museum of Havre de Grace,* where you can learn just about everything you need to know about the southern terminus of the Susquehanna and Tidewater Canal. There's a restored lockhouse and a pivot bridge. Admission is free, although donations are accepted. The museum is open from 1:00 to 5:00 P.M. Friday through Sunday May through October. The museum is located at the Lock House, 817 Conesto Street, Havre de Grace; (410) 939–5780 or (866) 939–5780; www.hdgtourism.com/do_museums.html.

Concord Point Light

A self-guided historic walking-tour brochure is available from the ***Havre de Grace Visitor Center*** on Pennington Avenue. It highlights a sample of the 800 structures that contribute to the ***Havre de Grace Historic District.*** The buildings range in period from the 1780s through the Canal era (1830–50) and the Victorian era (1880–1910) to the contemporary.

trivia

Edwin Booth's first theatrical performance was in the original Harford County Courthouse.

Havre de Grace is the self-proclaimed decoy capital of the world, and the ***Havre de Grace Decoy Museum*** has complete collections of decoys by Madison Mitchell and Paul Gibson among the 1,200 decoys and decorative carvings. An annual Decoy Festival is held about the first weekend of May at the museum and at the Havre de Grace Middle and High Schools. The Decoy Museum is open daily from 9:00 A.M. to 5:00 P.M., except major holidays. Admission is $6.00 for adults, $5.00 for those age 65 and older, and $2.00 for children ages nine to eighteen. The address is 215 Giles Street, Havre de Grace. Call (410) 939–3739; www.decoymuseum.com.

Crossing the Susquehanna River north of Harve de Grace via U.S. Highway 40 is the ***Thomas J. Hatem Memorial Bridge,*** between Harford and Cecil Counties (nice to know about when the bridge on I–95 is backed up). It opened in 1940 as the Susquehanna River Bridge and was renamed in 1986 to honor Hatem, a prominent Harford County resident who devoted his life to public and civic service. The bridge is 1½ miles long and rises 89 feet above the river, connecting the communities of Havre de Grace and Perryville. More than nine million vehicles use the bridge each year. The toll is $4.00 (eastbound only) for passenger cars.

South of Havre de Grace is Aberdeen, once known primarily for its military base, the Aberdeen Proving Grounds. On the grounds of the base is the ***U.S. Army Ordnance Museum,*** with a comprehensive collection of small arms and just about everything else military you'd want to see that would be too small to fit in a parade or would not be suitable for exterior display. After being closed for awhile due to security issues, the museum is once again accessible. Enter through the Maryland Avenue gate and request a one-day museum pass.

The museum is open daily from 9:00 A.M. to 4:45 P.M.; it is closed on major holidays except Memorial Day, Fourth of July, and Veterans Day/Armed Forces Day. There is no admission charge. Call (410) 279–3602 for a museum pass and additional information. The Web site is www.ordmusfound.org.

The other big gun from Aberdeen is Cal Ripken Jr., the Iron Man, the one who broke Lou Gehrig's record of 2,130 consecutive baseball games played.

Unfortunately the **Ripken Museum** in Aberdeen—which opened in 1996 and was hailed as a "repository of baseball and other Ripken family memorabilia"—is temporarily closed while its directors conduct a fund-raising campaign for its new home on the grounds of the Ripken Youth Baseball Academy, also in Aberdeen. In the meantime, some of the items can be seen at the club level of Ripken Stadium (see below). If you just can't wait until the museum reopens, call Jay Moskowitz (410–297–9292); or check the Web site, www.ripkenmuseum.org, for updates.

trivia

The town of Dublin, in Harford County, is named after Dublin, Ireland. In the eighteenth century it was a Scots-Irish settlement.

West of I–95 is the **Ripken Baseball Stadium,** which opened in June 2002. The minor league baseball team, the Aberdeen Ironbirds, plays thirty-six home games in this new stadium. Special events are almost always scheduled, including a number of theme nights when they give away such promotional items as baseballs, caps, and T-shirts. Fireworks displays are a frequent item on the calendar. Plans for the complex include several youth-size stadiums modeled after famous ballparks and a baseball academy that will house up to 200 youngsters and coaches for weeklong camps, clinics, and tournaments, and, eventually, the Cal Ripken World Series. Ripken Stadium is located at 923 Gilbert Road, Aberdeen; (410) 297–9292; www.ironbirdsbaseball.com.

Northwest of Aberdeen is Bel Air, the Harford county seat, and there you'll enjoy the pleasures of **Liriodendron,** a Palladian-style mansion with Greek columns, French doors, marble walls in the kitchen and bathroom, and thirteen fireplaces. Built as a palatial summer home in 1898 for Dr. Howard A. Kelly, one of the "big four" founders of Baltimore's Johns Hopkins Hospital and Medical School, the Kelly Mansion is now on the National Register of Historic Places. This historic house museum features changing exhibits and art displays as well as a permanent exhibit of memorabilia from the Kelly Collection.

trivia

Johns Hopkins Hospital in Baltimore was the site of the first use of silk sutures and the first use of rubber gloves to reduce the risk of surgical infection.

It also serves as a cultural center for Harford County, with superb facilities for exhibitions, lectures, and concerts. The museum is open for tours from 1:00 to 4:00 P.M. on Sunday from March through December. A donation is suggested. Call (410) 879–4424 for a tour schedule. The address is Liriodendron, 502 West Gordon Street, Bel Air; www.liriodendron.com.

For additional tourism information on Harford County, contact the Harford County Office of Tourism; 1250 Bulle Rock Parkway, Havre de Grace 21078; (410) 939–6631 or (800) 597–2649; www.harfordmd.com.

Howard County

South and west of Baltimore City, out I–70 or down I–95, is Howard County, a place offering tremendous contrasts in lifestyles, from Ellicott City, a former mill town, with its original stone buildings, antiques and specialty shops, historic sites, and Ellicott City B&O (Baltimore and Ohio) Railroad Station Museum, to Columbia, the planned community, with its Merriweather Post Pavilion, huge mall, and Columbia Welcome Center. As usual, I will cover some of the less visited and more countrified places.

If you travel from Baltimore County to Howard County, just off U.S. Highway 1, you can spot a bridge of note that is for trains rather than cars, known as the ***Thomas Viaduct*** (1833). Crossing the Patapsco River, eight elliptical arches support a 60-foot-high granite block structure, which allowed tall ships to pass under. Just as the Ellicott City Railroad Station has endured as a landmark to the growth of railroading in Maryland, so does the viaduct. When B&O Railroad officials began looking to expand the railroad south to Washington, D.C., they faced a monumental problem: how to cross the Patapsco River. They solved it with a monumental structure, the Thomas Viaduct. Named for the first president of the B&O Railroad, Philip Thomas, it was designed by Baltimorean Benjamin Latrobe, and it was the first curved, stone-arched bridge in America. Construction began July 4, 1832, and it was completed exactly three years later at a cost of a little more than $142,000. It still carries passenger and freight trains. The viaduct is off Levering Avenue at 6086 Old Lawyers Hill Road, Elkridge. Picnic areas are in nearby Patapsco Valley State Park, which is open from sunrise to sunset; (410) 796–3282.

trivia

Ellicott Mills, in Howard County, was started in 1772 by three Ellicott brothers from Bucks County, Pennsylvania. By 1774 it was said to be the greatest gristmill in colonial America, with seven mills in operation at its peak. Besides producing animal feed, flour, iron nails, oil, lumber, paper, wagons, and wool, the first commercial electricity in the county was produced in 1891 in a mill on Tiber Alley.

Another bridge of interest, at Savage, is the ***Bollman Truss Bridge*** (1869). The red cast-iron, open railroad bridge is the only one of its type in the world. It is said to be the first bridge constructed of iron, as opposed to wood or stone. Restoration of the bridge took place in 1974, near Savage Mill (which is now filled with antiques shops and artists' studios), and there is a nice little park and hiking trails around the bridge. You can find the bridge off US 1, at Savage, near Savage Mill. Call (410) 792–2820, or (800) 788–MILL.

Howard County is home to a few farms that are open for pick-your-own fruits and vegetables and lots of family fun.

Thousands of children ventured through the **Enchanted Forest** between 1955 and the late 1980s. It was a magical world that delighted (and enchanted) the imagination. Although there were several attempts to revive the Forest, there was no way to compete with today's theme parks or rising real estate values. Fortunately Mary Clark at **Elioak Farm** obtained the very large orange Cinderella pumpkin coach from the Enchanted Forest and displayed it on her farm so a younger generation could be enchanted, as well. That led to an agreement with Kimco Realty, the Enchanted Forest Shopping Center owners, who said Elioak could remove other items, too. In 2005 they moved Mother Goose and her gosling, the black duck, the six mice that pulled Cinderella's pumpkin coach, papa bear, the giant mushrooms, the bell-shaped flowers, two giant lollipops, a number of gingerbread men, a large candy cane, the little red schoolhouse, the crooked house and the crooked man, and more. Additional items were displayed in 2006. The farm staff and volunteers have spent hours and more than a few dollars restoring these treasured items. There's also a petting farm ($4.00), hayrides ($2.00), pony rides ($2.00), and a Halloween pumpkin patch on the 540-acre farm that's been in operation since 1797. Visit the farm at 10500 Clarksville Pike, Ellicott City; (410) 730–4049; www.clarkland farm.com.

Larriland Farms has a pick-your-own season starting in late May or early June with strawberries and ending with a cut-your-own season for Christmas trees in December. In addition, the farm has succulent and delicious fruits and vegetables and beautiful flowers. The market is in a 125-year-old post-and-beam barn. Larriland Farms, owned and operated by the Moore family, also offers hayrides, evening campfires, and other programs that let city folk enjoy the pleasures of rural life. Farm operating hours vary by season, so call or check the Web site for details. The address is 2415 Woodbine Road, Woodbine. Larriland Farms is 3 miles south of I–70 (exit 73) on State Route 94, near Lisbon. The phone number is (410) 489–7034; in season you can call (410) 442–2605 or (301) 854–6110 for a recording of what fruits and vegetables are available. Their Web site is www.pickyourown.com.

Toby's Dinner Theatre of Columbia celebrates the creative genius of Toby Orenstein and her dedication to fine theatrical productions. All the time she is working to entertain you, she is working to teach her "kids" the hows

trivia

In 1820 Amos Williams and his three brothers borrowed $20,000 from friend John Savage to start a textile-weaving business on the banks of the Little Patuxent River. With water flowing over a huge 30-foot water wheel, Savage Mill, named after their friend, was in use from 1822 through 1947. It is now a complex filled with artisans and antiques dealers. Find it at 8600 Foundry Street in Savage; (301) 498–5751 or (410) 792–2820.

and whys of show business so they can go on to professional careers in entertainment if they wish.

The most interesting aspect of Toby's is the theater, which has performances in the round. You are never far from the action.

The productions may be an outstanding Broadway show from years gone by, such as *Funny Girl* or *Singin' in the Rain,* or an entirely new attraction, such as a musical version of *It's a Wonderful Life,* which was created at Toby's and offered during the 1989 holiday season. Other selections have included *The Pirates of Penzance, Sunday in the Park with George,* and *Ain't Misbehavin'.* In other words, it's good family entertainment.

Dinner at Toby's is an all-you-can-eat buffet that features prime roast beef, steamed shrimp, fresh salad and vegetables, and a dessert table.

Toby's is at 5900 Symphony Woods Road, Columbia, ½ block east of Little Patuxent Parkway. The phone numbers are (410) 730–8311; (301) 596–6161 (in Washington); (410) 995–1969 (in Baltimore); and (800) 88–TOBYS (in Maryland and surrounding states). On the Internet, go to www.tobysdinnertheatre.com.

For additional information on Howard County, write to Rachelina Bonacca, Executive Director, Howard County Tourism, 8267 Main Street, Ellicott City 21043; www.visithowardcounty.com.

Places to Eat in Central Maryland

ABERDEEN

New Ideal Diner,
104 South Philadelphia Boulevard,
(410) 272–1880

ANNAPOLIS

Buddy's Crabs and Ribs,
100 Main Street,
(410) 626–1100

Chick and Ruth's,
165 Main Street,
(410) 269–6737

49 West,
49 West Street,
(410) 626–9796

Ports of Call,
210 Holiday Court,
(410) 573–1350,
www.portsofcallannapolis.com

Pusser's Landing,
80 Compromise Street,
(410) 626–0004

BALTIMORE

Brewer's Art,
1106 North Charles Street,
(410) 547–9310,
www.thebrewersart.com

Cafe Hon,
1002 West 36th Street
(Hampden),
(410) 243–1230,
www.cafehon.com

City Lights Seafood,
924 North Charles Street,
(410) 547–8480,
www.brasselephant.com

Crabby Dick's,
606 South Broadway,
(410) 327–7900,
www.crabbydicks.net

Hampton's Restaurant,
Harbor Court Hotel,
550 Light Street,
(410) 234–0550

Henninger's Tavern,
1812 Bank Street,
(410) 342–2172,
www.henningerstavern.com

Obrycki's Crab House,
1727 East Pratt Street,
(410) 732–6399,
www.obryckis.com

Pier 4 Kitchen & Bar,
The Pier 4 Building,
621 East Pratt Street,
(410) 659–1200

Royal Kosher Restaurant,
7002 Reisterstown Road,
(410) 484–3544,
www.royalkosherrestaurant
.com

Ruth's Chris Steak House,
600 Water Street,
(410) 783–0033,
www.ruthschris.com

Sabatino's,
901 Fawn Street,
(410) 727–9414,
www.sabatinos.com

Samos Restaurant,
600 Oldham Street,
(410) 675–5292

Theresa's Deli,
700 South Broadway,
(410) 732–8736

Timothy Dean Bistro,
1717 Eastern Avenue,
(410) 534–5650,
www.tdbistro.com

Valentinos Restaurant,
6627 Harford Road,
(410) 254–4700,
www.valentinosdiner.com

BEL AIR

**Manny's Family
Restaurant,**
1433 Rock Spring Road,
(410) 879–6976,
www.mannysrestaurant.com

COLUMBIA

Blue Cow Café,
5134 Thunder Hill Road,
(410) 772–8999

Kings Contrivance,
10150 Shaker Drive,
(410) 995–0500

Strapazza,
8775 Centre Park Drive,
(410) 997–6144

Tomato Palace,
10221 Wincopin Circle,
(410) 730–2828

EDGEWOOD

Giovanni's Restaurant,
2101 Pulaski Highway,
(410) 676–8100,
www.giovannis-rest.com

ELLICOTT CITY

MiCasa Mexican,
3355 Saint Johns Lane,
(410) 480–2900,
www.micasmd.com

ESSEX

Mr. Bill's Terrace Inn,
200 Eastern Boulevard,
(410) 687–5994

HAMPSTEAD

**Greenmount Station
Restaurant & Lounge,**
1631 North Main Street,
(410) 239–0063,
www.greenmountstation.com

HANOVER

Kelsey's,
8480 Baltimore National
Pike,
(410) 418–9076,
www.kelseysrestaurant.com

Timbuktu,
1726 Dorsey Road,
(410) 768–4331,
www.timbukturestaurant.com

HAVRE DE GRACE

Price's,
654 Water Street,
(410) 939–2782

ODENTON

Bangkok Kitchen,
1696 Annapolis Road,
(410) 674–6812

PERRY HALL

**DeSantis Gourmet Pizza
Grill & Bar,**
9638 Belair Road,
(410) 256–2770

WESTMINSTER

**Hoffman's Ice Cream &
Deli,**
934 Washington Road,
(410) 857–0824,
www.hoffmansicecream.com

Maggie's,
310 East Green Street,
(410) 848–1441,
(877) 816–1900

Places to Stay in Central Maryland

ANNAPOLIS

Doubletree,
210 Holiday Court,
(410) 224–3150,
www.doubletree.com

Loews Annapolis Hotel,
126 West Street,
(410) 263–7777,
(800) 526–2593,
www.loewsannapolis.com

Maryland Inn,
16 Church Circle,
(410) 263–2641

1908—William Page Inn,
8 Martin Street,
(410) 626–1506,
(800) 364–4160,
www.williampageinn.com

BALTIMORE

Admiral Fell Inn,
888 South Broadway,
(410) 522–7377,
(800) 292–INNS,
www.admiralfell.com

Celie's Waterfront B&B,
1714 Thames Street,
(410) 522–2323,
(800) 432–0184,
www.baltimore-bed-breakfast.com

Harbor Court Hotel,
550 Light Street,
(410) 234–0550,
(800) 824–0076,
www.harborcourt.com

Marriott Inner Harbor,
110 South Eutaw Street,
(410) 962–0202,
www.marriott.com

Pier 5 Hotel,
711 Eastern Avenue,
(410) 539–2000,
(877) 207–9047,
www.harbormagic.com

Tremont Grand Hotel,
222 Saint Paul Street,
(800) TREMONT,
www.tremontgrand.com

ELLICOTT CITY

Turf Valley Resort and Conference Center,
2700 Turf Valley Road,
(410) 465–1500,
(888) TEE–TURF,
www.turfvalley.com

LINTHICUM

Sheraton BWI Airport Hotel,
1010 Old Elkridge Landing Road,
(443) 577–2100,
www.sheraton.com

Westin Baltimore Washington Airport,
1012 Old Elkridge Landing Road,
(443) 577–2300,
www.westin.com

LINWOOD

Wood's Gain Bed & Breakfast,
421 McKinstry's Mill Road,
(410) 775–0308,
www.woodsgain.com

LOTHIAN

Butterfly Fields Bed and Breakfast,
320 Frank Moreland Place,
(410) 271–1435,
www.butterfly-fields.com

NEW WINDSOR

Yellow Turtle Inn Bed & Breakfast,
111 Springdale Avenue,
(410) 635–3000,
www.yellowturtleinn.net

SYKESVILLE

Inn at Norwood,
7514 Norwood,
(410) 549–7868,
www.innatnorwood.com

TANEYTOWN

Antrim 1844 Country Inn,
30 Trevanion Road,
(410) 876–0237,
(800) 858–1844,
www.antrim1844.com

WESTMINSTER

The Boston Inn,
533 Baltimore Boulevard,
(410) 848–9095,
(800) 634–0846,
www.222.thebostoninn.com

WOODBINE

Ramblin' Pines RV Park & Campground,
801 Hoods Mill Road,
(410) 785–5161,
www.ramblinpines.com

OTHER ATTRACTIONS WORTH SEEING IN CENTRAL MARYLAND

African Art Museum of Maryland,
Columbia,
(410) 730-7106,
www.africanartmuseum.org

American Visionary Art Museum,
Baltimore,
(410) 244-1900,
www.avam.org

B&O Railroad Museum,
Baltimore,
(410) 727-2490,
www.borail.org

Babe Ruth Birthplace and Orioles Museum,
Baltimore,
(410) 777-1539,
www.baberuthmuseum.com

Baltimore and Annapolis Trail/BWI Trail,
Severna Park,
(410) 222-6244,
www.accpl.net/rp

Baltimore Museum of Art,
Baltimore,
(410) 396-7100,
www.artbma.org

Bear Branch Nature Center,
Westminster,
(410) 848-2517,
http://ccgov.carr.org/hashawha/
index.html

Benjamin Banneker Historical Park and Museum,
Oella,
(410) 887-1081,
www.thefriendsofbanneker.org

Cascade Lake,
Hampstead,
(410) 374-9111,
www.cascadelake.com

CENTERSTAGE,
Baltimore,
(410) 332-0033,
www.centerstage.org

Ellicott City B&O Railroad Station Museum,
Ellicott City,
(410) 461-1944,
www.ecbo.org

Enoch Pratt Free Library,
Baltimore,
(410) 396-5430,
www.epfl.net

Esther Pringley Rice Gallery,
Westminster,
(410) 857-2595

Helen Avalynne Tawes Garden,
Annapolis,
(410) 974-3717

Joseph Myerhoff Symphony Hall,
Baltimore,
(410) 783-8000,
(800) 442-1198,
www.baltimoresymphony.org

Jug Bay Wetlands Sanctuary,
Lothian,
(410) 741-9330,
www.aacpl.lib.md.us/rp/parks/jugbay

Lacrosse Museum/National Hall of Fame
Baltimore,
(410) 235-6882,
www.lacrosse.org

Ladew Topiary Gardens,
Jarrettsville,
(410) 557-9466,
www.ladewgardens.com

(continued on next page)

Lexington Market,
Baltimore,
(410) 685–6169,
www.lexingtonmarket.com

Lyric Opera House,
Baltimore,
(410) 685–5086,
www.baltimoreopera.com/xlyric.html

M&T Bank Stadium,
Baltimore,
(410) 547–8100,
www.baltimoreravens.com

Maryland Science Center,
Baltimore,
(410) 586–5225,
www.mdsci.org

Maryland State House,
Annapolis,
(410) 974–3400

Maryland Zoo in Baltimore,
Baltimore,
(410) 396–7102,
www.baltimorezoo.org

Merriweather Post Pavilion,
Columbia,
(410) 730–2424,
www.merriweathermusic.com

Morris A. Mechanic Theatre,
Baltimore,
(410) 625–4230,
www.themechanic.org

National Aquarium,
Baltimore,
(410) 576–3800,
www.aqua.org

National Cryptologic Museum,
Fort Meade,
(301) 688–5849,
www.nsa.gov

National Museum of Dentistry,
Baltimore,
(410) 706–0600,
www.dentalmuseum.org

Peabody Conservatory of Music,
Baltimore,
(410) 659–8100,
www.peabody.jhu.edu

Port Discovery,
Baltimore,
(410) 727–8120,
www.portdiscovery.org

Pride of Baltimore II,
Baltimore,
(410) 539–1151,
www.pride2.org

Shot Tower,
Baltimore,
(410) 837–5424

Sykesville Gate House Museum of History,
Sykesville,
(410) 549–5150,
www.sykesville.net/gatehouse.html

Union Mills Homestead and Grist Mill,
Westminster,
(410) 848–2288,
http://tourism.carr.org/unionmil.htm

Walters Art Gallery,
Baltimore,
(410) 547–9000, ext. 337,
www.thewalters.org

Capital Region

Prince George's, Montgomery, and Frederick Counties make up the Greater Washington area. Washington, D.C., is at the center of a huge suburban megalopolis formed by the blending of these three counties and northern Virginia. Although there are areas of dense population, and seemingly miles upon miles of row or town houses, there are also miles and miles of parkland, green spaces, and open spaces. Because so many people who live here come from other places, such as places where it never snows, traffic seems to get jammed as soon as the TV and radio weather forecasters think about snow. Forget about what happens when it actually does snow. If you should be here when it snows, tune in to a radio or TV station, and go for public transportation. Or find a nice fireplace and cuddle up with a good book.

As a native of this area, I have received a steady stream of visitors over the years who want to tour Washington. I take them to the subway station, and the Metro Rail takes them downtown to the many Smithsonian buildings, galleries, the zoo, or anything else they want to see. The Washington Metro is as clean and safe as any subway system around and at last count was the second busiest subway in the country.

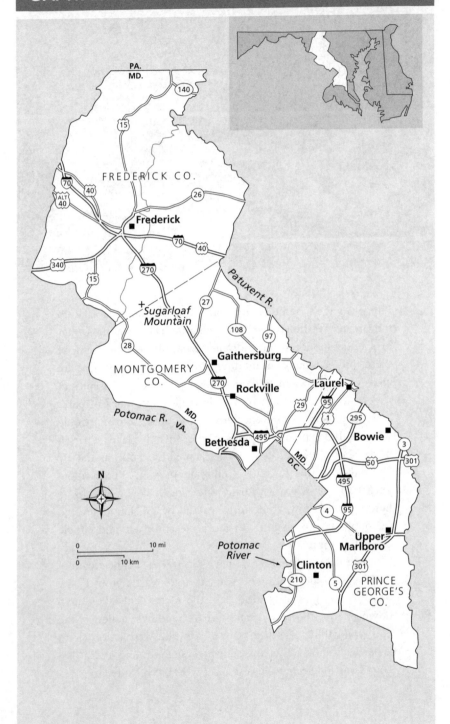

Three lines run in Prince George's County: the Green, the Orange, and the Blue. Green Line stations are at Greenbelt, College Park, Prince George's Plaza, West Hyattsville, Branch Avenue, Suitland, and Naylor Road; Orange Line stations are at New Carrollton, Landover, and Cheverly; and Blue Line stations are at Addison Road, Capitol Heights, Morgan Boulevard, and Lasgo Town Center.

There's one line with two branches running in Montgomery County: the Red Line, with stations at Shady Grove, Rockville, Twinbrook, White Flint, Grosvenor, Medical Center, Bethesda, and Friendship Heights going in toward Washington on the northwestern branch, and Takoma Park, Silver Spring, Forest Glen, Wheaton, and Glenmont coming out the more northerly route.

Trains run 5:30 A.M. to midnight Monday through Thursday, 5:30 A.M. to 3:00 A.M. on Friday, 7:00 A.M. to 3:00 A.M. on Saturday, and 7:00 A.M. to midnight on Sunday. Trains run about every five to fifteen minutes, depending on the time of day. Fares are based on time and distance, with rush hour (5:30 to 9:30 A.M. and 3:00 to 7:00 P.M., weekdays) costing more than off-peak times. The minimum fare is $1.35 to a maximum of $3.90. A one-day pass, good for unlimited rides from 9:30 A.M. (weekdays) or all day (weekends) until closing, is $6.50. For a bicycle permit, call (202) 962–1116. For general information about Metro Rail and Metro Bus (such as how to get from your door to your destination), call (202) 637–7000. This number is operational weekdays from 6:00 A.M. to 10:30 P.M. and weekends from 8:00 A.M. to 10:30 P.M. You must have a SmarTrip card to exit a Metro

trivia

In the spring and the fall, the Mary Surratt Society sponsors a "Booth's Trail" tour that follows the path of John Wilkes Booth from Ford's Theatre in Washington, D.C., to Dr. Mudd's home, to the Garrett Farm in northern Virginia. These fascinating tours fill up very quickly, and reservations are essential. Call (301) 868–1121 for tour dates and information.

JUDY'S FAVORITE ATTRACTIONS IN THE CAPITAL REGION

College Park Aviation Museum

Mount Olivet Cemetery

Patuxent Research Refuge

Roddy Road Covered Bridge

U.S. Department of Agriculture Research Center

White's Ferry

parking facility. Be sure to buy one before you exit the station. Visit www
.wmata.com.

Public art can be found at other Metro stations thanks to the **MetroArts**
program. In Montgomery County, stop at the Glenmont station to see Deirdre
Saunder's glass mosaic frieze *Swallows and Stars* (2001) and the Wheaton station to see Marcia F. Billig's bronze sculpture *The Commute* (1994). Prince
George's County Metro stations include art by Heidi Lippman with Ben Van
Dusen, who created the glass and stone mosaic frieze *Dawn and Dusk* (1999)
at the New Carrollton station; Ray King, who made the stainless steel and glass
sculpture *Largo Beacon* (2004) at the Largo Town Center Station; Athena Tacha,
who fashioned the sculpture *Stop & Go For Garrett A. Morgan* (2004) at the Morgan Boulevard station; George Peters and Melanie Walker, who did the neon
wall sculpture *Light Wheel* (2004); and Clark Weigman, whose painted metal
and glass sculpture *Departure* (2004) is at the Branch Avenue station. Oh, by
the way, Garrett Morgan is credited with inventing a type of traffic signal.

Prince George's County

People hear more about Prince George's County in the news than they realize.
A marriage is performed on the old wooden roller coaster at the Six Flags (formerly Adventure World) theme park outside Kettering; space flight information
is reported from the Goddard Space Flight Center (and Museum) in Greenbelt,
the hub of all NASA tracking activities; or the president or a visiting dignitary
arrives at Andrews Air Force Base, the home base for Air Force One.

Of course, Prince George's County is rarely mentioned, but all of this commerce and history is taking place here on a day-to-day basis. Prince George's
County is a place of "firsts" and "lasts."

Not far from Andrews, in the Clearwater Nature Center in Clinton, is the
Suitland Bog, which technically is a fen. It's home to some interesting and
rare plants (twenty species are on Maryland's rare, threatened, or endangered
list), as well as the occasional carnivorous plant, such as the spatulate-leaved
sundew and the Northern pitcher plant. The Suitland Bog is the last undisturbed Maryland coastal plain bog in Prince George's County. A short, winding
wooden boardwalk cuts a shaded path through the area, and signs are placed
by the rarer plants. Call the Clearwater Nature Center for a guided tour reservation from May to September. The center is located at 11000 Thrift Road, Clinton. Call (301) 249–6203; or log on to www.pgparks.com.

Upper Marlboro is the county seat for Prince George's. Understanding
that Prince George's County was and still is a very agrarian county, you will
appreciate the work of W. Henry DuVall. A lifelong Prince Georgean, DuVall

had the foresight to save tools from the nineteenth century, whether it was a scythe, can opener, carpenter's plane, or foot-operated dental drill. This was the beginning of the *DuVall Tool Museum.* There is even a white building block that is blackened on one side, which apparently was obtained during a nineteenth-century architectural revision of the White House. The dark stains are said to be soot from the burning of the building during the War of 1812. DuVall's collection, which he started in the 1930s, had more than 1,200 items by the time he died in 1979.

The Maryland–National Capital Park and Planning Commission bought the agglomeration so that it would not be lost to the twentieth or twenty-first century. More tools are accepted, so if you have something tucked away in your attic or out in the garage—particularly if it is unique to southern

trivia

Andrews Air Force Base was named Andrews Field (formerly Camp Springs Army Base) on March 31, 1945, in memory of Lt. Gen. Frank Maxwell Andrews. During the early stages of World War II, Andrews was the Commander of all Air Forces in Europe, serving with Gen. Dwight D. Eisenhower. An outspoken proponent of air power, Andrews was born on February 3, 1884, in Nashville, Tennessee. He was killed in an aircraft accident in Iceland on May 3, 1943, and buried in Section 3 of Arlington National Cemetery.

Maryland history—donate it here instead of to the dump. You can return to yesteryear by visiting the museum, located in the Patuxent River Park, Sunday from 1:00 to 4:00 P.M. and by appointment. The address is 16000 Croom Airport Road, Upper Marlboro. Call (301) 627–6074 or visit www.pgparks.com/places/historic/duvall.

Just south of Upper Marlboro is the old-turned-to-new Prince George's Equestrian Center and the newer *Show Place Arena*. Once a functional horse racetrack, it was closed and converted to fringe parking for county employees before it was reborn as an architectural masterpiece and the home of the annual county fair, concerts, and other special events. There are even a few days of horse racing now and then. You'll find the center and arena at 14900 Pennsylvania Avenue, Upper Marlboro, at the intersection of U.S. Highway 301 and State Route 4. Call (301) 952–7900 or visit www.showplacearena.com.

To the west of Upper Marlboro is Largo, the home of the former USAirways Arena, formerly the Capital Centre and the USAir Arena (if McDonald's had bought it, would it be the McArena?). It's now the home of the FedEx Field, where the Washington Redskins play.

Northwest of Largo is Bladensburg and the *Bladensburg Dueling Grounds,* a small, wooded glen in the northeastern corner of Fort Lincoln

Crain Highway

State Route 3, running between U.S. Highway 50 and the Potomac River, is also known as Crain Highway, named after Robert Crain, a Charles County farmer and lawyer who persuaded the state to fund a highway so farmers could transport their crops from southern Maryland to northern cities. The highway had its official opening ceremonies in October 1927, with 20,000 people in attendance.

Cemetery, adjacent to Colmar Manor. It was a court of last resort for nearly fifty years for offended gentlemen and politicians, who faced each other at ten paces with pistols and muskets. As noted on the historical marker placed by the Maryland–National Capital Park and Planning Commission, one of the most famous was that between Commodores Stephen Decatur and James Barron, which was settled here on March 22, 1820. Commodore Decatur, who had gained fame as the conqueror of the Barbary pirates, was fatally wounded by his antagonist.

trivia

On June 17, 1784, the first documented unmanned balloon flight in the United States took place in a field near the town of Bladensburg. Peter Carnes, the balloon owner, sent the manned balloon aloft a week later in Baltimore.

Although Congress passed an antidueling law in 1839, duels continued here until just before the Civil War. The dueling grounds are in Anacostia River Park near the intersection of Bladensburg Road and Thirty-eighth Avenue in Bladensburg. Also at Anacostia River Park is the Maryland–National Capital Park and Planning Commission Interpretive Center at the site of the old Bladensburg Marina.

Clements Pastry Shop, a Washington, D.C., institution since 1928, still lives. Really. That's sure to be a delight for dessert lovers far and wide. Started by Italian-born and classically trained pastry chef Clement Maggia and his brother Theo, Clements developed a steady and loyal following, including Presidents Eisenhower and Truman, Tony Curtis, and Kate Smith. Those customers followed the aromas from the original location to a storefront on 13th Street in 1957 and then again to G Street in 1965. It moved one more time, to this Hyattsville location, in 2000. Now operated by Richard, Matthew, and John Barrazotto, you can feast on the cakes, similar to the one made for Lynda Bird Johnson's wedding, or your fondest memory cake. There is no storefront through which you can amble, but you can call in your order (with two days' notice and

TOP ANNUAL EVENTS IN THE CAPITAL REGION

JANUARY

Winter/Spring Display Spring Has Sprung,
Wheaton,
(301) 949–8230,
www.clark.net/pub/mncppc/montgom/parks/brookside

MARCH

Maple Syrup Demonstration and Mountain Heritage Festival,
Thurmont,
(301) 271–7574,
www.dnr.state.md.us

APRIL

John Wilkes Booth Escape Route Tour,
Clinton,
(301) 868–1121,
www.surratt.org

MAY

Andrews Air Force Base Open House,
Camp Springs,
(301) 568–5995

Colesville Strawberry Festival,
Colesville,
(301) 607–8770

JUNE

Montpelier Summer Concert Series,
Laurel,
(301) 776–2805

AUGUST

Wings of Freedom over Frederick,
Frederick,
(301) 898–3761,
(301) 639–2656,
www.wingsoffreedomoverfrederick.com

SEPTEMBER

Great Frederick Fair,
Frederick,
(301) 663–5895,
www.thegreatfrederickfair.com

John Wilkes Booth Escape Route Tour,
Clinton,
(301) 868–1121,
www.surratt.org

OCTOBER

Butler's Orchard Pumpkin Festival,
Germantown,
(301) 972–3299

Taste of Bethesda,
Bethesda,
(301) 215–6660,
www.bethesda.org

NOVEMBER

Gaithersburg Railroad and Transportation Show,
Gaithersburg,
(703) 536–2954,
www.gserr.com

Garden of Lights,
Wheaton,
(301) 962–1453,
www.brooksidegardens.org

a credit card), see the products online, or ask your bakery to order for you. And, if you remember an old-time favorite (ours is the mocha rum cake, not the Italian rum), you can ask if they'll make it for you. According to Mary Jo Barrazotto, mother of the three men mentioned above, the chocolate truffle or strawberry short cake (yellow cake with whipped cream and strawberries in the middle and whipped cream and strawberries on top) are tied for favorites. The shop is at 3355 52nd Avenue, #B, Hyattsville; (301) 277–6300; www.clementspastry.com.

At the junction of the Beltway (Interstates 95 and 495) and John Hanson Highway (U.S. Highway 50) is the New Carrollton Metro station, a MARC and AMTRAK railroad station, a first in intermodal transportation stops.

The city of Bowie, east of New Carrollton, has several museums that let you explore the history of the area, and even some more modern electronic history. The **Belair Mansion,** circa 1745, is a five-part Georgian plantation house that was home to Samuel Ogle, provincial governor of Maryland. For several years it belonged to William Woodward, a noted horseman, and it was after his death in 1955 that suburban developer William Levitt bought the property and started building his Maryland version of a "Levittown." Objects on view range from paintings by Philippe Mercier (1689–1760) to a bronze statue of 1932's Triple Crown winner Gallant Fox, who spent his yearling season at the Belair Stables. Open Wednesday through Sunday from noon to 4:00 P.M. and for groups of ten or more by appointment, the mansion is located at 12207 Tulip Grove Drive, Bowie; (301) 809–3089; www.cityof bowie.org/museums.

trivia

The original events upon which the movie *The Exorcist* was based took place in Mount Rainier, Maryland, starting on January 18, 1949, when weird noises were heard from the home at 3210 Bunker Hill Road. Father Albert Hughes came from nearby St. James Catholic Church to perform the exorcism, but four months later he still had not been successful. Okay, so Hollywood changed a few things, and the movie was set in the Georgetown area of Washington, D.C. The original home has been demolished.

Also spending their yearling seasons at the Belair Stables were Nashua, the Horse of the Year in 1955, and Omaha, Gallant Fox's son. It's said that the first Thoroughbred horse, Selima, was stabled on the Belair Farm, making her the mother of all American Thoroughbred stock today. Until its closing in 1957, Belair was the oldest continually operating horse farm in the United States. Learn this and more at the **Belair Stables Museum,** open Wednesday through Sunday noon to 4:00 P.M., 2835 Belair Drive, Bowie; (301) 809–3089; www.city ofbowie.org/museum.

Reading Is Fun-damental

Special library collections abound in Prince George's County. As the Belair Estate in Bowie claimed to be the "Cradle of American Racing," it seems entirely appropriate that the Bowie Library has the Selima Room, with its extensive collection of horse-racing records and materials. Selima was one of the original mares who started the bloodline that flows in almost every racehorse in this country. Other special collections in the Prince George's County library system include the Tugwell Room in the Greenbelt Library, the Sojourner Truth Room in the Oxon Hill branch, the Kerlan Room children's collection in the Hyattsville branch, and the Documents Library in the County Administration Building in Upper Marlboro, which appears to have every document pertaining to Prince George's County that was ever printed or penned.

Genealogists will want to stop by the **Prince George's Genealogical Library** with its 4,000 volumes, periodicals, surname files, family group sheets, Bible records, and microfilms. The library, at 12219 Tulip Grove Drive, Bowie, is open every Wednesday from 10:00 A.M. to 7:00 P.M., except the first Wednesday of the month when it's open only until 1:00 P.M. It's also open on the last Saturday of the month from 1:00 to 5:00 P.M. Call (301) 262–2063 or log on to www.rootsweb.com/~mdpgeorg/text/pggensoc.html.

The **Bowie Railroad Station and Huntington Museum** in "Old" Bowie is housed in buildings constructed in the early 1900s. This is the place to learn about railroading in this area, and watch today's trains zoom past on their way to New York, Boston, Washington, and across the country. Check out the old photographs and equipment from Bowie's bygone railroading days. The station is open Tuesday through Sunday 10:00 A.M. to 4:00 P.M. It's located at 8614 Chestnut Avenue. Call (301) 809–3089; www.cityofbowie.org/comserv/museums.htm.

There's no historical reason that the **Radio and Television Museum** is located in Bowie; it's just that the Radio History Society needed space, and Bowie had it in the form of a home originally built around 1906, then rebuilt

Hoofbeats Heard on the Bridge

The newest **covered bridge** in Maryland is in Bowie. There's nothing historic about this bridge, as far as its age goes, for it was built in 1988, but its use could be unique. It's located at the Bowie Race Course, which is now an equestrian center rather than a racetrack. The bridge is used to move horses from the stables to the track for their workouts, not for people or cars.

in the mid-1980s after a fire. Inside the two-story structure are perhaps hundreds of pieces of radio and television history. Everyone of a certain age (there's no need to say what age that is) will recognize something in this collection, whether it's a crystal set (didn't every Boy Scout make one?) or a cathedral-shaped radio of the '30s and '40s. There are also several examples of Nipper, the RCA mascot. If you were around the D.C. area in the 1960s and 1970s, you may remember *The Joy Boys of Radio* on WRC. Ed Walker, one of the Joy Boys, has donated a number of items to this collection. Those who weren't around in those days may know his partner, Willard Scott, from NBC's *Today* show. The museum, at 2608 Mitchellville Road, Bowie, is open Friday from 9:00 A.M. to 5:00 P.M. and Saturday and Sunday from 1:00 to 5:00 P.M.; (301) 809-3089; www.radiohistory.org.

None of these museums charges an admission fee, but contributions definitely are welcome.

Details about 316 historic sites (including eleven archaeological sites) are contained in a 208-page spiral-bound book published by the Maryland–National Capital Park and Planning Commission. Thirty sites are in the Bowie–Mitchellville area. *Illustrated Inventory of Historic Sites: Prince George's County, Maryland* is available for $5.00 at the county Administration Office in Upper Marlboro (301–952–3520) or at gift shops of several of the county's historic house museums.

Take US 50 west, then head north around the Beltway, and you'll come to College Park, home of the University of Maryland and near there, the **College Park Airport,** where the first military training in a military-owned airplane took place in October 1909. The plane was designed by Orville and Wilbur Wright. College Park claims to be the "world's oldest continually operated airport," and today it is the only operating airport within the Capital Beltway. Pilots say they get a kick out of flying from the same airfield that the Wright brothers used almost a century ago.

trivia

Mrs. Ralph H. Van Deman said, "Now I know why birds sing," after becoming the first woman in America to fly as a passenger in an airplane, when she went aloft with Wilbur Wright in College Park on October 27, 1909.

Budding aviators are sure to enjoy the 26,000-square-foot **College Park Aviation Museum,** which opened in 1998. Tours, movies, and special events are scheduled throughout the year, including an annual AirFair in September.

The airport and museum are at 1985 Corporal Frank Scott Drive (named for the first civilian killed in an air accident), College Park. Admission is $4.00

for adults, $3.00 for seniors, and $2.00 for children and students. It is open from 10:00 A.M. to 5:00 P.M. daily. Call (301) 864–6029; www.pgparks.com.

The huge buzz around Adelphi in late 2006 wasn't a low-flying plane from the nearby College Park Airport, but a visit to **Ledo Restaurant** by *The Oprah Winfrey Show*. This pizzeria has been around since 1955 and has always been a favorite of University of Maryland students and faculty. Gayle King, Winfrey's friend, attended the U of M and had fond memories of the rectangular-shaped pies with the sweet sauce, flaky crust, and abundant toppings. Now you can find the famed pizza in nine states, but this University Boulevard location is the original. The restaurant is at 2420 University Boulevard, Adelphi; (301) 422–8622.

Just minutes from College Park is a planned city whose history starts in the 1930s. If you think planned cities are something new, then visit **Greenbelt.** From its inception, Greenbelt had a sense of history about it. It has been chronicled, cataloged, dissected, scrutinized, and studied many times over in thorough detail. Although the town is now surrounded by town house communities for Washington commuters, you still can see the core of the town, its art deco architecture, and its attempts to retain its identity.

Greenbelt is one of three planned greenbelt towns that were to be satellite towns on the edge of larger urban cores (the other two are Greenhills, Ohio, and Greendale, Wisconsin, outside of Cincinnati and Milwaukee, respectively). The town was built around an inner core, allowing residents to walk everywhere they had to go on pedestrian paths so that people on foot would not have to intermingle with cars. The town was superorganized and highly democratic, and residents met to discuss everything. (In fact, at one point they met to declare a moratorium on meetings.)

For a more thorough explanation and visual interpretation, stop by the **Greenbelt Museum** on Sunday between 1:00 and 5:00 P.M. There's no admission charge. The museum is located at 10 B Crescent Road, Greenbelt. Call (301) 507–6582 or visit www.otal.umd.edu/lvg/virtual-gb/gbtis.html. Greenbelt is at the northwest corner of the intersection of the Baltimore-Washington Parkway (Interstate 295) and the Capital Beltway (I–495). Log on to www.ci.green belt.md.us/About.Greenbelt/the_greenbelt_museum.

Head north up Baltimore-Washington Parkway (I–295) and you'll come to the outskirts of Laurel, the Montpelier Cultural Arts Center, and the Montpelier Mansion.

The **Montpelier Cultural Arts Center** is noted for its visual arts, serving as a home for eighteen professional resident artists. A rather full curriculum of visual arts classes is offered. The arts center is at 12826 Laurel-Bowie Road, Laurel. Call (301) 953–1993 or visit www.pgparks.com.

Next door is the **Montpelier Mansion**, built in 1783 by Maj. Thomas Snowden, a significant landowner in Prince George's County. At one point the Montpelier site was about 10,000 acres of gently rolling parkland. Among the famed guests who stopped here were George and Martha Washington and Abigail Adams.

William Breckinridge Long, undersecretary of state in the Franklin Roosevelt administration and U.S. ambassador to Italy from 1933 to 1936, was the twentieth-century owner, and his guests also were notable, including Presidents Roosevelt and Wilson. Long's daughter, Christine Long Wilcox, donated the house in the late 1950s to the Maryland–National Capital Park and Planning Commission. The mansion and other buildings sit on about seventy-five acres of the original estate.

Many original Snowden pieces are still in the mansion, and other furnishings are period antiques. You may take a tour through almost a dozen rooms of the historic mansion Sunday through Thursday from noon to 3:00 P.M. March through November and at 1:00 and 2:00 P.M. on Sunday the rest of the year. Admission is $3.00 for adults, $2.00 for seniors age fifty-five and older, and $1.00 for children ages five to fifteen.

And, if you wish, enjoy a lovely afternoon tea at the mansion, with a choice of teas and some delicious nibbles, usually on the second and fourth Friday of the month, at 2:00 or 4:00 P.M., for $15. Reservations and prepayment are required. Call (301) 498–8486 for reservations.

That phone number will get you to the Little Teapot at Montpelier, a gift shop that's open during the summer season from 10:00 A.M. to 6:00 P.M. Tuesday through Saturday, and from noon to 4:00 P.M. on Sunday. Call for winter hours.

Montpelier Mansion is located at 9401 Montpelier Drive, Laurel; (301) 953–1376; www.pgparks.com.

If you like murals as much as I do, you will be curious about Prince George's County's post office murals. The **Laurel Post Office mural** of the *Mail Coach at Laurel,* painted by Mitchell Jamieson in 1939, reportedly was taken down during a General Services Administration restoration of the building and has not been returned.

Oops

Many of the WPA murals that supposedly depicted area activities were more figments of imagination or expressions of scenes from other parts of the country or world than a reflection of local reality. The Prince George's County mural in Upper Marlboro, Maryland, for example shows a type of tobacco that's not grown in Maryland, but in North Carolina. And it's shown being harvested the way it's done in North Carolina, not the way it's done in Maryland.

Situated on 4,700 acres, the ***National Patuxent Wildlife Research Center, Patuxent Research Refuge*** specializes in research on endangered species, migratory birds, and environmental contaminants. Established in 1839 as America's first national wildlife experiment station, the center is charged with protecting and conserving the nation's wildlife and natural habitats through research and critical debate. Throughout the years, the center has been involved in history-making discoveries, including the detrimental effects of DDT. Rachel Carson did most of her research here for her book *Silent Spring*. Currently the center is working to save the endangered whooping crane, California condor, Mississippi sandhill crane, and masked bobwhite. It has successfully completed a program of repopulating America's proud symbol, the bald eagle.

Scientists from more than fifteen countries conduct research at the center on a regular basis. Patuxent is the largest wildlife research center in the world, and it is an exciting place to learn about global concerns, be a field researcher and travel through the five full-scale habitat areas, view acres of natural wildlife habitat, and see dramatic dioramas of wildlife. The center is open from 10:00 A.M. to 5:30 P.M. daily. A tram ride is available daily during summer months and on weekends in spring and fall. The cost is $2.00 for adults, $1.00 for children twelve and younger and seniors fifty-five and older. A gift shop offers a variety of environmental books, gifts, and educational materials.

A special committee of the Prince George's County Parks and Recreation Foundation, Inc., facilitates a public/private partnership to raise funds on a national basis for the multimillion-dollar National Wildlife Visitor Center. The visitor center's mission is to "educate the public, especially students, about wildlife conservation from a global perspective." The research center is located off Powder Mill Road, 2 miles east of the Baltimore/Washington Parkway, at 12100 Beech Forest Road, Laurel. Call (301) 479–5500 at least several days in advance to arrange a tour. Online, visit www.pwrc.usgs.gov.

A little south of Laurel is Beltsville and the home of the ***U.S. Department of Agriculture Research Center,*** with a visitor center in the Log Lodge. Built by the Civilian Conservation Corps during the 1930s, it contains a Hall of Fame of agriculture scientists.

Approximately half of the 125 pounds of potatoes you eat each year are found in processed foods, a lot of which are instant potato flakes, developed in 1954 to use up a surplus of potatoes. Approximately 400 million pounds of potato flakes are produced each year in the United States. John F. Sullivan is honored for that invention and other works.

He's one of forty-four scientists honored for their contributions to our agricultural well-being. Herbert J. Dutton is enshrined for pioneering research leading to the establishment of soybean oil as the predominant edible vegetable oil in the world. And James H. Tumlinson III is celebrated for his research leading to the eradication of the boll weevil from the southeastern United States.

The visitor center, in Building 186 (East), is open weekdays from 8:00 A.M. to 4:30 P.M. Guided tours are available by appointment. Call (301) 504–9403. The mailing address is U.S. Department of Agriculture, National Agriculture Library, Second Floor, 10301 Baltimore-Washington Boulevard, Beltsville 20705. The Web site is www.barc.usda.gov. There is no admission charge.

Travel down US 1 into Hyattsville and you'll discover Eugene Kingman, a noted muralist, painter, and museum director who created the five panels in the **Hyattsville Post Office** in 1938, jointly entitled *Hyattsville Countryside*. Kingman was born in 1909, attended Yale University College of Fine Arts, and received an honorary Ph.D. from Creighton University. His work is in the Library of Congress collection and at the Philbrook in Tulsa, Oklahoma, among many other places. He also created murals in Wyoming, Rhode Island, and the lobby of the New York Times Building in New York City.

The Hyattsville post office murals depict the working man in heroic proportions. They reflect the remains of the agricultural and pastoral quality of the Hyattsville lifestyle that still existed in 1937, when Kingman used such muralist techniques as stylized horses, foreshortening, and a decorative cornstalk border.

The Hyattsville Post Office is at 4325 Gallatin Street, Hyattsville. Call (301) 669–8905.

For additional information about Prince George's County, from events to lodgings, contact Matt Neitzey and his staff at the Prince George's County Conference and Visitors Bureau, Inc., 9200 Basil Court, Suite 101, Largo 20774. Call (301) 925–8300.

Montgomery County

Northwest of Prince George's County and north and west of Washington, D.C., Montgomery County goes from really high-density suburbia at the south end to gorgeous open country with huge landed estates and farms in the middle and then into a mixture of town house developments set in the rolling countryside nearing the foothills of the Appalachian Mountains.

Start at the D.C./Maryland border, where the unincorporated area known as Silver Spring is about to see a long-promised redevelopment. (I remember when the first department store opened out there and when the bus cost 5 cents, but you could never stand at a bus stop long enough to catch a bus, because a neighbor would drive by and give you a ride into town.)

Just blocks from the D.C./Maryland line, just off Georgia Avenue, is the **Silver Spring Acorn.** It is easy to spot this little park, located near the spring from which the area received its name, with its gazebo shaped by pillars and a "hat" with the configuration of an acorn. Benches are provided for a lunch break or a moment of rest. Francis Preston Blair—a wealthy and prominent eighteenth-century landowner, power broker, newspaper owner, and member of President Andrew Jackson's Kitchen Cabinet—and his daughter were out riding one day when they found this spring. The sunlight reflecting off the sand or mica in the bottom made the minerals look like silver, and thus was born the name of his estate and the area, Silver Spring. In 1942 the park was acquired by a local citizens

Silver Spring Acorn

group, and it was restored in 1955. The Silver Spring Acorn is on Newell Road at the intersection of East-West Highway and Blair Mill Road, 1 block south of Georgia Avenue (across the street from the Canada Dry bottling plant).

Read a George Pelacanos book and you're almost certain to see a mention of the 1945 ***Baltimore & Ohio Railroad station,*** just west of Georgia Avenue. He even mentions the conversion from train station to museum and now you can see the station, the only building in downtown Silver Spring to be on the list of the National Register of Historic Places. This is the station where my family and I would catch a train and it is where my daughters disembarked after their first train ride from Washington, D.C.' s Union Station. The station has

MBHS Alums

The humongous building behind the noise-barrier walls along the outer loop of the Beltway (Interstate 495) between the Colesville Road and University Boulevard exits is Montgomery Blair High School, home to approximately 2,500 students. It has all the bells and whistles one would like in a high school that saw its first students in September 1998. Its predecessor stands at Dale Drive and Wayne Avenue near downtown Silver Spring, maybe a mile away as the crow flies. That school opened in 1935, and I graduated from there a few years later (quite a few, thank you). Among the other students attending Blair (go Blazers!) a few years before, after, and during my time there were Goldie Hawn, Ben Stein, Carl Bernstein, Sylvester Stallone, and former Baltimore Orioles pitcher Steve Barber.

been restored, after an automobile crashed into its front door in 1997 and then its owner, CSX, wanted to demolish the building. Montgomery Preservation accepted the station from CSX in 1998, complete with leaking roof, falling plaster, filthy floors and tile, and graffiti. Restoration was complete in late 2002 with the help of numerous people, organizations, and businesses, and with the experienced eye of Robert B. Davis, the former stationmaster. A plaque is on the trackside bench commemorating his forty-two years of service. *Class Acts Arts, Inc.,* a Silver Spring performing arts organization (301–588–7525; www.classactsarts.org), now occupies the former baggage area and the agent/operators office. The passenger waiting room is available for rentals and will serve as a visitor center and museum as part of the planned Metropolitan Branch Hiker/Biker trail.

An open house is held at the station the first Saturday of each month, from April through December. The station is at 8100 Georgia Avenue; (301) 495–4915; www.montgomerypreservation.org/BOStation.html.

For years a *post office mural* sat in the Silver Spring Post Office on Georgia Avenue. Nicolai Cikovsky (of the Towson transportation mural incident) painted *The Old Tavern* in 1937 and it reflects the life in the area during and after the antebellum period. The mural has been moved to the Silver Spring Library, 8901 Colesville Road, Silver Spring; (240) 777–0910.

Continuing out Georgia Avenue, which parallels the railroad and subway tracks, you'll come to the intersection of Georgia and Colesville Road, and the Silver Spring subway station. A mural, 100 feet long and 8 feet high, was installed as part of the MetroArt I arts project (see also Prince George's County). Created by Sally Callmer of Bethesda, who previously was a miniaturist, the *Penguin Rush Hour Mural* was meant as a temporary installation but has become such an integral part of the community that the Montgomery County Department of Transportation has purchased the twenty-five panels as a permanent fixture. The penguins are about to figuratively ride the rails again and the newly restored panels should be installed by summer of 2007. The construction you see around the Silver Spring Metro station is the new Silver Spring Transit Center (combining WMATA, Montgomery County Ride-On, MTA regional commuter bus, Van-Go shuttle, Inter-city buses, the University of Maryland shuttle, and MARC services), which should be completed in 2010.

In 1887 a resort hotel and retreat was built in the Forest Glen area of Silver Spring. Over the years it also served as a finishing school for girls and a

trivia

Incidentally, the area, which is not incorporated, is called Silver Spring, not "springs" as in the Florida town.

convalescent center for World War II soldiers. Known as the **National Park
Seminary,** it has a number of exotic
buildings in a variety of architectural
styles. The building was neglected for
years and has been a passion for preservationists. It received a $20,000 grant
from the Maryland Commission for Cele-
bration 2000 to help fund exterior restoration of the pagoda for a visitor center
and museum. Check out the Web site: www.saveourseminary.org.

A new **Silver Theater** has risen on Colesville Road in Silver Spring rekin-
dling fond memories of its earlier days when it was "kool inside." It has three
sections, one with 400 seats and a 70mm screen, one with 200 seats, and one
with 75 seats. There is also a gallery, a cafe, concession stands, and a lobby. In
addition to classic, foreign language, and art movies, there will be musical performances and lectures.

When the art deco–style Silver first opened in October 1938, FDR was
president. Within the early years, such movies as *Little Miss Broadway, Boys
Town, Snow White and the Seven Dwarfs, The Wizard of Oz,* and *Gone with the
Wind* were shown. It's now the home of the **American Film Institute** (AFI)
and known as the AFI Silver Theatre and Cultural Center. It's located at 8633
Colesville Road in Silver Spring; (301) 495–6720; www.afi.com.

Just off the east side of Georgia Avenue, in Silver Spring, is a statue of Nor-
man Lane (1911–1987), known as the "unofficial mayor" of Silver Spring. The
bronze statue honors Lane who spent some twenty years walking the streets,
doing odd jobs, taking blooms from the Bell Flowers dumpster and giving them
to women, sleeping on the street or in back of nearby auto body repair shop,
and just being nice to people. The statue was created by his friend, artist Fred
Folsom, and was dedicated in 1991. The plaque quotes Lane's most oft-said
remark, "Don't worry about it."

The city of Bethesda lies west of Silver Spring, and longtime area residents
(anyone who's been here for more than fifteen years) can tell you about the
awkward, sprawling image of the **Bethesda Triangle** intersection of Wisconsin Avenue, Old Georgetown Road, and East-West Highway. Personally, I
remember it from when we used to hang out at the Hot Shoppes restaurant on
Saturday after high school football games between archrivals Montgomery Blair
and Bethesda Chevy Chase.

Known as the **Bethesda Urban District,** this area has nearly 200 restaurants, from traditional to trendy, from down-home to deluxe. There are more
than fifty sculptures and murals tucked into little nooks and crannies or out in

plain sight in the district. One of these is the **Pioneer Lady** *statue,* or Madonna of the Trail, symbolizing the importance of these roads even in their early days. Harry Truman dedicated the statue on April 19, 1929, in honor of the pioneer spirit and the National Pike, which connected the country from this spot on the East Coast to the town of Upland, California, on the West Coast. This was the last of twelve statues to be installed. The other statues were erected (chronologically) in Springfield, Ohio; Wheeling, West Virginia; Council Grove, Kansas; Lexington, Missouri; Lamar, Colorado; Albuquerque, New Mexico; Springerville, Arizona; Vandalia, Illinois; Richmond, Indiana; Washington, Pennsylvania; and Upland, California. The memorial (which faces east, whereas most of the other statues face west) is dedicated to the pioneer mothers of the covered-wagon days.

trivia

Wheaton, a few miles north of Silver Spring, is the twelfth and most recently (2005) designated Arts and Entertainment District. Joining Silver Spring and Bethesda, it's the third district in Montgomery County. Wheaton is known as a hub of music and culture, with its many ethnic and family-owned restaurants and Chuck Levin's Washington Music Center. An Arts Network of seventy-plus members identifies local arts and entertainment resources and develops programs that enhance the arts base. Two reasons this designation is so valuable is that artists working in the districts can receive an income tax break and developers who create art space can be exempt from paying certain property taxes.

The engraving reads: OVER THIS HIGHWAY MARCHED THE ARMY OF MAJOR GENERAL EDWARD BRADDOCK, APRIL 14, 1755, ON ITS WAY TO FORT DUQUESNE, AND [THIS IS] THE FIRST MILITARY ROAD IN AMERICA, BEGINNING AT ROCK CREEK AND POTOMAC RIVER, GEORGETOWN, MARYLAND, LEADING OUR PIONEERS ACROSS THE CONTINENT TO THE PACIFIC.

The *Pioneer Lady* statue is located between the post office and the Hyatt Regency Hotel at the corner of Wisconsin Avenue, East-West Highway, and Old Georgetown Road in Bethesda. The statue was reinstalled in 1986, after years in storage due to subway and hotel construction.

Then, perhaps like the pioneers before her, who settled and moved, moved and settled, the poor Pioneer Lady or Madonna of the Trail statue had another unsettling moment. In December 2004 she began to lean. A little forward and a little to the port. Off to storage, again, while the statue's owners, the Maryland State Society of the Daughters of the American Revolution, and other government bodies determined that a sinkhole from a water main break had caused the sudden Pisa-like appearance. She's safely back in place now. At least until the next problem comes along.

For more information about the public art, contact the Bethesda Urban Partnership and request a copy of the *Discovery Trail* brochure, 7906 Woodmont Avenue, Bethesda 20814; (301) 215–6660; www.bethesda.org.

The Montgomery Farm Women's Cooperative Market is the subject of the **Bethesda Post Office mural** painted by Robert Gates in 1939. This definitely represents a Montgomery County tradition, unlike the transportation scene painted in the Towson Post Office. The Bethesda mural was restored in 1967 with funds provided by the Montgomery Farm Woman's Cooperative Market. The post office is at 7400 Wisconsin Avenue.

Take Old Georgetown Road west out of Bethesda, just outside the Beltway, and you can stop by the **Dennis and Phillip Ratner Museum,** a walk through the Hebrew Bible via visual arts. Phillip is a multimedia artist (sculpture, painting, etched glass, tapestry, drawing, and graphic arts) and native Washingtonian; his work is in the permanent collections of the Smithsonian Institution, the U.S. Supreme Court, the Library of Congress, the White House, and many other places. His cousin Dennis is the founder and chairman of the Hair Cuttery, the nation's largest privately owned salon chain with more than 800 salons internationally. He—and therefore his corporation—is heavily involved in community and cultural affairs.

The museum's collection includes examples of Phillip's sculptures, drawings, paintings, and graphics, and exhibits of the works of professional and student artists, from various institutions and from seminars in the museum. This facility is open 10:00 A.M. to 4:30 P.M. Monday through Thursday and to groups by appointment, with no admission fee charged. The Ratner Museum is located at 10001 Old Georgetown Road, Bethesda. Call (301) 897–1518; www.ratnermuseum.com.

For years the locals knew that **Uncle Tom's Cabin,** of Harriet Beecher Stowe fame, sat behind a wall of trees on Old Georgetown Road in Bethesda. The 13-by-17-foot, eighteenth-century cabin was the home of Josiah Henson (1789–1883), but it was attached to a privately owned three-bedroom house sitting on an acre of land, and few people had a chance to see it. When Hildegarde Mallet-Prevost died in 2005, at the age of one hundred, the Montgomery County Planning Board bought the home and had a deed transfer celebration on January 16, 2006. It was attended by Joseph Henson, a distant relative of Josiah's, and Greg Mallet-Prevost (Hildegard's son), as well as a number of local elected officials and about one hundred interested bystanders—the first members of the public to see the inside of the home and cabin.

There's no money even for a sign or to do any of the necessary renovation work, however the cabin was open for Heritage Weekend (lines out the driveway!) and should continue to be open for future Heritage Weekends. For now, all you can do is walk or drive by and take a peek at history at 11420 Old

Georgetown Road, Bethesda; Maryland National Capital Park and Planning Commission, Historic Preservation office; (301) 563–3400.

If you like nature or have children who have excess energy to burn (and how many children fit into that category?), be sure to visit the **Cabin John Regional Park,** part of the Maryland–National Capital Park and Planning Commission park system. (There's also Wheaton Regional, in Wheaton; Watkins Regional, in Kettering; and Cosca Regional, in Clinton.)

Cabin John covers more than 500 acres, with an ice skating rink (with Monday night curling, at least as of this writing), hiking trails, sports fields, indoor and outdoor tennis courts, picnic tables and pavilions, a nature center, and most important for the moment, an Action Playground. Designed by Heidi Sussman, this playground is an elaborate obstacle course covering more than a half acre of ground. There's a section for toddlers, one for preschoolers, one for older children, and places for parents to sit. Among the challenges are a 40-foot net tunnel, a 30-foot tire bridge, and a 50-foot tunnel slide. What's really nice about this playground is if you can lose your inhibitions for a few moments, you can enjoy the swings, slides, and challenges, too. Well, at least some of them. Sussman also designed the play area for Wheaton Regional Park. Cabin John is at 7400 Tuckerman Lane, Rockville; (301) 299–4555; www.mncppc.org.

The **Rockville Post Office mural** was done by New York artist Judson Smith in 1940 and is of *Sugar Loaf Mountain.* Supposedly, it was painted from the porch of an estate called Inverness, which was built in 1818 by Benjamin White. The view includes fields and farm buildings, and the mural hangs over the wall where the lock boxes used to be located. The Rockville Post Office is at 2 West Montgomery Avenue.

trivia

F. Scott and Zelda Fitzgerald, once residents of the area, are buried in the St. Mary's Church cemetery in Rockville, located at the corner of Viers Mill Road and State Route 355 (Rockville Pike); (301) 762–0096.

Northeast of Rockville is the little town with the theater that has the big reputation. The **Olney Theatre Center** opened in 1942 as a stop on the summer "straw hat" circuit, closed because of the war, and then reopened in 1946 with Helen Hayes starring in *Good Housekeeping.* Other luminaries who have graced its stage include Tallulah Bankhead, Gloria Swanson, and Bea Lillie. The late Reverend Gilbert Hartke, head of Catholic University's drama department, took over the management in 1953, providing exposure for his students as well as for Carol Channing, John McGiver, and Frances Sternhagen.

Also known as the State Summer Theatre of Maryland, Olney Theatre Center started a new tradition in 1989 with the annual production of *The Butterfingers Angel, Mary & Joseph, Herod the Nut,* and *The Slaughter of 12 Hit*

Carols in a Pear Tree, a Christmas entertainment by noted playwright William Gibson. The theater also is known for the elected officials it attracts, particularly on opening night, both to see the outstanding presentations and to be seen. The Victorian farmhouse (circa 1880) next door is the Actors' Residence, where housing is provided for the cast in season. Actually, two casts stay there at one time, one for the show in production and one for the show in rehearsal. On opening night post-performance festivities take place here.

Olney Theatre is at 2001 Olney-Sandy Spring Road, Olney; (301) 924–3400; www.olneytheatre.org.

When you tell someone you're going to **Roy's Place,** they think you're talking about that old cowboy movie star. But this Roy's Place is in Gaithersburg, northwest of Rockville, and it is far from fast food and fast eating. In fact, the menu tells you that if you are in a hurry, go someplace else. No, it is not fine dining. It is just sandwiches and more sandwiches—some of the weirdest sandwiches you've ever imagined. How would you like a sandwich with roast beef, fried oysters, and a side serving of tartar sauce? Would you prefer provolone cheese, anchovies, blue-cheese dressing, onions, and lettuce? Or would you like something else?

The menu features more than one hundred different sandwiches, or you can start at the front page with a salad selection and skip to the back page for a simple hamburger, if you do not feel like reading the equivalent of a novella before you eat. Roy's has been open since 1971, and several local and national celebrities have had sandwiches named after them. The decor is just as interesting and offbeat as the menu, with posters, old advertisements, and a sign by the skylight that says THIS WAY OUT.

COMSAT Charrette

As you travel Interstate 270 through Montgomery County, you might catch sight of the silver-colored **COMSAT** building in Clarksburg. Constructed in 1969 from a design by renowned architect Cesar Pelli, the building (now occupied by Lockheed Martin) has an aluminum and glass skin, and is an early example of "high-tech" architecture. It sits on about two hundred acres of rolling countryside and is the target of a huge preservation vs. teardown battle. Public hearings have been held, Pelli was in town in 2006 for a charrette about the building, and the debate continues. A movement is afoot to have it named as a Montgomery County landmark, with it and thirty-three acres protected from the ever-expanding suburban housing landscape. Lockheed Martin has the rights to the property now and probably through 2012, but it's worth taking time to look at it, just in case preservationists lose this fight to LCOR, a Pennsylvania company that wants to develop the property. The building is at 22300 Comsat Drive; www.montgomerypreservation.org.

Roy's Place is at 2 East Diamond Avenue in Gaithersburg; call (301) 948–5548; www.roysplacerestaurant.com. Hours are Monday through Thursday 11:00 A.M. to 11:00 P.M., Friday and Saturday 11:00 A.M. to midnight, and Sunday noon to 11:00 P.M. Reservations are not accepted.

White's Ferry, well west of the Beltway, is the only remaining ferry system on the Potomac River, connecting White's Ferry, Maryland, to Leesburg, Virginia. It probably is more important these days than when it began operation in 1828, for it is the only river crossing between the American Legion Bridge on the Washington (or Capital) Beltway to the south and east, and the Point of Rocks bridge to the north and west. Regular commuters and tourists can easily tell when there is a major backup on the Beltway because these back-country roads become filled with drivers escaping the jam. The ferry *General Jubal Early* (named for a Confederate leader) runs the 1,000-foot crossing on a cable propelled by a diesel tug in about three minutes. It can hold fifteen cars and operates all year, weather and river conditions permitting, on a demand basis. A country store selling sundries and souvenirs is open on the Maryland side spring through fall. The ferry is off Route 107 at 24801 White's Ferry Road, Dickerson. Call (301) 394–5200 for information.

Just up the ramp from White's Ferry landing is the ditch that was once the **Chesapeake & Ohio Canal** and is now the longest and thinnest National Historical Park in the country, narrowing to less than 50 feet at one point. There was a time when there were twenty trading posts along the 185-mile canal, which ran from Cumberland to Washington, D.C., roughly paralleling the Potomac River. In 1988 conservationists spent three months clearing away foliage and found the 150-foot foundation of a nineteenth-century depot and the Granary. From the Civil War until 1924, canal boats headed down to Washington, D.C., where they would tie up to a three-story wooden storage build-

Panning for Gold

Minute quantities of gold have been found along the Potomac, near Great Falls, and in the Piedmont regions. If you'd like to try your hand at panning, or at least see where some gold has been mined, stop by the Chesapeake and Ohio (C&O) Canal Park and Great Falls Tavern Museum, near the intersection of MacArthur Boulevard and Great Falls Road. Park in the C&O Canal parking area and follow the unmarked trail to the **Maryland Gold Mine,** which was worked until the 1920s. No one has become rich with Maryland gold, but one can try. For more information about the history of gold finds in the state and rules and regulations about prospecting, write to the Maryland Geological Survey, 2300 St. Paul Street, Baltimore 21218.

Take Father Hurley, Then Turn Left

As you travel along Interstate 270, you may see a sign for Father Hurley Boulevard and wonder who he is to deserve such recognition. Actually, he's now Monsignor Leonard Hurley, founding pastor of Mother Seton Parish in Germantown, which is located on the forenamed road.

Hurley, now in his late-70s, worked with the county (or maybe they worked for him) in the 1980s on development controls and ordinances. In 1987 the county renamed Germantown Drive in his honor.

ing called the Granary to load up with grain from area farms. In the more than sixty years since the canal closed, the Granary and canal have been neglected and overgrown by trees and shrubbery.

Other parts of the canal are alive and thriving, although hurricanes often wreak havoc upon the waterway. About four million people visit some part of the park, with May through October the busiest time. The 14 miles between Georgetown (in Washington, D.C.) and Great Falls sees the most visitors, so if you're looking for solitude in your nature walks, biking, or horseback riding expeditions, aim toward the upper areas. Primitive camping areas are located approximately every 5 miles, from Swain's Lock (mile 16) to Evitts Creek (mile 180), on a first-come, first-served basis, no permits needed (except for a group area at mile 12). Each site has a chemical toilet, pump water (May to November), picnic table, and fire ring with cooking grill.

The park is open from sunrise to sunset and there are six visitor centers, Georgetown, Great Falls Tavern, Brunswick, Williamsport, Hancock, and Cumberland. There's a $4.00-per-car entrance fee that's good for three days (an annual pass is $15.00) and $2.00 for cyclists and pedestrians at the Great Falls area of the canal. Golden Eagle and Golden Access passes are honored. Commercial vehicle fees are $25 for one to six people, $40 for seven to twenty-five people, and $100 for more than twenty-five people. Mule-drawn canal boat rides are available at Georgetown and Great Falls spring through fall. Besides the canal towpath, there are other hiking trails at Great Falls, including the Gold Mine, River, Woodland, Berma Road, Angler's Spur, and the appropriately named Billy Goat Trail. For information contact the C&O Canal Headquarters, 16500 Shepherdstown Pike, Sharpsburg; (301) 739–4200.

For additional Montgomery County tourism information, write to the Visitors Center Manager, Conference and Visitors Bureau of Montgomery County, MD Inc., 12900 Middlebrook Road, Suite 1400, Germantown 20874; call (301) 428–9702 or (800) 925–0880, or visit www.visitmontgomery.com.

Frederick County

Abutting the northwest border of Montgomery County and going north to the Pennsylvania state line, with the Potomac River on its southern border, Frederick County is renowned in certain circles for the antiques shops in New Market and the city of Frederick. Steeped in history, the county also is home to the restored train depot and museum at Brunswick; the Barbara Fritchie and Roger B. Taney homes; wineries and orchards; the Catoctin Mountains (where Camp David, the presidential retreat, is located); the Grotto of Lourdes and the National Shrine of St. Elizabeth Ann Seton; the Lilypons Water Gardens; Gov. Thomas Johnson's Rose Hill Manor and Schifferstadt Architectural Museum; many churches and steeples; and, of course, that picturesque stopping point, Sugar Loaf Mountain.

Frederick, about equidistant from Washington, D.C., and Baltimore—or about an hour's drive from either city—is another of the state's designated Arts and Entertainment Districts. The city's leaders and citizens have worked hard to revitalize the downtown area, preserving a fine collection of Federal, Georgian, and Victorian buildings. Among the highlights is the Weinberg Center for the Arts, housed in a renovated 1926 movie theater. The city has museums, photography studios, and about a dozen art galleries. As mentioned elsewhere, the Arts and Entertainment District designation provides a property tax credit for developers and business owners who renovate buildings for arts-related purposes. The National Trust for Historic Preservation also has chosen Frederick as a Distinctive Destination.

A few words about **_churches in Frederick._** There are ten of note and one synagogue, and their histories and architectural styles date from the colonial, revolutionary, and Civil War eras. Tours are available during the year, and a brochure is available from the Frederick Visitor Center that details the history of each

When Is a Stone Bridge Not a Stone Bridge?

The **Community Bridge mural project** created the illusion of 3,000 stones, none of which are alike, a gate, a fountain, and numerous other items suggested by the community, both nearby and from afar. William M. Cochran was the primary muralist in this 2,500-square-foot trompe l'oeil, but many others helped. Pam Jaffee painted almost all of the ivy, a feat that took her almost six months to finish. The project started in February 1993 and took five years to complete. You will find the mural at South Carroll Street in Frederick; (301) 644–4047; www.bridge.skyline.net.

house of worship. A special event for all the houses of worship is the Candle-light Tour held in December; each is decorated for the holiday and hosts are on hand to greet visitors and answer questions. Special music and presentations are provided at various churches throughout the evening, and free parking is available. Hospitality rooms are located at a number of places, and the one at Trunk Hall in the Evangelical Lutheran Church is wheelchair accessible.

Many prominent Marylanders now reside in **Mount Olivet Cemetery,** including Francis Scott Key, Barbara Fritchie, and Gov. Thomas Johnson, along with veterans of the American Revolution, the Civil War (more than 800 Confederate soldiers), and World War II, as well as more than 30,000 other people. A statue of Key stands more than 9 feet tall on a monument that is 16 feet high and 45 feet around; you can't miss the statue because it welcomes you at the main entrance. The U.S. flag standing by him flies twenty-four hours a day in honor of his writing the words to "The Star-Spangled Banner." Much of the money collected for the $25,000 monument was donated in dimes and dollars by people all over the country.

Little green-and-white signs direct you to the graves of Governor Johnson and Barbara Fritchie, which are across the road from each other. Johnson was a Revolutionary War patriot, born in Frederick County in 1732 (the same year as George Washington), and was a prominent member of the Continental Congress. He was the first governor of the state of Maryland and associate justice of the U.S. Supreme Court. Fritchie was made immortal by John Greenleaf Whittier's poem about her bravery against Gen. Stonewall Jackson, when she flew the Union flag and dared soldiers to "Shoot if you must, this old gray head, but spare your country's flag." A monument of Maryland granite with the Whittier poem on a bronze tablet was unveiled on September 9, 1914. The cemetery is considered one of the most beautiful and distinguished in this part of the country. Mount Olivet Cemetery, 515 South Market Street, Frederick; (301) 661–1164.

Between Frederick and Thurmont is the old **Catoctin Furnace.** For 125 years Catoctin Village was a prosperous iron-making community. Started by a group of men that included the future first governor of Maryland, Thomas Johnson, the stack went into blast in 1776 to produce pig iron, tools, and household items, including the popular ten-plate stove. Bombshells for 10-inch mortars were produced toward the end of the Revolutionary War. By the mid-eighteenth century, the owner of the furnace had eighty

trivia

Thurmont originally was called Mechanicstown because Jacob Weller, a mechanic of German descent, settled here with his family in 1751.

Rosebud Salve

Those of you who've used Rosebud Salve, made by the Rosebud Perfume Co., will be delighted to know that its home offices are in an old three-story hotel in Woodsboro, north of Frederick. The company was started in 1892 by pharmacist George F. Smith, and it's now run by two of his granddaughters and other family members. Items about the balm have appeared in *Glamour, Allure, Woman's Day,* and *Self* within the past year or two, keeping sales at a brisk pace. Check in beauty salons and Walgreen's in the States or in stores as far away as London. Rosebud Perfume Co., 528 Trail Avenue, Frederick 21701.

houses for his workers, a sawmill, gristmill, company store, farms, ore railroad, three furnace stacks (including an anthracite coal stack), and more than 11,000 acres of land. By 1903 the furnace ceased to operate, although ore was taken out of this area until 1912.

For additional information write to the Catoctin Furnace Historical Society, Thurmont 21788, or call Cunningham Falls State Park, (301) 271–7574. The furnace, remaining houses in Catoctin Village, and Harriet Chapel can be seen along State Route 806, on the east side of U.S. Highway 15, about 12 miles north of Frederick.

There's just enough winter in Frederick County that covered bridges were desirable to assure safe passage over waterways. Bridges otherwise would have become frozen, slick, and impassable.

Welcome to the ***Mason & Dixon Discovery Center,*** formerly the Welcome Center, where you can discover all kinds of travel information, Civil War items, a scenic overlook, picnic area, walking trails, and a playground. The center is located on US 15, 1 mile south of the Pennsylvania and Maryland border; (301) 447–2553.

There are three covered bridges in Frederick County. The first is ***Loy's Station.*** This 90-foot-long bridge, built between 1850 and 1860, crosses Owens Creek and is surrounded by a five-and-a-half-acre park. It's located on Old Frederick Road, off State Route 77, about 3 miles from Thurmont. (301) 271–1843.

Roddy Road Covered Bridge (1856), north of Thurmont off US 15, is considered the best looking of the state's remaining bridges by covered-bridge fans. It is a single span, about 40 feet long, with a 13⅔-foot roadway. It is a fine example of basic king-post truss design, though steel stringers were installed later. Surrounding the bridge, which crosses Owens Creek, is a seventy-acre natural area for picnicking and gentle afternoon outings. (301) 271–1843.

The ***Utica Covered Bridge,*** at 101 feet, is the largest of the three. Built in 1850, it was moved in 1889 and has been structurally reinforced with concrete piers and steel-beam supports. The bridge crossed the Monocacy River until a summer flood in 1889 lifted the span from its abutments and placed it down on the river several yards away. Instead of replacing the still-intact bridge on its supports, it was dismantled, moved, and reassembled over Fishing Creek at Utica Mills. The bridge is located on Utica Road off Old Frederick Road, which is off US 15. For more information about the covered bridge, call (800) 999–3613 or (301) 228–2888; www.visitfrederick.org.

Frederick County's fertile ground attracted many settlers, and you can still see and enjoy the fruits of many hard workers at a number of orchards.

Catoctin Mountain Orchard is known for its diversity and quality of all types of berries, soft fruits, apples, and vegetables. Cortland, Red and Golden Delicious, Stayman, York, and Ida Red apples are available in autumn. You can pick your own blackberries, black raspberries, sour and sweet cherries, and strawberries, but call ahead for picking days and hours. Catoctin Mountain Orchard also offers preserved fruit and jam, packed in appealing, reusable containers, freshly baked pies, cobblers, and turnovers.

The orchard is open 9:00 A.M. to 5:00 P.M. daily June through January, and Friday and Saturday January through March. The orchard is on US 15, 15036 North Franklinville Road, and the mailing address is 15307 Kelbaugh Road, Thurmont 21788. Call (301) 271–2737; www.catoctinmtorchard.org.

Bell Hill Farm Market and Orchard is a hundred-acre farm, and the family-run fruit stand sits by a pre–Civil War home and stone springhouse. The McKissick family orchard features the traditional Red and Yellow Delicious and Stayman apples, as well as some older varieties, including Grimes Golden, York, Jonathan, and Winesap. In season you can buy peaches, plums, pears, nectarines, watermelons, cantaloupes, raspberries, corn, beans, cucumbers, potatoes, and other produce.

Bell Hill Farm is 1½ miles north of Thurmont on US 15 and is open daily from 9:00 A.M. to 5:00 P.M. Call (301) 271–7264.

Pryor's Orchard has a modern storage facility housed in a rustic barn-type market, complete with racks of antlers and an antique cider press. Pryor's seventy-three-acre orchard is one of the oldest in the Thurmont area and a favorite of local canning enthusiasts. Pryor's is noted for its many varieties of peaches, summer and fall apples, and pears. You can pick your own blueberries and sour and sweet cherries.

The orchard is closed in the winter. It is ½ mile west of Thurmont on Pryor's Road (take a left off Route 77). Call (301) 271–2693.

Scenic View Orchard has a fine selection of produce, including peaches, plums, nectarines, pears, apples (and cider), melons, sweet corn, green beans, and other vegetables. It is open daily 10:00 A.M. to 6:00 P.M. July 15 through

November 1. It's located 5 miles north of Thurmont on State Route 550 at 16239 Sabillasville Road, Sabillasville; (301) 271–2149.

Thurmont is not only the gateway to the mountains but also the gateway to *Camp David,* which was originally called High Catoctin and was one of three camps built by the Civilian Conservation Corps during the Depression. The other two camps, still in existence, are Misty Mount, used for group camping, and Greentop, used by the Baltimore League of the Handicapped since 1937. The camp buildings were constructed from local timber. High Catoctin was renamed Shangri La by Franklin Delano Roosevelt and then renamed Camp David by Dwight D. Eisenhower.

You can't visit Camp David, but you can stop by the Cozy restaurant and see the *Camp David Museum* in Thurmont. The camp's history is revealed here, with pictures and memorabilia of presidents, from Hoover to today, including campaign buttons and coffee mugs. Almost all of the items were given to the Cozy by the press corps and foreign dignitaries. The *Cozy,* started by Wilbur R. Freeze in 1929, is the oldest family-owned restaurant in the state, and contains an inn, shops, and, of course, a restaurant. It is located at 103 Frederick Road; (301) 271–4301; www.cozyvillage.com.

Footprints in the Park

Frederick County is considering a park to showcase Maryland's earliest dinosaur footprints, on a two-acre lot near Emmitsburg. That's where 200-million-year-old footprints of three ancient reptiles were found, according to paleontologist Peter M. Kranz. The footprints are believed to be the tracks of atreipus, a 4-foot-long herbivore; coelophysis, a carnivore that was a little larger than the atreipus; and a prosauropod, a vegetarian that was an ancestor of the brontosaurus and the *Astrodon johnstoni,* Maryland's official state dinosaur. They're the only footprints in Maryland from the Triassic period.

There are numerous campgrounds where you can spend a night or two, and Frederick is close enough to Washington and Baltimore to be used as a base, if you wish. One of the better-known private campgrounds is ***Crow's Nest Lodge Campground,*** owned and operated by Ned and Renna Haynes. It has 110 campsites located along Big Hunting Creek, a mountain trout stream that flows through the Catoctin Mountains. Each spacious campsite is designed to accommodate a large tent, tent trailer, or travel trailer. Most of the sites are shaded, and many have water and electricity. At the campground you can enjoy a spring-fed freshwater pond for swimming and wading, 10 miles of scenic foot trails that wind through the Catoctin Mountain Park, fishing, nature study, and a half dozen action sports. Pets are welcome, as long as they are on a leash at all times.

The address is Crow's Nest Lodge Campground, P.O. Box 145, Thurmont 21788. Call (301) 271–7632.

For additional tourism information, write to the Tourism Council of Frederick County, 19 East Church Street, Frederick 21701, or call (301) 644–4047 or (800) 999–3613. Online, log on to www.visitfrederick.org.

Places to Eat in Greater Washington

BETHESDA

There are nearly 200 restaurants in and around the Bethesda Triangle (at the intersection of Old Georgetown Road, Wisconsin Avenue, and East-West Highway), catering to just about every taste you can imagine. Because of this competition, it's easy to find an excellent place to eat within your budget, from inexpensive to extremely pricey. Here are a few suggestions:

Bean Bag,
10400 Old Georgetown Road,
(301) 530–8090

Benihana of Tokyo,
7315 Wisconsin Avenue,
(301) 652–5391

Tastee Diner of Bethesda,
7731 Woodmont Avenue,
(301) 652–3970

BOWIE

Chessie Chesapeake Grille,
4500 Crain Highway,
(301) 464–4586

Grace's Fortune,
15500 Annapolis Road,
(301) 805–1108

CLINTON

Wayfare,
7401 Surratts Road,
(301) 856–3343

COLLEGE PARK

Moose Creek Steak House,
1000 Baltimore Avenue,
(240) 542–1231

94th Aero Squadron,
5240 Paint Branch Parkway,
(301) 699–9400

R.J. Bentley's,
7323 Baltimore Avenue,
(301) 277–8898

CROFTON

Jasper's,
1651 Route 3 North,
(301) 261–3505,
www.jaspersrestaurants.com

DUNDALK

Salty Dog's Crab House,
4011 North Point Boulevard,
(410) 388–0515

OTHER ATTRACTIONS WORTH SEEING IN THE CAPITAL REGION

Antique Carousel,
Watkins Regional Park,
Kettering,
(301) 218–6757,
www.pgparks.com

Barbara Fritchie House and Museum,
Frederick,
(301) 698–0630

Beltsville Agricultural Research Center,
Beltsville,
(301) 504–9403,
www.ars.usda.gov/is

Brookside Gardens,
Wheaton Regional Park,
Wheaton,
(301) 949–8230,
www.brooksidegardens.org,
www.clark.net/pub/
mncppc/montgom/park/
brookside/index.htm

Clara Barton National Historic Site,
Glen Echo,
(301) 492–6245,
www.nps.gov/clba

Clearwater Nature Center,
Clinton,
(301) 297–4575,
www.pgparks.com

Darnall's Chance House Museum,
Upper Marlboro,
(301) 952–8010,
www.pgparks.com

Frederick Keys Baseball,
Frederick,
(301) 662–0013,
www.frederickkeys.com

Glen Echo Park,
Glen Echo,
(301) 492–6282,
www.nps.gov/glec

GAITHERSBURG

O'Donnell's,
311 Kentlands Boulevard,
(301) 519–1650,
www.odonnellsrestaurants
.com

GREENBELT

Jasper's,
7401 Greenbelt Road,
(301) 441–8030,
www.japsersrestaurants.com

HYATTSVILLE

Adelis,
6495 New Hampshire
Avenue,
(301) 559–4100

LARGO

Gladys Knight & Ron Winans Chicken & Waffles,
860 East Capital Centre
Boulevard,
(301) 627–5990

Jasper's,
9640 Lottsford Court,
(301) 883–2199,
www.jaspersrestaurants.com

LAUREL

Brass Duck Lounge,
15101 Sweitzer Lane,
(301) 776–5300

Tapatios Mexican Restaurant,
13485 Baltimore Avenue,
(301) 210–0950

Huntington Railroad Museum,
Bowie,
(301) 805–4616,
(301) 262–6200

Lilypons Water Gardens,
Buckeystown,
(301) 874–5133,
(800) 999–5459,
www.lilypons.com

Monocacy National Battlefield,
Frederick,
(301) 662–3515,
www.nps.gov/mono

Montpelier Cultural Arts Center,
(301) 953–1993,
www.smart.net/~parksrec/montarts.htm

National Archives at College Park,
College Park,
(202) 501–5205,
www.nara.gov

National Capital Trolley Museum,
Silver Spring,
(301) 384–6088,
www.dctrolley.org

**National Shrine–
St. Elizabeth Ann Seton,**
Emmitsburg,
(301) 447–6606,
www.setonshrine.org

Sandy Spring Museum,
Sandy Spring,
(301) 774–0022
www.sandyspringmuseum.org

Schifferstadt Architectural Museum,
Frederick,
(301) 663–3885,
www.fredericklandmarks.org

Strathmore Hall Arts Center,
North Bethesda,
(301) 530–0540,
www.strathmore.org

Watkins Regional Park,
Upper Marlboro,
(301) 390–9258

OXON HILL

Gallant Fox,
6400 Oxon Hill Road,
(301) 749–9400

RIVERDALE

Calvert House Inn,
6211 Baltimore Avenue,
(301) 864–5220

ROCKVILLE

Amada Amante,
9755 Traville Gateway Drive,
(301) 217–5900,
www.amadaamante.com

Places to Stay in Greater Washington

Most hotels and motels in the Greater Washington area belong to the major hotel chains, including Best Western, Days Inn, Doubletree, Econo Lodge, Holiday Inn, Marriott, Ramada Inn, Red Roof Inn, and Susse Chalet Inn. If, for some strange reason, you're bypassing all the wonderful things you can do and see in Maryland and you're headed toward the attractions of Washington, you'll probably be staying in Prince George's or Montgomery County, and you'll want one that's either on or near a subway line, or that provides shuttle service to a subway.

BRADDOCK HEIGHTS

Haydn's Tavern,
5018 Old National Pike,
(301) 371–9189,
www.frederick.com/dining/
haydntavern.htm

BRANDYWINE

Cedarville State Forest,
10201 Bee Oak Road,
(301) 888–1410,
(888) 432–2267,
www.dnr.state.md.us

CLARKSBURG

**Little Bennett Regional
Park,**
23701 Clarksburg Road,
(301) 972–9222,
www.mc-mncppc.org

DERWOOD

**Reynolds of Derwood Bed
& Breakfast,**
16620 Bethayres Road,
(301) 963–2216,
www.reynolds-bedbreak
fast.com

CLINTON

Cosca Regional Park,
11000 Thrift Road,
(301) 868–1397,
www.pgparks.com

COLLEGE PARK

Cherry Hill Park,
9800 Cherry Hill Road,
(301) 937–7116,
(800) 801–6449,
www.cherryhillpark.com

GAITHERSBURG

Gaithersburg Inn,
104 Russell Avenue,
(301) 330–1331,
www.gaithersburginn.com

GREENBELT

Greenbelt Park,
6565 Greenbelt Road,
(301) 344–3948,
(800) 367–2265,
www.nps.gov/gree/

ROCKVILLE

Cabin John Regional Park,
7701 Tuckerman Lane,
(301) 495–2525,
www.mc-mncppc.org

Parklawn Campsites,
12724 Viers Mill Road,
(301) 495–2525,
www.mc-mncppc.org

TAKOMA PARK

Davis Warner Inn,
8114 Carroll Avenue,
(301) 408–3989,
(888) 683–3989,
www.daviswarnerinn.com

THURMONT

**The Cozy Restaurant
and Village,**
103 Frederick Road,
(301) 271–4301,
www.cozyvillage.com

UPPER MARLBORO

Watkins Regional Park,
301 Watkins Park Drive,
(301) 249–6900,
www.pgparks.com

Southern Maryland

Although civilization (or at least suburban sprawl) has entered Southern Maryland, parts of Charles, Calvert (sometimes pronounced "Cawlvert" or "Calvit" by the locals), and St. Mary's Counties probably have changed more because of avulsion and accretion (erosion and accumulation of land) than because of developmental encroachment since the first English colonists settled here in the mid-1600s.

As you drive down these roads, you will see signs of early settlements established by brave men and women who came seeking new lives, religious freedom, and adventure. Dozens of churches, some dating from the early seventeenth century, dot the historic landscape.

Water has made its influence felt, of course; there are many waterside communities, places to buy and eat fresh seafood, and aquatic research centers. In Southern Maryland I looked for markets that keep a community alive, and I found several community craft centers and talented artisans. I hope you will take the time to enjoy the maritime influence and the fine and unusual dining surrounding, or perhaps surrounded by, this rich coastal area.

Bikers particularly enjoy the terrain of Southern Maryland, and a bicycle map has been created just for you, highlighting

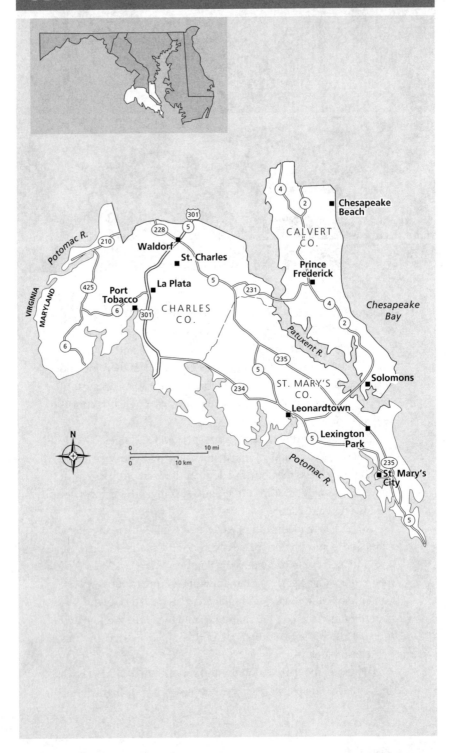

the sights through ten loops. The loops range from 7 to 58 miles. Bike stores and points of interest are designated along the various routes. Contact any of the tourism offices for a copy.

Calvert County

The ***Battle Creek Cypress Swamp Sanctuary*** is one of the northernmost stands of bald cypress trees in the country and the only one on Maryland's western shore. Forget the images of cypress trees and the Old South, for there is neither Spanish moss hanging from these boughs nor Southern belles in hoop skirts. The cypress in this swamp are thought to be descendants of trees growing here some 5,000 to 15,000 years ago, shortly (relatively speaking) after the glaciers started receding. Some of the trees reach more than 100 feet in height and are 4 feet in diameter.

Within this one-hundred-acre nature sanctuary is an interpretive center and a great place for nature photography in the spring (when violets, mayapples, and pink lady's slipper orchids are in bloom) and early summer when the blooms are most profuse. Bring fast film and a tripod, because the light is heavily filtered through the canopy. With its rich wetlands, look for such species as sweet gum, ash, southern arrowwood, and spicebush. You'll also see tulip tree, mountain laurel, and Virginia pine.

Just take the 1,700-foot boardwalk through the swamp to get really close to nature. However, you don't want to get too close to some of it. Those thick, fuzzy vines climbing the trees along the boardwalk through the swamp are poison ivy, and they are just as dangerous as their cousin with the three shiny leaves if you are allergic to it.

The sanctuary, the first Nature Conservancy preserve in Maryland, is at 2800 Grays Road off Sixes Road (State Route 506) in Prince Frederick. Call (410) 535–5327 or visit www.calvertparks.org. It's open Tuesday through Saturday from 10:00 A.M. to 4:00 P.M. and Sunday from 1:00 to 4:30 P.M. It is closed on Monday, and on Thanksgiving, Christmas, and New Year's Day.

JUDY'S FAVORITE ATTRACTIONS IN SOUTHERN MARYLAND

Battle Creek Cypress Swamp Sanctuary	Flag Ponds Nature Park
Calvert Marine Museum	Historic St. Mary's City

If you want to hobnob and brush shoulders with the movers and shakers of Calvert County, you probably should find your way to **Stoney's Seafood House** at the Fox Run Shopping Center, 545 Solomons Island Road North in Prince Frederick (410–535–1888). Sit down for a crab cake or oyster sandwich (you might hear that pronounced "arester," but no matter how you say it, they'll understand you). For more information and opening dates of the Broomes Island restaurant, call (410) 586–1888. A third has now opened in Solomons (410–394–0236; www.stoneysseafoodhouse.com).

Francis and Ann Koenig donated the thirty-acre park known as **Annmarie Garden** to the people of Calvert County, but it's there for everyone to enjoy. Located at the headwaters of St. John Creek in Solomons, the park was dedicated in October 1993. There's a range of sculpture and botanical treasures here, starting with the glazed ceramic gateposts, perhaps the largest and most complex hand-built enterprise ever attempted by a U.S. pottery studio. It consists of seven tons of ceramics in 630 pieces.

trivia

Solomons was named for Isaac Solomon who opened an oyster cannery here in 1867.

The first major permanent installation was a tribute to the oyster tonger, without whom we wouldn't have those succulent morsels. Maryland artist Antonio Tobias Mendez created the statue that was dedicated at Artsfest '94, an annual weeklong September event that combines the visual and performing arts. There's also the holiday Garden in Lights. Among the flora attractions are more than 460 azaleas. Another special treat is the Surveyor's Map, a floating walkway that's more than 300 feet long, ending at a lookout within the tree canopy.

Annmarie Garden is open from 9:00 A.M. to 5:00 P.M. daily; it is located on Dowell Road, Solomons. Call (410) 326–4640.

Contained within the 327-acre park known as **Flag Ponds Nature Park** are wooded uplands, ponds, swamps, freshwater marshes, sandy beaches, and part of Chesapeake Bay. Here you can clearly see the difference between the uplands and the wetlands, between the Cliffs of Calvert and Chesapeake Bay. Wildlife abounds, including fox, muskrat, otter, turkey, whitetail deer, and pileated woodpecker. Special facilities include 3 miles of gentle hiking trails, rare plants such as the blue flag iris (from which the park derives its name), pond observation decks, picnic sites, a beach, a fishing pier, and a visitor center with wildlife exhibits.

One building remains from what was once a thriving "pound net" fishery that supplied trout, croaker, and herring to the bustling Baltimore markets during the first half of the twentieth century. There is a daily vehicle charge of

$4.00 for residents and $6.00 for nonresidents April 1 through October 1, or a seasonal pass for $15.00 and $20.00, respectively. November through March the charge is $3.00 for both residents and nonresidents.

Flag Ponds is open from 9:00 A.M. to 6:00 P.M. daily and 9:00 A.M. to 8:00 P.M. on weekends during the summer. From Labor Day through Memorial Day the park is open from 9:00 A.M. to 6:00 P.M. on weekends and closed during the week. It's located on North Solomons Island Road and Flag Pond Parkway, Lusby. For additional information call (410) 586–1477 or visit www.calvert parks.org.

Instead of being a day late and a dollar short, Otto Mears and a group of Denver railroad financiers decided in 1890 that they'd build a new resort on the Chesapeake Bay so Washingtonians could escape the notoriously hot and humid summers. They built the railroad to Chesapeake Beach, a 1,600-foot boardwalk that had a band shell, dance pavilion, roller coaster, and a mile-long pier for tourist boats from Baltimore. The resort opened on June 9, 1900. A carousel opened in 1929 and it's believed that Gustav A. Dentzel, the premier carousel maker, created many of the carved animals. North Beach, a mile to the north, was created to house the workers.

The Depression was one factor that led to the resort's demise, and that was compounded by the introduction of the automobile, then World War II, gas rationing, and the rest is history. You can learn more about the history at the *Chesapeake Beach Railroad Museum* and see old photos, a diorama, archaeological finds, a carousel animal, railroad equipment, and the amazing growth that has now come to this area. The museum is open weekends from 1:00 to 4:00 P.M. in April and October, and by appointment. It is at 4155 Mears Avenue; (410) 257–3892; www.cbrm.org.

Jefferson Patterson Park and Museum always offers something interesting about the history and archaeology about the area, the War of 1812, and the environment, so it's no surprise that still another attraction has been added. "Patuxent Encounters: The Patuxent Indians and Captain John Smith" is part of the regional observation of Smith's voyages of the Chesapeake Bay. Additions to the Woodland Indian hamlet are in the works so you can learn more about the traditional and contemporary American Indian ways of life.

The 560-acre park that covers 9,000 years of human history is set along 2½ miles of the Patuxent River and St. Leonard Creek. There's an active calendar of events, including heritage celebrations, children's activities, tours, concerts, dances, lectures, and education programs. The park is open Wednesday through Sunday, from 10:00 A.M. to 5:00 P.M. from April 15 through October 15. It is located at 10515 Mackall Road, St. Leonard; (410) 586–8500; www.jefpat.org.

TOP ANNUAL EVENTS IN SOUTHERN MARYLAND

MARCH

Maryland Day,
St Mary's City,
(301) 862–0990,
(800) 762–1634

APRIL

**John Wilkes Booth
Escape Route Tour,**
Clinton,
(301) 868–1121,
www.surratt.org

MAY

Criterium Bicycle Races,
Leonardtown,
(410) 394–2770,
www.paxvelo.com

**Piney Point Lighthouse Waterfront
Festival,**
Piney Point Lighthouse Museum and
Park,
Piney Point,
(301) 769–2600,
www.stmarysmd.com/recreate/museum

Quilt and Needlework Show,
Sotterley Plantation,
Hollywood,
(301) 373–2280,
(800) 681–0850,
www.sotterley.org

Shad Bake,
Bryans Road,
(301) 908–1985,
http://somd.com/detailed/3429.php

JUNE

**African-American Family
Community Day,**
St. Leonard,
(410) 586–8501

Blue and Gray Days,
Point Lookout State Park,
(301) 872–5688

North Beach House and Garden Tour,
North Beach,
(410) 257–6127

Southern Maryland Soap Box Derby,
Leonardtown,
(301) 863–2561

St. Mary's County Crab Festival,
Leonardtown,
(301) 475–5236,
www.leonardtownsomd.com

JUNE/JULY

**St. Mary's College of Maryland River
Concert Series,**
St. Mary's City,
(240) 895 4107,
www.riverconcertseries.com

A little south of the Calvert Cliffs power plant is *Calvert Cliffs State Park,* a 1,460-acre wooded area that brings you to cliffs formed more than 15 million years ago. The cliffs hold more than 600 species of fossils. To seek your own 15-million-year-old fossils, take the approximately 2-mile hike down to the beach (and 2 miles back up, of course). The park, at 1650 Calvert Cliffs Parkway, is open from sunrise to sunset. Admission is $5.00 per car. Call (301) 872–5688 or log on to www.dnr.state.md.us/publiclands/sounterhn/calvert cliffs.html.

JULY

Calvert County Jousting Tournament,
Port Republic,
(410) 586–0565,
www.christchurchcalvert.org

AUGUST

Bassmaster Elite,
Smallwood State Park,
Marbury,
(301) 645–0558

Jousting Tournament,
Port Republic,
(410) 535–1710

SEPTEMBER

Calvert County Fair,
Barstow,
(410) 535–0026,
www.calvertcountyfair.com

Charles County Fair,
La Plata,
(301) 932–1234

St. Mary's County Fair,
Leonardtown,
(301) 475–8434,
www.somd.com/smcfair

OCTOBER

Blessing of the Fleet,
Colton's Point,
(301) 769–2222,
www.blessingofthefleet.org

St. Mary's County Oyster Festival,
Leonardtown,
(301) 863–5015

NOVEMBER

Lighthouse Open House,
Point Lookout State Park,
(301) 872–5688,
www.dnr.maryland.gov

DECEMBER

Madrigals and Carols,
St. Mary's City,
(301) 862–0990 or (800) 762–1634

Maryland State Police Shiver in the River,
Newburg,
(410) 789–6677,
www.somd.org

Continuing south on State Route 2-4 will bring you to Solomons. A visitor center is open daily from spring through fall and on Friday, Saturday, and Sunday in the winter at 14175 Solomons Island Road South; (410) 326–6027. Across the street is the *Calvert Marine Museum* and *Drum Point Lighthouse;* parking is behind the administration building.

The Calvert Marine Museum is proof that a museum can be fun, fascinating, and fact filled. This museum has grown from a seed planted by LeRoy "Pepper" Langley in 1970, and it is certainly worth a visit for a number of reasons.

Drum Point Lighthouse

One reason is the Children's Discovery Room, where there is a pile of earth from Calvert Cliffs that you can dig in to find fossils. It can be difficult and time-consuming to search for fossils at outdoor sites, but not here. One shark's tooth per person, please. This room is more fun than a bushel of crabs that has just been dusted with seasoning.

Yet there is more, and you are on your own to enjoy, to be entertained, and to be educated. Even the more conventional exhibits about boating, the paleontology of Calvert Cliffs, and the estuarine biology of the Patuxent River and Chesapeake Bay are well handled.

The museum's second treasure is the Drum Point Lighthouse, one of the old screw-pile, cottage-style lighthouses that used to protect the adventuresome watermen of the bay. The two-story, hexagon-shaped structure was built in 1883 to mark the entrance of the Patuxent River from the Chesapeake Bay. A crane and barge moved the stilted cottage to its current location in 1975.

Take a few minutes to walk through the lighthouse (watch your head when going up and down the steps), and mentally transport yourself to the time when people lived here and tended the light. It is romantic to think of the "good old days" when there were lightkeepers, but most don't think this remote lifestyle is very attractive these days.

The third treasure is an old bugeye, the *William B. Tennison,* which takes people on cruises around the bay. This bugeye is a Chesapeake Bay sailing craft built in 1899 at Crabb Island by B. P. and R. L. Miles. Her hull is "chunk built," or made of nine logs, rather than by a plank-and-frame method of construction. Originally rigged for sailing, she was converted to power in 1907, and a new, larger cabin was added aft.

You can cruise on the *Tennison* and see the Governor Thomas Johnson Bridge, the Solomons Island and Chesapeake Biological Laboratory, and the U.S. Naval Recreation Center at Point Patience. This allows you to view the inner harbor and Patuxent River as you can never see them from land. The one-hour cruise starts at 2:00 P.M. Wednesday through Sunday (minimum of ten people required) between May 1 and October 30, or you can charter the boat for your own event. Fares begin at $7.00 per adult and $4.00 per child (five to twelve) per hour for the charter. Call (410) 326–2042 for additional information. The Web site is www.calvertmarinemuseum.com.

The Calvert Marine Museum is open daily 10:00 A.M. to 5:00 P.M. except New Year's Day, Thanksgiving, and Christmas. A wheelchair is available, but the lighthouse is not wheelchair accessible. Admission is $7.00 for adults, $2.00 for children five to twelve, and $6.00 for seniors fifty-five and older. The Calvert Marine Museum is at 14150 Solomons Island Road. Call (410) 326–2042 or visit www.calvertmarinemuseum.com.

Lighthouse lovers, rejoice! For years, there's been limited access to the Cove Point Lighthouse, but now the Calvert Marine Museum owns it and has regularly scheduled shuttle service from the museum to the lighthouse.

Cove Point was lit for the first time in December 1828, but it would be one hundred years before the light was converted from kerosene to electricity, and nearly another sixty years before it was fully automated, in 1986. The 40-foot tower and lightkeeper's house were constructed of locally made bricks.

After the Calvert Marine Museum Society acquired the light from the U.S. Coast Guard in 1996, there was a massive amount of repair work to be done on the buildings, fencing, grounds, security, and other facilities so it could be open for your visit. Because the light is still operational (it's the oldest continuously working lighthouse in Maryland), visitors are only allowed inside the base, but you can look up the spiral stairway to the lantern room.

The lighthouse is open daily from 10:00 A.M. to 4:00 P.M. June through August and on weekends and holidays in May and September. Admission is $3.00. Check with the Calvert Marine Museum for details about the shuttle bus schedule; (410) 326–2042.

For more information about Solomons, call (410) 326–6027 or log on to www.calvert.com.

For additional information about Calvert County, contact the Calvert County Department of Economic Development, Courthouse, 175 Main Street, Prince Frederick 20678; (410) 535–4583, (301) 855–1880, or (800) 331–9771.

Charles County

Most of the usual tourist attractions in Charles County are centered in La Plata and Port Tobacco (one of the oldest communities on the East Coast).

One of the mysteries of history can be found at **St. Ignatius Catholic Church** near Port Tobacco. Father Andrew White, who sailed with other Jesuits

Neighbor to Neighbor

On Sunday, April 28, 2002, an F-4 force tornado (with winds of 207–260 mph, strong enough to level well-constructed homes and hurl cars) touched down in the town of La Plata, killing four people and injuring about one hundred others. This tornado caused more damage than any storm since the 1926 tornado that killed fourteen schoolchildren. Dozens of businesses and a number of homes and churches in the storm's 26-mile path were damaged or destroyed. Business and personal papers were found 50 miles away, across the Chesapeake Bay in Dorchester and Talbot Counties. Many of the papers have been returned, many accompanied by personal notes of sympathy.

The entire community, including people living far beyond the La Plata boundaries, helped the town get back on its feet. On July 3, a little more than two months after the devastation, the Waldorf Jaycees sponsored a "Charles County Cares— Neighbor to Neighbor" dinner that netted $195,000 to be distributed to the American Red Cross, the Children's Aid Society, the Tri-County Youth Services Bureau, and the county's nonprofit relief fund. La Plata is bouncing back, supported by emergency funding and the great spirit and help of "neighbors" everywhere.

on the *Ark* and the *Dove* to help found a new colony, established St. Ignatius in 1641. Years later a tunnel was discovered leading from the basement of the servants' quarters to the Potomac River, 120 feet below. No one knows whether this was part of the Underground Railroad, a convenient way to load and unload boats from the river below (particularly during inclement weather), or an escape route in the days when Catholic priests had to make a fast departure.

Stop by the church and see a relic of the Cross now encased in glass and silver. It was brought over by Father White (who wore it around his neck). Also see a mahogany table made in Santo Domingo. Stroll around the grounds and see animals at the working farm run by the resident Jesuits. Catch the Way of the Cross garden, the historic herb and butterfly garden, and the outdoor Shrine of Our Lady. Also, view the needlepoint kneelers made by the parishioners to celebrate their one-hundredth anniversary.

Following the 1773–1805 suppression of Jesuits, the men who stayed at St. Ignatius took their vows again in 1805 under a White Russian superior, thus making St. Ignatius and the residence the oldest in the United States and probably the world. Father Sal Jordan, who grew up nearby, spent days at this Chapel Point spot during his youth. He now serves as the church's pastor.

Tours of the church, Manor House, and parish grounds may be arranged through the hospitality group. St. Ignatius Church, 8855 Chapel Point Road, Port Tobacco; (301) 934–8245; www.chapelpoint.org.

Settled in 1634, Port Tobacco was once Maryland's second-largest seaport and was even found on early world maps. The town was the original county seat.

A courthouse was constructed in Port Tobacco in 1729, but was replaced when the county seat moved to La Plata. The original **Port Tobacco courthouse** has been restored and is open April through October, Monday, Saturday, and Sunday from noon to 4:00 P.M. and by appointment. Chapel Point Road, Port Tobacco; (301) 934–4313.

Nearby is the **Port Tobacco One-Room Schoolhouse,** built in 1876 and used until 1953. The Charles County Retired Teachers' Association restored the building in the 1990s; it's furnished with items from the 1800s. The schoolhouse is open on weekends from noon to 4:00 P.M. April through October, and also on Monday from noon to 4:00 P.M. June through August, and by appointment. Chapel Point Road, Port Tobacco; (301) 932–6064 or (301) 934–8836.

A few miles southwest, in Welcome, is the home and workshop of Steve and Kris Crescenze, restorers and builders of all things related to carousels, including animals and decorations. They have also restored some of the creatures and features on the 1905 Dentzel carousel (formerly of Chesapeake Beach) at Watkins Regional Park in Largo.

Their love affair with carousels began in the late 1980s when the Crescenzes bought two carousel figurines to display in a curio cabinet. Now their home, with garage workshop called **Restorations by Wolf,** looks like a curio cabinet inside a never-ending carousel. There are figures in every nook and cranny, including a pig, a giraffe, a lion, and, of course, horses—everywhere except in one room filled with Coca-Cola memorabilia.

If you've ever picked up a copy of *The Carousel News & Trader* you may well have seen a picture of their work; they've been on more than a dozen covers. Yes, a carousel coffee-table book is on Steve's mind.

You can visit the animals on the first Saturday after Easter when there's an open house, or you can see them by appointment at 8480 Gunston Road, Welcome; (301) 932–2734; www.carouselrestorations.com.

On the easternmost tip of Charles County is the town of Benedict, named for Benedict Leonard Calvert, the fourth Lord Baltimore. It was a flourishing town at least three times. The first was a period between 1817 and 1937, when steamboats carrying freight and passengers stopped here on their way to and from Baltimore and ports on the Rappahannock and Potomac Rivers. The second time was when slot machines were legal in the county and people came to gamble from as far north as New Jersey and New York. The third time was in 1988, when the Governor Thomas Johnson Bridge from Solomons Island to St. Mary's was temporarily closed. Ferries were put in service, but many people detoured to Benedict and used the Patuxent River Bridge.

Today this waterside town, the farthest inland port on the Patuxent River, has a post office that is also a paperback lending library, a restaurant or two, and some "boatels" for storing boats.

Locals certainly know about the **Benedict Marina** with its floating docks, boatlifts, other nautical essentials, and even a seaplane base. Visitors should stop by for an extremely tasty bowl of Maryland cream of crab soup, crab cakes, and fresh catch of the day entrees. For those who can't decide, there's a captains platter (fried seafood and shellfish) and a mariners platter (steamed). David and Stephanie Davidson, who bought the Benedict Marina and pier and restaurant in 2002, provide a DJ every Friday and Saturday night. The marina is at 19311 Wilmott Street; (301) 274–2882; www.benedictmarina.com.

Mount Carmel Monastery was the first convent for religious women in colonial America, founded on October 15, 1790. It was started by four Carmelite nuns, three of whom—Ann, Ann Theresa, and Susan Mathews—along with the Reverend Charles Neale were natives of Charles County. The group set up temporary quarters at Chandler's Hope, then owned by the Neale family.

Father Neale donated 860 acres to the Carmelites to build their monastery. Two of the original convent buildings have been restored and are open to visitors during the summer season. The other buildings are still used as an active convent.

If you are driving in from U.S. Highway 301 on Mitchell Road, Mount Carmel Monastery is on the left about ½ mile past Charles County Community College at 4035A Mount Carmel Road, La Plata. The monastery is open in the summer from 9:00 A.M. to 4:00 P.M. Mass is said daily at 7:15 A.M. and on Sunday at 8:00 A.M. Call (301) 934–1654 or log on to www.erols.com/carmel-of-port-tobacco.

In your travels through the county, you may see evidence of tobacco, an important (and maybe the most important) crop in this area for 300 years. It takes 250 man-hours to produce one acre of tobacco (less labor-intensive crops

British Invasion

Benedict is also notable as the landing site for 4,500 British troops in August 1814. Local historians say it is the only small town on U.S. soil that has been invaded by foreign troops, for these were the troops who marched on to the nation's capital. The British troops returned to Benedict with their wounded, and two of their soldiers were buried at Old Fields Chapel cemetery in Hughesville. During the Civil War, Camp Stanton was established here for recruiting and training African-American infantrymen to serve in the Union Army.

Bass-ically Speaking

For the past dozen years or so, Smallwood State Park has been the home of the *National Bass Tournament,* attracting pros and amateurs from the United States, Canada, and other countries. In 1854 the Potomac River was stocked with thirty bass brought from Ohio, spawning a major industry. Today the Potomac ranks as one of the country's premier largemouth bass fisheries. Winning strings regularly exceed fifty pounds. Included in the challenge of the competition is the ever-changing hydrilla (an underwater plant that provides cover for the bass population) and the timing of the tides.

The year 2005 was a spectacular one for bass fishing, when the Forrest Wood (FLW) tour came to Smallwood and brought in tons of money (well, $4.6 million worth anyway) with food and lodging accommodations, souvenirs, and other necessary boat supplies. There is also another revenue source, says Joanne Roland, tourism director for Charles County and coordinator of the event: Several anglers arrive a week before the event, go to the nearby Maryland Airport to rent a pilot and plane, and fly over the Potomac River to see how the hydrilla is growing and to note any changes in the river.

The tournament returns in June 2007 for the fifth of the seven stops along the tour. If you can't catch the event in person, you can watch the highlights on cable television. See if you can snag some of Joanne's cookies (she's known as the "cookie lady"), and if you'd like to be the co-angler with one of these professionals (top prize for the co-angler in 2005 was $40,000; the top pro received $200,000), check the FLW Outdoors site at www.flwoutdoors.com.

As you may have read or heard, the Northern Chinese Snakehead was introduced into the Potomac and many feared they'd devour the bass fingerlings or feed on the same parts of the lower food chain. There were some who thought the bass might do that to the snakeheads. So far, neither one seems to be bothering the other, and Virginia and Maryland authorities are doing the best they can to eliminate this newest imported fish.

may take as little as four man-hours), and Maryland tobacco is air-dried in a "stick" of tobacco made up of individually harvested leaves. By contrast, in Virginia the entire tobacco plant is cut at one time and is flue-cured by heat in three days. During the three- to six-month drying or curing process, each stick of tobacco will lose more than one-and-a-half gallons of water.

However, Maryland initiated a tobacco-farm buyout program and nearly 75 percent of the tobacco growers in the state, primarily in the southern counties, have agreed to the buyout. This means they get paid for not growing the tobacco while the state helps them find other productive cash crops. Some farmers are experimenting with vineyards, Christmas trees, and fruit orchards.

Generally speaking, only the Amish farmers, who don't want a government handout, are still growing tobacco. If you want to attend one of the few spring tobacco auctions, contact the Charles County tourism office for dates, times, and locations.

Pope's Creek is the best place to go for crabs and a view of the Potomac River. The 3-mile drive off US 301 down Pope's Creek Road is also a little history lesson, for it was along this route that John Wilkes Booth found refuge after assassinating Abraham Lincoln. Two historical markers designate where he stopped along Pope's Creek Road for three days and where he crossed the Potomac into Virginia.

Down at Pope's Creek are the shells of oysters eaten over the centuries, first by Charles County Native Americans, then by settlers, and today by travelers. These shells cover some thirty acres to a depth of 15 feet in some places.

If you prefer eating crabs and oysters to looking at old shells, stop by ***Captain Billy's*** for some crabs served in a traditional style. The tables are covered with paper and piles of those tasty crabs; a pitcher of beer accompanies the feast. Here you can learn why Maryland is called the Land of Pleasant Living. You may have seen Captain Billy's featured on an episode of *The Best of* on The Food Network or check the restaurant's Web site for the history of this traditional eatery. Call Captain Billy's at (301) 932–4323; www.captbillys.com.

trivia

On January 1, 1873, the first trains started running on the Pope's Creek Line of the Baltimore & Potomac Railroad. Although it was created so goods could be transported from Charles and Prince George's Counties to Baltimore and is used today to transport coal to the power plant on the Potomac, the line also allowed a "spur" to be run from Bowie to Washington, D.C., something that would otherwise have been prohibited because this new line provided competition to the Baltimore & Ohio line between the two cities.

The old building on your right as you drive along Pope's Creek Road to the water is an old Rural Electrification Administration powerhouse with lovely arched windows reminiscent of the Palladian style.

The bridge across the Potomac, 3 miles downriver, is the Governor Harry W. Nice Bridge. It opened in 1940, replacing Laidlow's Ferry, and was the first crossing of the Potomac River south of the nation's capital. The 1938 groundbreaking was presided over by President Franklin D. Roosevelt. The bridge is 1¾ miles long, rises 135 feet above the water, and carries nearly four million vehicles yearly. Passenger cars pay a $3.00 southbound toll (no toll northbound).

Dr. Samuel A. Mudd's house, where John Wilkes Booth was treated by the country doctor after Booth shot President Abraham Lincoln, is now a museum with costumed docents leading tours. The two-story, three-part early Victorian frame farmhouse, built about 1754, is furnished with original and family pieces from that period. It is open for tours April through November from noon to 4:00 P.M. on weekends, from 11:00 A.M. to 3:00 P.M. on Wednesday, and by appointment. There is a $3.00 admission charge for adults. 14940 Hoffman Road, Beantown; (301) 645–6870.

For additional tourism information write to the Charles County Office of Tourism, P.O. Box 2150, La Plata 20646; call (301) 645–0558 or (800) SOMD–FUN; or visit www.visitcharlescounty.com.

St. Mary's County

There are some counties in Maryland that are off the beaten path even when you are on their most-traveled roads. St. Mary's is one of them. The county offers many different attractions that draw thousands of people each year, yet it remains primarily historic and underdeveloped. From the Naval Air Test and Evaluation Museum (connected with the Naval Air Station, Patuxent River), to the Old Jail Museum, to Point Lookout State Park with its terrific camping area and beaches, to the crafts at Cecil's Old Mill, you can spend a good deal of time down here.

The *Three Notch Trail,* a 28-mile recreational (pedestrian, bicycle, and equestrian) trail along a railroad right-of-way, was begun in June 2006. Starting from Hughesville (in Charles County) and running to Lexington Park (to the Patuxent River Naval Air Station), the trail will connect the Northern County Senior Center in Charlotte Hall, the Charlotte Hall Library, St. Mary's County Farmers' Market, Charlotte Hall Veterans Home, the new St. Mary's County Welcome Center, the Northern Senior Center, and link the villages of New Market and Charlotte Hall. The first two phases are constructed of asphalt and are 10 feet wide in most sections. Split-rail fencing and various plantings offer buffers for the trail in some sections. Benches are provided along the way and the trail complies with the Americans with Disabilities ACT (ADA). The third phase is awaiting funding and should be completed by 2008.

You have a chance to "adopt" part of the trail or sponsor mile-marker signs, so call the Department of Recreation, Parks, and Community Services if you're interested; (301) 475–4200, ext. 1811; they're also looking for volunteers for trail upkeep and other functions. Call Jim Swift at (301) 862–1695 or Mary Wood at (301) 934–1330 for additional information; www.co.saint-marys.md.us/recreate/facilities/threenotchtrail.asp.

Historic St. Mary's City was the first proprietary colony in America and the first capital of Maryland. There are still numerous traces of colonial times in and around this area, including *Sotterley Plantation,* an eighteenth-century Tidewater plantation overlooking the Patuxent River.

The Sotterley tale is one of inspiration, for it has gone from America's most endangered historic site to its most promising. This plantation, the only remaining Tidewater plantation in Maryland open to the public with a number of visitor and educational programs, is older than Mount Vernon and Monticello. Over the years the property had decayed, and it was feared it would have to be shut down. However, John Hanson Briscoe, great-grandson of a Sotterley slaveholder, and Agnes Kane Callum, great-granddaughter of a Sotterley slave, spearheaded the campaign for funds and restoration, and with the help of people across the country and the foundation's trustees, Sotterley is returning to its former impressive self.

Sotterley's grounds are open Tuesday through Sunday from 10:00 A.M. to 4:00 P.M. The manor house, off State Route 245 at 44300 Sotterly Lane, Hollywood, is closed from October 31 to May 1, although special tours may be arranged and the grounds remain open the rest of the year. Admission is $2.00 per person Monday through Friday during the off-season. In-season admission rates are $7.00 for adults and $5.00 for children six through sixteen to tour on Saturday and Sunday. Call (301) 373–2280 or (800) 681–0850; or visit www.sotterley.com.

trivia

There are plenty of movies supposedly set in Maryland (remember *Annapolis?*), but 2006 saw a movie made at Sotterley Plantation that stood in for the deep south during the time of slavery. *Prince Among Slaves* follows the life of Abdul Rahman, an African prince who was sold into slavery in 1788. A ninety-minute documentary was shot for PBS, airing in the fall of 2007, and the production crew was definitely enamored with the area on the water, without modern skyscrapers in the background, plenty of horses and antique equipment available, and some terrific talent.

The *Old Jail Museum and Visitor Information Center,* located on the Courthouse lawn in Leonardtown, has exhibits of artifacts and memorabilia, a "lady's cell," and Dr. Phillip Bean's office as it was when he practiced here from 1914 to 1980. The museum is open weekdays from noon to 4:00 P.M. Call (301) 475–2467.

The *Patuxent River Naval Air Museum* is the country's only museum highlighting naval aviation research and development, and testing and evaluation. Seventeen aircraft tested at the station are exhibited outside. Inside is a collection of 1,300 models, samples of helmets used over the years, and displays of crew systems, cockpits, and a time line of aviation history. A library is available for research. State Route 235 and Pegg Road, Lexington Park, adjacent to Gate 1 of the Naval Air Warfare Center–Aircraft Division; (301) 852–7418; www.paxmuseum.com.

At the *St. Clements Island Potomac River Museum* you can discover the landing site of Maryland's first European settlers. St. Mary's City is actually a small town—just St. Mary's College, a post office, Trinity Episcopal Church, and *Historic St. Mary's City,* an outdoor living-history museum. Scant development and modernization has meant that St. Mary's is the only early permanent English settlement that has remained largely undisturbed; thus it is a favorite of archaeologists, who have uncovered millions of artifacts in a relatively short time.

George McWilliams III (a former area native who recently moved to West Virginia) created the 20-by-8-foot oil-on-canvas mural depicting the landing of the first colonists to found the colony of Maryland in 1634. However, the people in the painting are more modern residents, including Kim Cullins, marketing and program specialist for the St. Clements Museum (she's standing in the group of three behind the men carrying the cross), and the two people standing next to her are McWilliams' parents. McWilliams went to St. Clements Island in March and took pictures so he'd know how the sky and trees looked at that time of the year. Including research, it took him a year to complete the painting. Visit www.stmarysmd.com/recreate/museums.

You can see the replica of the square-rigged **Maryland Dove,** one of the two ships that brought the first settlers and supplies from England; the reconstructed State House of 1676; the Godiah Spray Tobacco Plantation; archaeological excavations; the Margaret Brent Memorial Garden; and a visitor center with an archaeology exhibit hall, guided walking tours, and museum gift shop.

Be My Loveville Valentine

In 1989 Eva C. Hall decided the postmark from her zip code, 20656, should be red and have a cherubic arrow-shooter aiming toward a heart, particularly around the first half of February. It's understandable; 20656 is Loveville, named after Kingsley Love, the town's first postmaster. Hall has worked at the post office for thirty years, and she receives mail from around the world so special cards and letters will have a special stamp for Valentine's Day. About 30,000 pieces of mail will be hand-stamped at this post office, which normally sees about 400 pieces a day. Most come from visitors from nearby Washington, Virginia, Pennsylvania, and, of course, Maryland, but other letters have come from as far away as Japan. The post office is at 27780 Point Lookout Road, Loveville 20656. Call (301) 475–5243.

It's difficult to believe you're barely an hour from Washington, D.C. (well, depends on the traffic), while walking through this seventeenth-century capital. The 800 acres of unspoiled tidewater landscape whisper tranquillity.

The exhibits are open March 24 through the last weekend in November, Wednesday through Sunday 10:00 A.M. to 5:00 P.M. Call (240) 895–4990 or (800) SMC–1634, or log on to www.stmaryscity.org.

With more miles of shoreline than square miles of land and a college campus full of students, you know this has to be a good party town (the college shudders at that reputation). One can study only so long. St. Mary's College was formerly St. Mary's Female Seminary, and it is considered one of the best buys in education, with an excellent teacher-student ratio and a small enrollment of about 1,300 students. Of course, as a student or parent of a student, that is the reputation that should interest you.

One of the major social and sailing events of the year is the annual August overnight **Governor's Cup Yacht Race** down the Chesapeake from Annapolis to St. Mary's (current capital to first capital). When the race is over and the boats have been rafted, there's live music, food vendors, and an awards ceremony. Among the crew members on the 148 boats in 2006 were Maryland Special Olympics sailors who joined the thrill of this oldest and longest race on the Chesapeake. None of them had ever participated in an overnight race before. For information call (240) 895–3039 or (240) 895–2000; www.smcm.edu/govcup.

National sailors consider the annual Governor's Cup one of the ten best sailing parties of the year. The water is also perfect for those interested in sailboarding. With St. Mary's mild winters, students can enjoy boating about six months of the school year.

The **Freedom of Conscience** *Statue* at the entrance to the college was erected by the counties of Maryland and symbolizes the religious freedom on which the state was founded. In 1649, at the request of town officials from St. Mary's City, a guarantee of freedom of conscience to all Christians (freedom of other religions came later) was enacted by the state legislature.

The Potomac and Patuxent Rivers, the creeks, the streams, and the Chesapeake Bay are ideal for biology and marine-science studies. But the bay also makes this area ideal for sailing, so it is frequently invaded by sailors seeking a home port.

On the banks of the St. Mary's River is a 40-foot *circle labyrinth,* with a path that leads to the center, or rosette, and back out again. It's modeled after one on the floor of Chartres Cathedral in France. Labyrinths have been around for thousands of years, as seen in the Hopi medicine wheel. The labyrinth emphasizes tranquillity while you clear your mind and meditate. Unlike a maze, there's only one path and you can't get lost. Call (301) 863–8403 for more details. The labyrinth is on private property, next to the Historic St. Mary's City Visitor Center, 18751 Hogaboom Lane, St. Mary's City. Call (301) 862–0990.

All is not water, water, everywhere, in St. Mary's County; some of the area is devoted to produce farms. One of the major enticements of the county is the *Charlotte Hall Farmers Market,* with its Amish goods, produce, antiques, and curios. As with most farmers' markets, the earlier you arrive, the better the selection.

The market, open year-round Monday through Saturday, April through October, from 8:00 A.M. to 5:00 P.M., is on State Route 5 in Charlotte Hall. Call (301) 475–4200, ext. 1402.

The *Captain Tyler passenger ferryboat* runs between Point Lookout State Park and Smith

Freedom of Conscience Statue

Island, on weekends May through October. The cost is $24 for the cruise or $315 per couple, with overnight accommodations at the Cove or the Paddlewheel Motel. For more information call Tyler's Cruises at (410) 425–2771, or visit www.smithislandcruises.com.

For a picturesque view, you'll want to stop at *Point Lookout State Park* at the confluence of the Potomac River and the Chesapeake Bay. The light-

Buzzy's Country Store

As you head toward Point Lookout, at the very southern tip of St. Mary's, you're likely to find Ridgell's Country Store and its proprietor, Clarence "Buzzy" Ridgell. This is the place to find beer, souvenirs, pennants, bait, wine, and other "stuff." You'll also see, plastered, after a fashion, on the ceiling, his collection of more than 400 hats, from as far away as Australia and Russia. If you have a cap you want to donate, feel free to do so. You can find Buzzy at 12665 Point Lookout Road, Scotland; (301) 872–5430.

Tasty Treat

Stuffed baked ham is a traditional meal in these parts and one of the best places to try it is at Raley's Town and Country Market in Ridge. An average twenty-pound ham will include about ten pounds of cabbage, a pound or so of kale, three pounds of onions, some crushed red pepper, and some black pepper. The fat is trimmed off, the bone is removed, and slits (about 1–2 inches deep) are made in the ham. Then the shredded veggies are stuffed into the slits and where the bone was. The stuffed ham is baked for about five hours. It's usually very salty, so eat with fresh biscuits to cut the salty taste. Raley's Town and Country Market, Point Lookout Road, Ridge; (301) 872–5121.

---

house here is unique and was the first permanent light built on the Potomac River. This is a great spot for picnicking, fishing, and enjoying the nearby campground (if you're really crazy about mosquitos). The six-acre park is open daily from sunrise to dusk. The park's phone number is (301) 872–5688; www.dnr.state.md.us.

The *Piney Point Lighthouse Museum* is where you can see exhibits describing the construction and operation of the lighthouse (which was in use from 1836 through 1964) and the role of the U.S. Coast Guard. The museum, maritime exhibit, lighthouse, and store are open Friday through Monday from 10:00 A.M. to 5:00 P.M. from May through October. The lighthouse tower is open for climbing. Admission is $3.00 for adults, $1.50 for children six to eighteen, free for children under five. Located on Lighthouse Road, Piney Point; (301) 769–2222; www.co.saint-marys.md.us/recreate/museums/ppl.asp.

trivia

The Piney Point Lighthouse was known as the Lighthouse of Presidents because starting with James Madison, presidents and other notables spent their summers at Piney Point.

The **Black Panther** is a U-1105 German submarine from the World War II era that featured a rubber coating that made it "invisible" to the detection devices of the day. The sub was captured at the end of the war, and after going over it with a fine-toothed comb, the United States Navy sank it off the coast of Piney Point. Now it's Maryland's first Historic Shipwreck Diving Preserve and a National Historic Landmark. For more information, call the St. Clement's Island Potomac River Museum at (301) 769–2222 or log on to www.co.saint-marys.md.us/recreate/museums.

While driving through Great Mills, stop by *Cecil's Old Mill,* one of Maryland's first industrial districts (circa 1900). You'll find locally made crafts and original artworks. It's open from 10:00 A.M. to 5:00 P.M. Thursday through Sunday March through October and November 1 through December 24; located on State Route 5; (301) 994–1510.

For additional tourism information write to St. Mary's County Division of Tourism, P.O. Box 653, Leonardtown 20650. Call (800) 327–9023 or log on to www.stmarysmd.com.

trivia

The old sailor's rhyme was "Point Lookout, Point Lookin, Point no Point, Point Again." I've seen the first three on a map, but not the fourth. Perhaps it was just rhyme or had some deeper, older meaning I never learned.

Places to Eat in Southern Maryland

ABELL

Morris Point Restaurant,
38869 Morris Point Road,
(301) 769–2500,
www.morris-point.com

BENEDICT

Chappelear's,
7350 Benedict Place,
(301) 274–9828

BROOMES ISLAND

Stoney's Seafood House,
39393 Oyster House Road,
(410) 586–1888

CALIFORNIA

Tavern at the Village,
23154 Wetsone Lane,
(301) 863–3219,
www.thetavernatthevillage
.com

CHESAPEAKE BEACH

Rod-N-Reel,
Route 261 and Mears Avenue,
(410) 257–2735,
(301) 855–8351

COBB ISLAND

Captain John's Crab House,
16215 Cobb Island Road,
(301) 259–2315,
www.cjcrab.com

LA PLATA

Casey Jones Restaurant,
417 East Charles Street,
(301) 932–6226

LEONARDTOWN

Café des Artistes,
41655 Fenwick Street,
(301) 997–0500,
www.cafedesartistes.ws

LEXINGTON PARK

Johnny D's Barbecue,
22380 Three Notch Road,
(301) 855–0995,
www.johnny-ds-bbq.us

Peking Restaurant,
21775 Great Mills Road,
(301) 863–6190,
www.pricestomper.com

LUSBY

Catamarans Restaurant,
12504 Algonquin Trail,
(410) 326–8399,
www.catamarans-restaurant.com

Vera's White Sands,
1200 White Sands Drive,
(410) 586–1182,
www.veraswhitesands.com

MECHANICSVILLE

Bert's 50s Diner,
28760 Three Notch Road,
(301) 884–3837

POPE'S CREEK

Capt Billy's Crab House,
Pope's Creek Road,
(301) 932–4323

PRINCE FREDERICK

Adams, the Place For Ribs,
2200 Solomons Island Road
North,
(410) 586–0001

RIDGE

Spinnaker's Restaurant,
16244 Millers Wharf Road,
(301) 872–5020,
www.pointlookoutmarina
.com

SOLOMONS

Dynasty Restaurant,
13322 HG Trueman Drive,
(410) 394–1185

Lighthouse Inn,
14636 Solomons Island
Road South,
(410) 326–2444,
www.lighthouse-inn.com

**Naughty Gull Restaurant
and Pub,**
Lone Road, Spring Cove
Marina,
(410) 326–4855
www.naughtygullpub.com

Places to Stay in
Southern Maryland

CHESAPEAKE BEACH

**Chesapeake Beach Hotel &
Spa,**
4165 Mears Avenue,
(410) 257–5596,
www.chesapeakebeach
hotelspa.com

DUNKIRK

**Haven's Rest Bed &
Breakfast,**
1961 Haven Lane,
(301) 855–2232

FAULKNER

**Town and Country Motel-
Faulkner,**
10870 Crain Highway,
(301) 934–8252,
(800) 408–7650,
www.towncountry.com

HUGHESVILLE

Shady Oaks of Serenity,
7490 Serenity Drive,
(301) 932–8864,
(800) 597–0924,
www.bnbweb.com/shady
oaks.html

LA PLATA

Linden B&B,
8530 Mitchell Road,
(301) 934–9003,
www.lindenfarm.com

Part of Plenty B&B,
8664 Port Tobacco Road,
(301) 934–0707,
(800) 520–0708,
http://partofplenty.com

LEXINGTON PARK

The Miller House,
46090 Wilson Court,
(301) 863–5730

MECHANICSVILLE

**Wide Bay Cottage at
Dameron,**
28170 Old Village Road,
(301) 884–3254

NORTH BEACH

Bay Views B&B,
9131 Atlantic Avenue,
(410) 257–1000,
www.bayviewsbb.com

PINEY POINT

**Camp Merryelande
Vacation Cottages,**
15914 Camp Merryelande
Road,
(301) 994–1722,
(800) 382–1073,
www.campmd.com

PORT REPUBLIC

**Cottages of Governors
Run,**
2847 Governors Run Road,
(410) 586–2346,
(877) 586–1793,
www.baycottages.com

Enchanted Bayfront Home,
10 Governors Run Road,
(703) 620–6472,
www.chesapeakebayrentals
.com

PRINCE FREDERICK

Baycliff B&B,
168 Windcliff Road,
(410) 535–2278,
www.chesapeake.net/~bay
graff/bedandbreakfast

Cedar Hill Plantation B&B,
455 Barstow Road,
(410) 474–4684,
www.cedarhillplantation.com

Cliff House,
156 Windcliff Road,
(410) 474–4684,
www.bbonline.com/md/
cliffhouse

RIDGE

Bard's Field B&B,
15671 Pratt Road,
(301) 872–5989

Scheible's Motel,
48342 Wynne Road,
(301) 872–5185,
www.scheibles.homestead
.com

Woodlawn Historic Bed & Breakfast,
16040 Woodlawn Lane,
(301) 872–0555,
www.woodlawn-farm.com

ST. LEONARD

Chesapeake Bay Vacation Rentals,
6040 Bayview Road,
(410) 495–8674,
www.lovethebay.com

Matoaka Beach Cabins,
4510 Matoaka Lane,
(410) 586–0269,
www.matoakabeachcabins
.com

ST. MARY'S CITY

Brome-Howard Inn,
18281 Rosecroft Road,
(301) 866–0656,
(888) 801–0656,
www.bromehowardinn.com

SCOTLAND

Hale House B&B,
49644 Potomac River Drive,
(301) 872–4558

St. Michael's Manor B&B,
50200 St. Michael's Manor
Way,
(301) 872–4025,
www.stmichaels-manor.com

SOLOMONS

Back Creek Inn B&B,
210 Alexander Lane,
(410) 326–2022,
www.bbonline.com/md/back
creek

Bowen's Inn, Inc.,
14630 South Solomons
Island Road,
(410) 326–6790

Locust Inn Rooms,
14478 South Solomons
Island Road,
(410) 326–9817

Solomons Holiday Inn Select,
155 Holiday Drive,
(410) 326–6311,
(800) 356–2009,
www.ameritel.net/hisolomons

Solomons Victorian Inn,
125 Charles Street,
(410) 326–4811,
www.solomonsvictorianinn
.com

TALL TIMBERS

Potomac View Farm Bed and Breakfast,
44477 Tall Timbers Road,
(301) 994–2311,
www.erols.com/campmd

OTHER ATTRACTIONS IN SOUTHERN MARYLAND

Chesapeake Bay Field Laboratory,
St. George Island,
(301) 994–2245,
www.skipjacktours.com

Chesapeake Beach Railway Museum,
Chesapeake Beach,
(410) 257–3892

Chesapeake Beach Water Park,
Chesapeake Beach,
(410) 257–1404,
www.cal.md.us/cced/guide/
waterpark.htm

Jefferson Patterson Park and Museum,
St. Leonard,
(410) 586–8500,
www.jefpat.org

Joseph C. Lore & Sons Oyster House,
Solomons,
(410) 326–2042,
www.calvertmarinemuseum.com

Middleham Chapel,
Lusby,
(410) 326–4948,
www.chesapeake.net/~stpete

Patuxent River Naval Air Museum,
Lexington Park,
(301) 863–7418,
www.paxmuseum.com

Eastern Shore

Welcome to the Eastern Shore, the southern part of the **Delmarva Peninsula** (*DEL*aware, *MAR*yland, and *Virgini*A). This is where you see as well as hear about those unfamiliar boats, the skipjack, the bugeye, and the bungy. You will also see "June bugs," the thousands of kids who invade the ocean beaches and boardwalks every summer to work at jobs and on tanning.

Explore and enjoy the dissimilarities you will find within a few short miles. Stop by a library to see a mural painted by an artist who became so popular that the library could not afford another mural like it. Find budding artists at the Dorchester Arts Center. Search for bald eagles and great blue herons, mingle with area residents at the general store, and see centuries-old homes that have not needed restoration because they have been so well maintained over the years. Ride the ferryboats, eat at some of the best seafood restaurants in the country, examine the fine local examples of duck-decoy carving, and take a peek at some of the prettiest passenger boats and ferryboats being built these days.

Take time to locate the Mason-Dixon line; it surprises most people that the line not only separates Pennsylvania and Maryland, but it also delineates the Delaware-Maryland border. Last but not least, get some sand between your toes and contemplate

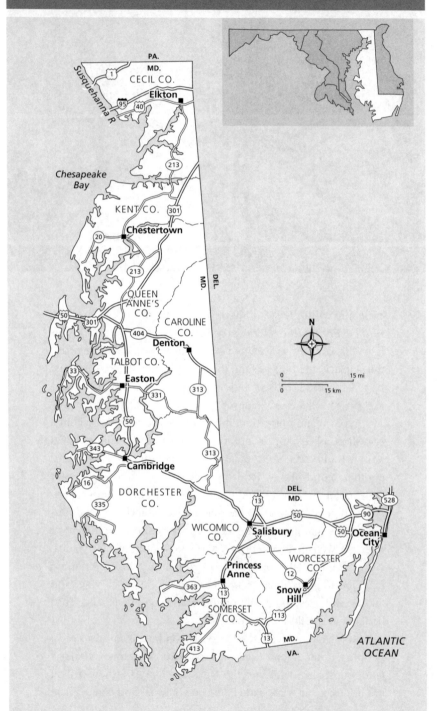

the treasures of America in Miniature. On the eastern side of the Chesapeake Bay lies the Eastern Shore, a very distinct and separate entity from the "western shore." People here are dedicated to the ways of the watermen and to the riches the land can bring, although farming here means just about anything that grows (except tobacco).

At the eastern end of the William Preston Lane Jr. Memorial Bridge—the Chesapeake Bay Bridge (U.S. Highways 50 and 301)—is Kent Island, where the first European settlement in Maryland was founded in 1631. When the settlers came, they found the Nanticoke and Choptank tribes, which are now immortalized by Indian lore exhibits and two rivers named after the tribes.

History surrounds the bay's little towns and 500 sheltered harbors. The bay is home to boatbuilders, sailors, fishermen (10,000 fishermen earn their livelihood from the bay), and sportsmen. The waterways are often as secluded as in the days when pirates and buccaneers hid in the bays and inlets. Some say there may still be buried treasure stashed in the sand dunes. At other times the waterways can compete with traffic-bound interstate freeways for congestion.

Hunters flock here every fall, for this is a major stop for migrating birds on the Atlantic flyway. To conserve and protect those birds that are not so abundant, nearly $2 million has been raised for conservation projects along the flyway.

On the flat-as-a-pancake terrain are farmlands, stately manors, and, once again, small towns. It seems that most of Maryland is filled with small towns. And, fortunately, the towns of the Eastern Shore are always sponsoring festivals celebrating the richness of the land or the sea.

Many crafters and artisans are located along the Lower Eastern Shore, and the *Lower Eastern Shore Heritage Committee* (LESHC) has prepared a brochure listing artists, galleries and museums, and a calendar of art-related events. For example, there are coppersmiths, paper makers, painters, and specialists in ceramics. How much better to pick up some memorable item for a souvenir or home decor item, than to buy a dirty-language T-shirt or to cocoon yourself in your room should it happen to rain for your entire vacation. You can contact the Committee at 11696 Church Street, Princess Anne 21853; (410) 651–4420; www.skipjack.net/le_shore/heritage.

JUDY'S FAVORITE ATTRACTIONS ON THE EASTERN SHORE

Blackwater National Wildlife Refuge

Ward Museum of Wildfowl Art

Plumpton Park Zoo

For the past few years Maryland has provided a booklet called *The Bay Game* to help youngsters (and their parents) spend meaningful and educational time while traveling from the Bay Bridge to the ocean. *The Bay Game* contains puzzles, a bookmark, games, and more. In 2002 the booklet introduced Cooper and Hanna, two water droplets that tell their story of traveling through the Chesapeake Bay watershed. The booklets are free at tollbooths and Eastern Shore welcome centers while quantities last. For more information, visit www.dnr.state.md.us/baygame or call (877) 620–8367, ext. 8016.

My Eastern Shore excursion starts at the top of the bay and works its way down and to the east, over to the Atlantic Ocean.

Cecil County

Starting at the top of the state, at the head of the Chesapeake Bay, we begin at Cecil County.

If you have seen such movies as *The Manchurian Candidate, Guys and Dolls, The Philadelphia Story, Pillow Talk,* and *Solid Gold Cadillac,* then you have heard people talking about eloping to Elkton or going to "that town in Maryland" to get married. Until the late thirties the town of Elkton was known as the Marriage Capital of the World. Some 10,000 people a year were wed here, and one assumes most of them were eloping. They came to Elkton because it was the first county seat south of New York that did not require a waiting period or blood test before the ceremony was performed.

Only one wedding chapel remains, the **Little Wedding Chapel.** This is where Babe Ruth and Joan Fontaine were married (no, not to each other), among dozens of notables, and this is where nearly 1,000 couples are still married each year. Stop by to talk with Barbara Foster and hear some of her many stories, witness a wedding or two, or plan for your own nuptials to be held here.

The Little Wedding Chapel is located at 142 East Main Street, Elkton. The phone number is (410) 398–3640.

Fair Hill Nature and Environmental Center is a facility located in the northern half of the 5,600-acre Fair Hill Natural Resources Management Area in northeastern Cecil County. One of the state's remaining covered bridges is at Fair Hill, which

trivia

You'll see Elk Neck State Park, North East, twice during Clint Eastwood's film, *Absolute Power.* He plays Luther Whitney, whose estranged daughter Kate (played by Laura Linney), regularly jogs in the park. And, if you happened to catch *Dead Man's Curve* (1998), the lighthouse scene was shot at the Elk Neck Lighthouse in Elk Neck State Park.

A Beloved Place

Fair Hill Nature and Environmental Center will look familiar to those of you who saw the Oprah Winfrey film *Beloved,* for about half of the movie was shot on the property. According to Carol Cebula, Fair Hill office administrator, the house was built from scratch and was "aged" for the movie. Only those rooms used in the movie were actually decorated; the rest were left bare. The back of the house was constructed of plywood so the cameras could have access for filming.

The movie's other buildings, particularly the log structures, were imported from North Carolina, where they had been dismantled and shipped to Maryland to be reassembled. The farm animals were brought in and the garden was planted.

A barn, smokehouse, outhouse, corn crib, carriage shed, and other farm structures were built, two wells were drilled, telephone cables were installed, the heating and air conditioning were upgraded, roadways were laid, and a new Chevy Tahoe was given to the center. In all, Fair Hill received about $1 million in cash and donated items.

All of this for about two weeks' worth of shooting! Ed Walls, the former Fair Hill manager, was in the movie as a ticket taker in the carnival scene and was the only staff member who had a part in the movie.

was a 7,000-acre estate owned by William DuPont Jr. The entire Maryland portion was purchased by the state as a Natural Resource Area. In the northern reaches of the property, near the Pennsylvania border, is the 1850s covered bridge. The headquarters building was formerly used by DuPont as his hunting lodge and is next to the covered bridge over Big Elk Creek. There are two Mason-Dixon line markers on the property.

This is an outdoor education school with programs designed to encourage awareness, understanding, and appreciation of the natural world, our natural resources, and the impact of people on the environment. The indoor and outdoor classrooms are open Monday through Friday and on occasional weekends and evenings for members of the Fair Hill Environmental Foundation Inc. (a private, nonprofit support group) and for groups by reservation.

Program subjects might include bird identification, wildflowers, marsh studies, landscaping, animal designs for survival, aquatic studies, basic entomology, clean water watch, ecology, forestry, and soil studies.

The Fair Hill Nature and Environmental Center is at 630 Tawes Drive, Elkton, and is open from 9:00 A.M. to 3:00 P.M. Monday through Friday from mid-March until mid-June and late August through November, and from 8:30 A.M. to 2:30 P.M. from mid-June until the end of July; closed the week of July 4. Call (410) 398–4909 for additional information or log on to www.fairhillnature.org.

trivia

Located in the northeastern corner of Maryland, midway between Baltimore and Philadelphia, Cecil County is the only Maryland county that is considered part of the Wilmington, Delaware, New Jersey, and Maryland primary metropolitan statistical area.

Across State Route 273 is the *steeplechase track at Fair Hill,* an exact replica of Aintree, where England's Grand National is held. Since it opened in 1933 there have been a number of steeplechase races annually, and the May event is the only steeplechase in the United States that permits pari-mutuel wagering. Fair Hill (410–620–3709; www.fairhillraces.org) is also the home of the National Steeplechase and Hunt Association, which moved from Belmont, New York, in June 1989.

Detouring a little before heading down the Eastern Shore, we can visit the other covered bridge (or "kissing" bridge) in Cecil. *Gilpin's Falls covered bridge* has a 119-foot span and a 13½-foot roadway, and it is adjacent to State Route 272 over Northeast Creek, ½ mile north of Bayview. Reportedly, the bridge's arches were made from single timbers, which were curved to shape by balancing them on stumps and pulling their ends down. The bridge was constructed in the 1850s, abandoned in the 1930s, and left to disintegrate until 1959, when it was restored. Traffic along Route 272 bypasses the bridge, which is within a few yards of the roadway.

Gilpin's Falls covered bridge is on State Route 272, 5 miles north of the town of North East, or 2 miles north of Interstate 95; (410) 996–6292.

Now, head west just a little more to visit the *Day Basket Factory.* Established in 1876 in the town of North East, the factory still makes oak splint baskets the old-fashioned way. Shortly after the Civil War, Edward and Samuel Day came to North East from Massachusetts to make their baskets because the

Water Power

The Susquehanna River separates the western border of Cecil County from the eastern border of Harford County. At one time there were two covered bridges crossing the Susquehanna River, but the last one was flooded with the construction of the *Conowingo Hydroelectric Plant.* Built in 1928, Conowingo is one of the largest hydroelectric plants in the northeast and the biggest fish lift in the United States. The enormous dam forms a freshwater lake 14 miles long, impounding some 105 billion gallons of water. It is a noted fishing spot. There's a public swimming pool, open from Memorial Day through Labor Day. The plant is located on U.S. Highway 1 in Conowingo. Call (410) 457–5011.

wood was plentiful, the transportation was good, and the demand for their wares, particularly from cotton pickers, was great. Business boomed, and during World War I the factory had thirty-five people on its payroll turning out 2,000 baskets a week. There are now four or five basket makers there who produce old-time baskets, from lunch and market styles to fruit and bread baskets. Antiques are tucked into nooks surrounding the baskets.

Depending on the wood supply, hobbyists will be pleased to know they have pliable number 1 oak strips, hand-split in any dimension, for chair seats or baskets or whatever you need. You can watch the process (you must be at least eighteen) Monday through Friday from 8:30 A.M. to 4:00 P.M. The shop is open from 10:00 A.M. to 6:00 P.M. Monday through Saturday in the summer and until 5:00 P.M. in the winter, but there are no workers in the factory on Saturday. Please call ahead (410–287–6100) to let them know if you want a tour. The factory is located at the corner of Irishtown Road and Mauldin Avenue, 714 South Main Street in North East; log on to www.daybasketfactory.com.

trivia

The Principio Iron Furnace on the shore of the Susquehanna River in Perryville was an important Cecil County ironwork site from 1725 until 1925. The Maryland Commission for Celebration 2000 gave $15,000 toward this site so the property can be protected and future development can be determined.

Plumpton Park Zoo, the second-largest zoo in Maryland, is a rural zoological garden that features plants as well as exotic and native animals, including emus, wallabies, llamas, bison, Persian sheep, Chinese deer, miniature donkeys, pygmy goats, wild turkeys, and Australian black swans in a country setting.

Eighteenth-century buildings and ruins are on the grounds, including the 1734 mill that houses the gift shop. The zoo has an adopt-an-animal program, with prices ranging from $25 for an Amazon parrot or Australian black swan to $250 for a giraffe or a Siberian tiger, with options in between.

Plumpton Park Zoo is open daily from 10:00 A.M. to 4:00 P.M. March 1 through September 30, and from 10:00 A.M. to 4:00 P.M. Wednesday through Sunday the rest of the year, weather permitting. It's closed on Thanksgiving and from December 1 through early March. Admission is $11.95 for adults, $10.95 for seniors sixty and over, and $7.95 for children two through twelve. Group tours are available by reservation. Contact the zoo at 1416 Telegraph Road (Route 273), Rising Sun 21911, or call (410) 658–6850. The Web site is www.plumptonparkzoo.org.

Heading farther south is Chesapeake City, where you'll come across the ***Chesapeake and Delaware Canal.*** On October 17, 1829, it made water

MARCH

Eagle Festival,
Blackwater National Wildlife Refuge,
Cambridge,
(410) 228–2677,
www.blackwater.fws.gov

St. Patrick's Day Parade and Festival,
Ocean City,
(410) 289–6156

APRIL

Daffodil Show,
Princess Anne,
(410) 651–9636,
www.visitsomerset.com/events.html

MD International Kite Festival,
Ocean City,
(410) 289–7855,
www.ococean.com

Salisbury Dogwood Festival,
Salisbury,
(410) 749–0144

Spocott Windmill Day,
Lloyds,
(410) 228–7090

**Ward World Championship
Wildfowl Carving,**
Ocean City,
(410) 742–4988, ext. 106,
www.wardmuseum.org

MAY

Antique Aircraft Fly–in,
Cambridge,
(301) 490–6759

Bay Bridge Walk,
(877) BAYSPAN,
www.baybridge.com

1800s Festival,
Fairmount,
(410) 651–3945,
www.visitsomerset.com/events.html

Kent Island Days,
Stevensville,
(410) 643–5358

Soft Shell Spring Fair,
Crisfield,
(410) 968–2500,
(800) 782–3913,
www.visitsomerset.com/events.html

Springfest,
Ocean City,
(410) 250–0125,
(800) OC–OCEAN,
www.ococean.com

JUNE

Bay Music Festival,
Centreville,
(410) 758–2538,
www.baymusicfestival.com

Crumpton Garden Tour and Auction,
Crumpton,
(410) 928–3860

Cypress Festival,
Pocomoke City,
(410) 957–1919,
www.pocomoke.com

EagleMan Ironman 70.3,
Cambridge,
(410) 964–1246,
www.tricolumbia.org

**Eastern Shore Chamber of Music
Festival,**
Easton, Queenstown, Chestertown,
(410) 819–0380,
www.musicontheshore.org

Eastern Shore Fishing Derby,
Salisbury,
(410) 548–4900, ext. 109,
www.wicomicorecandparks.org

Rock Hall Annual Rockfish Tournament,
Rock Hall,
(410) 639–6622

Scorchy Tawes Pro-Am Fishing Tournament,
Crisfield,
(410) 968–2500,
(800) 782–3913,
www.crisfieldchamber.com/events.htm

Youth Fishing Derby,
Blackwater National Wildlife Refuge,
Cambridge,
(410) 228–2677,
www.blackwater.fws.gov

JULY

J. Millard Tawes Crab and Clam Bake,
Crisfield,
(410) 968–2500,
www.visitsomerset.com/events.html

Kent County Fair,
Chestertown,
(410) 778–0416,
www.kentcounty.com

Somerset County Fair,
Princess Anne,
(410) 651–9689,
www.visitsomerset.com/events.html

Talbot County Fair,
Easton,
(410) 822–8007,
www.talbotfair.org

Tuckahoe Tractor Pull,
Easton,
(410) 822–9868,
www.tuckahoesteam.org

AUGUST

Great Pocomoke Fair,
Pocomoke City,
(410) 957–1919,
www.pocomoke.com

National Hard Crab Derby and Fair,
Crisfield,
(410) 968–2500,
(800) 782–3913,
www.crisfield.org

Pine'eer Arts and Craft Festival,
Ocean Pines,
(410) 208–3060

Queen Anne's County Fair,
Centreville,
(410) 758–0267

Seafood Feast-I-Val,
Cambridge,
(410) 228–1211,
www.seafoodfeastival.com

Summerfest,
Denton,
(410) 478–2050,
www.carolinesummerfest.com

Thunder on the Narrows,
Chester,
(410) 643–5764

Wheat Threshing, Steam and Gas Engine Show,
Federalsburg,
(410) 754–8422,
www.threshermen.org

(continued on next page)

White Marlin Open,
Ocean City,
(410) 289–9229,
(800) OC–OCEAN,
www.whitemarlinopen.com

Worcester County Fair,
Snow Hill,
(410) 957–4079,
www.worcestercountyfair.com

SEPTEMBER

African-American Heritage Festival,
Berlin,
(410) 641–3255

Autumn in Delmar Country Craft Fair,
Delmar,
(410) 228–6645,
(800) 239–6645

Berlin Fiddlers' Convention,
Berlin,
(410) 641–4775

**Eastern Shore Fall Festival
Championship Jousting Tournament,**
Ridgely,
(410) 482–2176

**Maryland State Surfing
Championships,**
Ocean City,
(410) 213–0515

National Hard Crab Derby and Fair,
Crisfield,
(410) 968–2500,
(800) 782–3913,
www.crisfieldchamber.com/events.htm

Port Deposit Heritage Day,
Port Deposit,
(410) 378–2121

Skipjack Races and Land Festival,
Deal Island,
(410) 784–2785,
www.webauthority.net/lions.htp

Sunfest,
Ocean City,
(410) 250–0125,
(800) OC–OCEAN,
www.ococean.com

**West Wicomico Heritage Ride Bike
Tour,**
Salisbury,
(410) 860–2447,
www.wicomicorecandparks.org

Yesterdays,
North East,
(410) 287–2658

OCTOBER

Artisan's Festival,
Centreville,
(410) 758–0835

transportation in the northern part of the bay even more important. At that time the canal had four locks, but the Corps of Army Engineers lowered the canal to sea level in 1927.

Receiving considerably less publicity than the C&O Canal, the 13-mile C&D Canal cuts off some 350 miles of water navigation for ships going between Philadelphia and Baltimore, and the 22,000 vessels that use it annually make it one of the busiest waterways in the world.

Autumn Walk at Leaf Thyme,
Elkton,
(410) 398–5566

Chesapeake Wildfowl Expo,
Salisbury,
(410) 742–4988, ext 106,
www.wardmuseum.org

Giant Pumpkin Party,
St. Michaels,
(410) 745–6073

J. Millard Tawes Oyster and Bull Roast,
Crisfield,
(410) 968–2501,
www.crisfieldheritagefoundation.org

Native American Indian Heritage Festival & Pow-wow,
Marion,
(410) 623–2660,
www.visitsomerset.com/events.html

Ocean City Oktoberfest,
Ocean City,
(410) 524–7020,
(410) 524–6440,
www.oceanpromotions.info

Olde Princess Anne Days,
Princess Anne,
(410) 651–2238,
(800) 521–9189,
www.teackle.mansion.museum

Upper Shore Decoy Show,
North East,
(410) 287–2675

Wye Grist Mill Day,
Wye Mills,
(410) 827–6909

NOVEMBER

Boat Barade,
Grasonville,
(410) 643–1977,
(410) 643–1858

OysterFest,
St. Michaels,
(410) 745–2916,
www.cbmm.org

Waterfowl Festival,
Easton,
(410) 822–4567,
www.waterfowlfest.org

DECEMBER

First Night Talbot,
Easton,
(410) 820–8822,
www.easternshore.com/firstnighttalbot

The *C&D Canal Museum* in Chesapeake City, located next to the canal, reviews its history. The museum is open Monday through Friday from 8:00 A.M. to 4:00 P.M. Call (410) 885–5622 for more information; or visit www.chesapeake city.com/about.htm.

South Chesapeake City is on the National Register of Historic Places, with picturesque Victorian architecture, antiques, waterfront restaurants, art galleries, and inns.

I find the other, or north, side of the canal equally interesting—at least the views are. During the ride or walk across the bridge, 135 feet in the air, you can see the canal's course for miles. From the north side you can see the pilots on their pilot boats going to and from the ships navigating the canal. Stop by the Pilot House for information and a schedule on ships coming through.

For additional information write to Tourism Coordinator, Cecil County Tourism, 1 Seahawk Drive, Suite 114, North East 21901, or call (410) 966–6290 or (800) CECIL–95.

Kent County

Kent County has the largest proportion of farmland to total acreage of the Upper Eastern Shore counties, yet it is bordered on the north by the Sassafras River, on the south and the east by the Chester River, and on the west by the Chesapeake Bay, so you can understand its multiple focal points. There might be an Old-Fashioned Fourth festival in Rock Hall, an Eastern Shore fish fry, and a Kent County Watermen's Association workboat race and docking competition, all on the same summer weekend. After the harvest, it is time for snow goose and deer hunting. For those who prefer architectural history to land and water sports, Chestertown, the county seat of the smallest county in the state, is said to be the tenth-favorite historic place in America because of the large number of restored eighteenth-century homes.

When driving through Kent County, it is wonderful to take time to see local sights such as the picturesque view of waterfront homes at Chestertown; the Eastern Neck National Wildlife Refuge; the Geddes-Piper House, a Philadelphia-style town house that serves as a museum and the home of the Kent County Historical Society; the Kitty Knight House; the 3,000-acre wildlife research and demonstration area known as Chesapeake Farms (formerly Remington Farms); the Rock Hall Museum, the Tolchester Beach Revisited Museum, and the Waterman's Museum; and Washington College, the tenth-oldest college in this country, which George Washington helped found.

At the *Kent County Museum* are indoor and outdoor exhibits of farm machinery from the last two centuries. The county gave a group of local farmers one hundred acres, twenty-five acres of which they ran on a volunteer basis to help defray the museum's operating costs. It was started about two dozen years ago, and people from the area and as far away as Pennsylvania have donated equipment to it. Two early farm tractors mark the entrance, so you can't miss it.

Inside and outside the 40-by-150-foot building are exhibits on equipment used in planting and harvesting corn, wheat, soy, and other grains. You will see threshers, tools from preindustrial days, and modern-day combines and reapers. Other exhibits explain the work done by hand planters, automated corn planters, and tractors (the earliest tractor on display is a 1947 model).

On the first Saturday in August is a threshing dinner. Of course, if you just happen by at other times of the year when workers are planting or otherwise tending to the fields, you can watch them at work then, too.

No admission is charged, but contributions are accepted. Kent Museum is open noon to 3:00 P.M. May through October, and it is located on State Route 448 at Turner's Creek Public Landing, near Kennedyville. Call Brian Quinn at (410) 348–5239 or visit kentcounty.com/farmmuseum for additional information.

Bicycle tours are popular in Kent County, and the Tourism Development Office has prepared a booklet, *The Kent County Bicycle Tour,* for your information. Included are nine routes developed by the Baltimore Bicycling Club that range from 11 to 81 miles in length.

Routes include the 11-mile Pomona Warm-Up, which follows winding country roads, along the Chester River, and the 81-mile Pump House Primer through northern Kent County and Cecil County. In addition to tourism information, specific directions, maps, and a listing of restaurants, hotels, motels, campgrounds, and bed-and-breakfast establishments are available from the Kent County Tourism Development Office.

The **Kent Manor Inn & Restaurant** is intimate enough to feel like a bed-and-breakfast and large enough to have the amenities of a fine country estate. The property sits on 220 woodland acres on a tributary of the Chesapeake Bay. Its public spaces and twenty-four rooms are lovingly decorated. The original wing of the house was built circa 1820, with the center portion added just prior to the Civil War. This is the perfect place for a romantic getaway, a corporate retreat, and, perhaps best of all, an ideal place for a wedding (there's a garden house with seating for 150 guests), for it's secluded without being remote. A visit here means there's time to stroll the grounds, take a ride on the inn's paddleboats, swim in the Olympic-sized swimming pool, or enjoy a fine meal on the glass-enclosed sun porch when the weather permits.

You can get to the Kent Manor Inn via Route 50 (12 miles from Annapolis), by plane (the Bay Bridge Airport is just across the street), or by boat (the dock is 38 57'50.34 North and 76 18'52.61 West on Thompson Creek, accessible via Cox Creek and Eastern Bay. The dock is 3½ feet at mean low water). It is located at 500 Kent Manor Drive, Kent Island, Stevensville; (410) 643–5757 or (800) 820–4511 (lodging) and (410) 643–7716 (dining); www.kentmanor.com.

If you'd like to see a full-size, exact replica of a 1768 schooner that plied the waters of colonial North America in the service of the Royal Navy, then head to the foot of Canon Street—Chestertown's waterfront—to see the **Schooner Sultana.** Built directly from original plans, *Sultana* was launched in 2001 and is considered to be one of the most accurate vessel replications in the world today. The *Sultana*'s mission is to provide unique, hands-on educational experiences in colonial history and environmental science throughout the Chesapeake Bay area.

So, if she's not at her home dock, she is probably sailing and visiting the ports of such neighboring Chesapeake Bay towns as Annapolis, Baltimore, and St. Michaels. *Sultana* also is available for a limited number of private charters each month, serving up to thirty passengers. She is suitable for events including private sailing charters from two hours to five days in length, dockside receptions, festivals, and reenactments. The vessel is Coast Guard certified and is staffed by a professional captain and crew. For more information, contact the Schooner *Sultana*–1768 Office, P.O. Box 524, Chestertown, MD 21620; (410) 778–5954; the Web site is www.schoonersultana.com.

If you travel through Rock Hall, in southwestern Kent County, you may notice **Tallulah's on Main,** a gallery/gift shop and a five-suite hotel, and wonder about the name. According to Jim Messersmith, owner of Tallulah's, the famed movie star Tallulah Bankhead used to shop at this location when it was a general store; she bought her meats and gourmet items next door when it was Myer's meat market. Many of the locals still remember her frequent visits, and her grandnieces visit the gift shop and gallery. Jim says they liked the name, but "most of all felt that she needed to be honored still as a great actress and woman of our time." The folks at Tallulah's have several books about her life and wonderful stories. Tallulah's also rents a house on the beach with a beautiful due-west sunset view all year long. It's located at 105 South Cross Street, Chestertown; (410) 778–5954; or log on to www.Tallulahsonmain.com.

For additional county information write to Kent County Tourism Development Office, 400 High Street, Chestertown 21620, call (410) 778–0416, visit www.kentcounty.com, or e-mail tourism@kentcounty.com.

Queen Anne's County

The **Old Wye Grist Mill** is the oldest business in Queen Anne's County, in operation since about 1682 and powered by water. At least three mills (two grist and one saw) have been located in this area for more than 300 years, giving the town of Wye Mills its name. Among its historic claims is the fact that Robert Morris, financier of the American Revolution, purchased ground cornmeal from this mill to be used as provisions for George Washington's Continental army at Valley Forge in 1778.

The Wye Mill is open Friday, Saturday, and Sunday from 10:00 A.M. to 4:00 P.M. and by appointment from mid-April through mid-November. There is no admission charge, but donations are appreciated. Located at 14296 Old Wye Mills Road (State Route 662); call (410) 827–6909; or log on to www.wmgristmill.htm.

Queen Anne's is known for its sprawling countryside and 410 farms, averaging 400 acres each, terrific access to the bay and bay tributaries, and the genteel lifestyle it promotes. Kent Narrows, formerly known for its horrendous weekend beach traffic jams, has become a minor destination of its own, with plenty of historic sites, fine boating, golf, and dining.

The meeting place of the Eastern Shore since 1955, however, has been **Holly's Restaurant,** noted for having the best milk shakes (with four scoops of ice cream and three ounces of milk) and fried chicken (cooked in peanut oil, I'm told) in the state. The tables are wooden and devoid of such frills as tablecloths, and the waitresses are friendly. You will find Holly's and all the Ewing family members off US 50 at 108 Jackson Creek Road, Grasonville. Call (410) 827–8711; the Web site is www .hollysrest.com.

Birdlife photographers and observers will enjoy the Wildfowl Trust of North America's **Chesapeake Bay Environmental Center** and the adjacent captive wildfowl collection in Grasonville. Surrounded by more than 500 acres of natural beauty, the center has a fascinating and colorful flock of wildfowl, including ducks, geese, and swans, and nearby are deer, red foxes, river otters, and bald eagles living in the brackish marsh, pine forest, shrub habitat, meadow, and shallow water impoundment. Special screening allows you to quietly enter blinds so you can observe wildlife without disturbing it. Nature trails, wetland boardwalks, the observation towers, and viewing blinds offer a variety of ways to see the wildlife and a panoramic view of Chesapeake Bay.

takemeouttothe ballgame

James or Jimmie "Double X" Foxx was born in Sudlersville. Known for pitching right-handed for the Philadelphia Athletics, he was enrolled in the National Baseball Hall of Fame in 1951. It's said the coach in the movie *A League of Their Own* was based on Foxx.

The Wildfowl Trust of North America, founded in 1979, is responsible for the center, and you can be sure of programs, guided walks, workshops, a wetland festival, and lectures promoting stewardship of our dwindling wetland resources. A gift shop and a shaded picnic area are also on-site.

The center is ½ mile from State Route 18, off Perry Corner Road. Admission is $5.00 for adults, $4.00 for seniors age fifty-five or older, and $2.00 for children age eighteen and younger. Dogs are not permitted. The center is open 9:00 A.M. to 5:00 P.M. daily. It is closed Thanksgiving, December 24 and 25, New Year's Day, and Easter. For more information write to the Executive Director, The Wildfowl Trust of North America, 600 Discovery Lane, P.O. Box 519, Grasonville 21638, or call (410) 827–6694 or (800) CANVASBACK. The Web site is www.wildfowltrust.org.

For more tourism information write to Queen Anne's County Department of Business and Tourism, 425 Piney Narrows Road, Chester 21619. Call (410) 604–2100 or (888) 400–RSVP; www.qac.org.

Talbot County

Tourists coming through this area on State Route 33—about 100,000 each year going to St. Michaels—stop to see the Chesapeake Bay Maritime Museum, the Customs House, St. Michaels Museum at St. Mary's Square, the Robert Morris Inn, and Tilghman Island. The Chesapeake Bay Maritime Museum receives by far the most tourists, and well it should.

The St. Michael's Museum at St. Mary's Square exhibits items of significance to the local history and culture, not just of St. Michaels, but of the land between Tilghman and Royal Oak, called the Bay 100—that portion of land that could be defended by one hundred armed men. Two buildings, originally part of a steam saw- and gristmill, are used for this museum, one of them dating from 1820 and one from 1860. The latter is referred to as the "Teetotum" building because it is shaped like a child's four-sided top of that name. In the 1820 building are artifacts from 1800 to 1850, in the kitchen area are items from 1850 to 1900, and in the Teetotum room are articles from colonial days to about 1950.

The Town That Fooled the British

The tale may be apocryphal, but the story of how St. Michael's got its nickname has been around for so long that people will swear on their mothers' graves that it's true. So you will hear that during the War of 1812, this town "was an important shipbuilding center of privateers, blockade runners, and naval barges. This activity caused an attempt by the British naval forces to destroy the shipyards and the boats under construction. On the morning of August 10, 1813, a number of British barges shelled the town and attacked a fort on the harbor side. Residents, forewarned, had hoisted lanterns to the masts of ships and the tops of the trees, causing the cannons to overshoot the town. This first 'blackout' was effective and only one house was struck. It is known as the 'Cannonball House.' St. Michaels is now known as 'The Town that Fooled the British.'"

The museum is open May through October on Saturday and Sunday from 10:00 A.M. to 4:00 P.M. and by appointment. There is no admission charge, but donations are accepted. For additional information call (410) 745–9561.

Graul's Supermarket, with stores in Annapolis, Parkton, Towson, Lutherville, and Cape St. Claire, has been a favorite grocery store since 1920, so you can imagine the delight when a new store opened in St. Michaels. All its customers who have lived on the western side of the bay can now enjoy their favorite shopping experience where they vacation.

The fourth generation of Grauls operates the six markets; John Evans Jr., a great-grandson of originators Fred and Esther Graul, runs this store. You'll find family recipes handed down through the generations, unmatchable friendly service, and incredibly delicious baked goods. Graul's is at 1212 South Talbot Street, St. Michaels; (410) 745–3537; www.graulsmarket.com.

If hot (and I don't mean weather) tempts your taste buds, then a stop in St. Michaels isn't complete until you've visited *Flamingo Flats.* Their motto is: "Where taste is paramount and life's too short to eat boring food." Opened in 1988, Flamingo Flats has hot sauce and salsa specialties; cigars; a tasting bar with more than 2,000 salsas, hot sauces, marinades, and barbecue sauces; more than 500 mustards; more than 75 jars with olives as a base; and hundreds of cookbooks, gifts, and jewelry items.

Among the sauces you'll find are Chile Today Hot Tamale, Gator Hammock Gator Sauce, Jump Up and Kiss Me, Lottie's Bajan Cajan, Matouk's Hot Calypso, Ring of Fire, and Rothschild's Fiery Raspberry Salsa. If you have an asbestos tongue, step up to the tasting bar and go to town. The shop specialty is its own Cannonball sauce. Cannonball is a combination of carrots, onions, lime juice, tomato, vinegar, and habanero peppers. It's a sauce more for tasting than for destroying your intestinal lining.

Flamingo Flats is located at 100 South Talbot Street in St. Michaels. It is closed on Tuesday and Wednesday during the winter. Call (410) 745–2053 or (800) HOT–8841; or log on to www.flamingoflats.com.

As you drive southwest out of St. Michaels, and the land becomes narrower and the waters become closer, aim toward Tilghman Island and the *Phillips Wharf Environmental Center.* You can catch a cruise, charter a boat, take a water tour, and with fun and education in mind you can see the last crab shanty on Knapp's Narrows, and meet up with a blue crab, a horseshoe crab, oysters, a sea star (formerly called starfish), and other bay critters.

Talk with Kelly Cox to learn more than you ever thought possible about the Bay and the area. The center is open Friday through Tuesday from 10:00 A.M. to 4:00 P.M. from May through November. Admission is $5.00 for adults and $3.00 for children from three through eleven. Or, take a cruise aboard the *Express Royale* or the *FUN4U* and be admitted to the center for free. (888) 312–7847; www.docksidexpress.com/phillips.html.

Bed-and-breakfast establishments seem to belong in large Victorian homes, and the ***John S. McDaniel House Bed and Breakfast,*** owned and operated by Mary Lou and Fran Karwacki, fits that description to a T. Built about 1890, the house has a high octagonal tower (a great sitting room), a hip roof with dormers, and a porch that runs across the front and part of the south side of the house. Each of the eight guest rooms is spacious and bright and equipped with air-conditioning and a ceiling fan. Fortunately, the house is located within walking distance of historic Easton.

The John S. McDaniel House Bed and Breakfast is located at 14 North Aurora Street, Easton. Call (410) 822–3704 or (877) 822–5702 for information and reservations; or visit www.nbnlist.com/md/mcdaniel/index.

One of the ten remaining ferries in service in Maryland is the ***Oxford-Bellevue Ferry,*** which crosses Tred Avon River and connects Oxford to Bellevue. It has been operating since 1683 and is said to be the oldest "free-running" (not cable-connected), privately owned ferry in the country.

Tom and Judy Bixler assumed ownership of the ferry in 2002. And in 2006 Judy, president, was named one of Maryland's Top 100 Minority Business Owners for the year. The program recognizes the state's best minority and women business owners and their achievements. She was cited for her business development, client satisfaction, professional affiliations, and community outreach. Besides being captain of the ferry, she's worn other hats, including president of the Oxford Business Association, a member of the advisory board of the Talbot County Board of Tourism, and a volunteer for the Festival of Trees, Oxford Invitational Fine Arts Fair, Oxford Day committee, Oxford Fire Department Building Fund, and the March of Dimes. Obviously, if you have a question about the area, good restaurants, or directions, Judy's the person to ask.

It operates from the first day of spring through the Sunday after Thanksgiving. Generally, the ferry schedule starts at 9:00 A.M. daily and runs until sunset, except during June, July, and August, when it runs until 9:00 P.M. The first ferry starts from the Oxford side.

It costs $8.00 for car and driver one-way and $12.00 round-trip, plus $1.00 per passenger each way. Bicycles are $3.00 one-way, $5.00 round-trip, and foot passengers are $2.00 each. Motorcycles are $4.00. This is a particularly photogenic ferry crossing at sunset, when the boats are all at their Oxford harbor moorings with their masts standing out against the skyline. To reach the Oxford-Bellevue Ferry from Easton, take State Routes 33 and 333; from Bellevue take State Routes 33 and 329 to Royal Oak and follow the signs. Call (410) 745–9023 for more information or log on to www.oxfordbellevueferry.com.

Next to the Oxford landing is the **Customs House,** a replica of the original built in pre–Revolutionary War days when Oxford was an official port of entry. It's open from 3:00 to 5:00 P.M. Friday through Sunday, April through October. Call (410) 226–5760.

For a quiet town, there's been a lot of activity in tiny Oxford. First, the film crew for *Wedding Crashers* (starring Owen Wilson, Vince Vaughn, Christopher Walken, Jane Seymour, and a number of local residents) came to town in 2004 and there was a perceptible surge in wedding bookings, particularly at the Inn at Perry Cabin. Then, the next year Matthew McConaughey and Sarah Jessica Parker were in town for the filming of *Failure to Launch.*

Most recently, and perhaps the event with the longest-lasting impact, Kathy Harig opened a second branch of her **Mystery Loves Company** bookstore in a century-old bank building. The store has frequent local author appearances, and as the only bookstore in Oxford, carries a full line of new and carefully read used books, not just mysteries, signed first editions, book gift baskets, and book-related gifts, children's books, and items about the Chesapeake Bay. Harig's first store is in the Fell's Point area of Baltimore, but she lives in Talbot County.

Nearby are the Oxford Museum, shops, and restaurants. If you're in the area on Friday mornings, tune in to WCEI radio, 96.7 FM from 8:10 to 8:15 A.M. for news about bestseller list books, favorite books, and upcoming events; or sign up for their monthly newsletter by writing to mlcnews@mystery lovescompany.com. The store is at 202 South Morris Street; (410) 226–0010; www.mysteryloves.company.com.

Almost as good as a platter of crabs are the biscuits from **Orrell House and Bakery.** Hundreds of dozens of these heavy biscuits, which started as a source of pin money for Mrs. Orrell about fifty years ago, go out to local stores and shops around the country. The recipe, which combines flour, water, salt, lard, sugar, and baking powder, originated in Southern Maryland and the Eastern Shore during plantation days. It produces a biscuit that is soft and doughy on the inside and hard on the outside. There are some who say these biscuits are not any good until they feel like hockey pucks, and many swear by them as teething biscuits.

trivia

There are more than 240,000 acres of public land in the Maryland State Forests and Parks system, meaning there is a state forest or park within forty-five minutes of nearly every Marylander.

Wye Is This Oak So Famous?

You have heard that big oaks come from little acorns, and, of course, the converse is true—little acorns come from big oaks. The Maryland Forest, Park, and Wildlife Service gathered the acorns from the Wye Oak, planting them, and letting them grow for a couple of years until they are established seedlings. You can purchase a Wye Oak seedling from the state for about $6.00 (plus tax if you live in Maryland) even though the famous oak no longer stands. They are shipped in March in time for spring planting. They cannot be shipped to Arizona, California, Florida, Louisiana, or Oregon due to quarantine restrictions. These are the cutest little trees, no bigger in diameter than your little finger, but they produce mature-size leaves, about six or seven of them the first year. They do not grow as rapidly as, say, a maple tree, but they are of substantial size within a decade. And, who knows, 400 years from now there may be a champion tree in your yard. To order Wye Oak seedlings, write to the Nursery Manager, Buckingham Forest Tree Nursery, Harmans 21077. You must give a full street address; a post office box number is inadequate for delivery.

Believe me, just because they feel hard does not mean they have gone stale. A special pick is used to prick the tops of the biscuits (in an O and cross design) so they will not blister and burn.

The bakery is open on Tuesday and Wednesday from 7:00 A.M. to 2:00 P.M., Thursday from 2:00 to 11:00 P.M., and Friday from 7:00 A.M. to noon. The address is 14124 Old Wye Mill Road (Route 662), Wye Mills. Call (410) 822–2065.

On June 6, 2002, a thunderstorm raged through Talbot County and felled the mighty Wye Oak. It was believed to be more than 450 years old and was 96 feet tall. In another word, it was HUGE. Considered to be the largest and finest white oak tree in the country, it stood in the middle of **Wye Oak State Park**. The state bought the tree and one acre around it in 1939—the first time any state ever purchased one tree just to preserve it. Over time, more land was added to make this a state park. It was the first state park to be fully accessible to the disabled.

Plans now include keeping the property as a state park, with the tree stump and a one-room schoolhouse. Fortunately, state foresters had gathered fresh buds from the tree to make clones of it. Two of the trees previously cloned from the Wye Oak have been planted at Mount Vernon, Virginia, and one probably will be planted to replace the tree that was felled.

What do you do with a downed tree that size? Well, movers built a frame around its circumference, hauled it away, and placed the remains in a warehouse (which had one of its walls removed for the tree to fit). Previously, when large branches broke off, they were carved into sculptures.

Oh, the new white oak state champion now stands in Harford County.

For more tourism information write to Talbot County Office of Tourism, 11 South Harrison Street, Easton 21601, or call (410) 770–8000.

Caroline County

Caroline County is the only Eastern Shore county not directly on the ocean or the bay, but there are calm waters, such as the Choptank and Tuckahoe Rivers and Marshyhope Creek, state parks for canoeing and fishing, and an active crabbing and fishing industry. The prime interest here is agrarian, and the crops are bountiful. Corn, soybeans, cucumbers, tomatoes, peas, beans, sweet corn, cantaloupes, peaches, and melons fill the fields and make a stop at a local produce stand an essential part of anyone's visit.

Across from the Caroline County Courthouse in Denton is the ***Museum of Rural Life.*** Even county residents realize that the farming folk who have populated Caroline for the past three centuries may as well have been "consigned to a black hole of obscurity." The county has produced no national leaders, scientists, engineers, patriots, or even notorious rogues. Tombstones are the only proof that people have indeed lived here throughout the history of the United States.

The museum combines one of the original dwellings on Court House Square with new construction. There's a reception area, a gallery for rotating exhibits, and an audiovisual room. The museum explores the various aspects and changes in rural life since European settlers arrived here in the 1600s. Hun-

The Green Garden County

According to George Sands of the Caroline County Library: "On March 24, 1981, the County Commissioners of Caroline County adopted a resolution establishing an official motto for 'Caroline the Green Garden County of Maryland.' This was carried out in conjunction with the library publication of an Agricultural Directory. The research showed that at that time, Caroline County was first in Maryland in production of vegetables for markets and processing. It is among the top 3 percent in the U.S. in acreage of garden vegetables and at or near the top in Maryland and the nation in a number of related vegetable production areas. The term was coined by Bud Hutton."

Ah, Sweet Caroline

What's in a name (to paraphrase the Bard)? Also called the Green Garden County, in the heart of the Eastern Shore, Caroline County was created in 1773 from Dorchester and Queen Anne's Counties. It's named for Lady Caroline Eden, the wife of Maryland's last colonial governor, Robert Eden (1741–1784). Lady Caroline was the daughter of Charles Calvert, Fifth Lord Baltimore, and the sister of Frederick Calvert, Sixth Lord Baltimore.

---

dreds of artifacts, documents, and photographs have been collected. You may even uncover some of the history behind the fireworks-induced conflagration of July 4, 1865.

The historical marker next to the **Choptank Electric Cooperative** on State Routes 404 and 328, just west of Denton, marks the modest but historic **Neck Meeting House.** Built in 1802 by members of the Society of Friends, the meetinghouse is believed to be the oldest house of worship in Caroline County. Most of the funds raised for the aluminum marker came from the recycling of aluminum cans by local residents.

trivia

George Martinak deeded land to the state in 1961 for preservation as a recreational facility and a natural area for the enjoyment of all. It was named Martinak State Park after him.

The Caroline County Historical Society is refurbishing the small building, and if you would like to look inside, stop by the cooperative for the key.

In June 1984, in the quiet hours of an early Sunday night, a thirty-five-ton limb from Maryland's former state tree crashed to the ground. Being practical, the state decided that some of the limb should be made into souvenirs, such as gavels; but 70,000 pounds of tree would make a lot of gavels. The Maryland Forest, Park, and Wildlife Service sent a two-ton chunk of wood to sculptor Steven Weitzman to create the **Wye Oak Sculpture.**

trivia

The Adkins Arboretum at Tuckahoe State Park, west of Denton, was conceived and funded by the late Leon Andrus of Cheston-on-Wye. He suggested that it be named in honor of the Adkins family, who has produced civic leaders for generations.

He carved the wood into a monument in his shop at Seneca Creek State Park in Gaithersburg. On April 3, 1985, his sculpture of two children leaning over a shovel in the act of planting a tree was moved to its permanent home at **Martinak State Park,** 2 miles east of Denton. The children, carved larger than life-size, are standing beneath a white oak tree in this 10-foot-tall statue that measures about 4½ feet from front to back.

Martinak is bordered by the Choptank River and Watts Creek, and you can drop a line for bass, perch, sunfish, and catfish (a Maryland Chesapeake Bay Sportfishing License is required), camp in one of the sixty-three campsites for tent or trailer camping April through October, stay in a year-round cabin, launch your boat, rent a boat, go hiking, picnic, enjoy a ball game, or recreate on the playground. You'll also be able to see the reconstructed hull of a wrecked bungy, a type of boat used on the bay in the early nineteenth century.

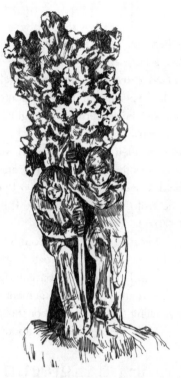

Wye Oak Sculpture

The park is open from sunrise to sunset daily, except Christmas week. Martinak State Park is at 137 Deep Shore Road, off Route 404, Denton. Call (410) 479–1619 or (888) 432–2267; www .dnr.state.md.us.

Seven miles west of Denton, off Route 404, is **Tuckahoe State Park.** Tuckahoe Creek meanders through this park, and a sixty-acre lake offers fishing and boating opportunities on twenty acres of open water. There are thirty-five campsites and four sites for youth groups. A central bathhouse with showers and toilet facilities is available. The Adkins Arboretum encompasses 500 acres of parkland and nearly 3 miles of walkways through the trees and shrubs. Canoes are available for rental from May to October. There are also other recreational options, including archery, a playground, a ball field, an equestrian center, hiking trails, a pet loop, and picnicking. Tuckahoe State Park is located in Queen Anne. Call (410) 820–1668 or (888) 432–2267; the Web site is www.dnr.state.md.us.

For additional tourism information write to Caroline Office of Tourism, 16 North Second Street, Denton 21629, or call (410) 479–0655; www.tour caroline.com.

Dorchester County

When you cross the Choptank River bridge, you'll see something that looks like a large sailing yacht. It's the **Dorchester County Visitor Center** at **Sailwinds Park East,** and the mistake is understandable because the center lies amid a spectacular 110-foot fiberglass sail. Here you will find visitor information on the Eastern Shore region, indoor and outdoor interpretive exhibits, a children's playground, a beach, and a boardwalk that links to the Choptank Fishing Pier. At the nearby Governors Hall at Sailwinds Park, such diverse events as the Seafood Festival and concerts with big name stars and more are held. Governors Hall is at 200 Byrn Street, Cambridge. Phone (410) 228–SAIL. The visitor center is at 2 Rose Hill Place, Cambridge. Phone (410) 228–1000 or (800) 522–TOUR.

Because Dorchester County is blessed with fairly flat terrain and lots of water, the county has created brochures of interest to boaters and birders. A bird watcher guide lists birding options at Blackwater National Wildlife Refuge and several wildlife management areas. Any of the brochures can be obtained by calling (410) 228–1000 or (800) 552–TOUR.

Years before I thought about writing this book, I stopped at the **Dorchester County Public Library** and admired a wonderful mural of Eastern Shore scenes being painted by Chesapeake Bay artist John Moll. That creation has stayed in my mental filing drawers all these years.

Moll's lithographs are known for their faithful characterizations of the skipjacks and bay lighthouses he loved. His Christmas cards with Oxford and Annapolis scenes or Baycraft portraits are still popular, and John Moll oils hang in the permanent collection of the Eastern Academy of Arts, in the **Visitor Center at Sailwinds Park East,** and in the historic Robert Morris Inn in Oxford. This gives you an idea how popular the artist is whose work is on the Dorchester County Public Library walls. The address of the library is 303 Gay Street, Cambridge. (410) 228–7331; www.dorchesterlibrary.org.

The **Dorchester Arts Center** was founded in 1970 and has between 400 and 500 members (mostly from the Cambridge area) including potters, pho-

a heartfelt greeting

Dorchester County is located in the center of Maryland's Eastern Shore, and if you look at the shape of the county, you'll realize it's heart-shaped. That's the rationale behind the county's promotion as "the Heart of Chesapeake Country," and the state's designation as the Heart of Chesapeake Country Heritage Area.

tographers, quilters, stained-glass artists, and basket makers. In addition to regular classes in these and other crafts, the center has two galleries where local work is exhibited and sold. Each month a new exhibit opens with a reception. During the year, the center sponsors a variety of music, dance, and educational programs, a number of which are free to the public.

Each September the sidewalks along historic, brick High Street, with its beautiful period homes, are festooned with the best work of 125 or more of Dorchester County artists at the Dorchester Showcase.

The center, located at 120 High Street, Cambridge, is open Monday through Friday from 10:00 A.M. to 2:00 P.M. and Saturday from 11:00 A.M. to 3:00 P.M. Call (410) 228–7782 or check out www.dorchesterartscenter.org for more information.

Interesting tours are conducted through the **Brooks Barrel Company,** one of the last remaining slack cooperages now operating in America and the only one in Maryland. Paul Brooks founded the company in 1950, making "hand-crafted wooden barrel product . . . Nature's Way" with equipment dating from the turn of the twentieth century. These planters, kegs, and barrels are made of natural yellow pine from Delmarva. Planning to grow strawberries next year? Try one of the 12-by-18-inch strawberry kegs with holes.

Tours (which can be very noisy) are available by appointment for $5.00. Brooks Barrel Company Inc. is at 5228 Bucktown Road in Cambridge. Call (410) 228–0790 or (800) 398–BROOKS; or log on to www.brooksbarrel.com.

Another place of interest is Bucktown, where Harriet Tubman lived as a child. Tubman has been called the Moses of her People because of her work in the Underground Railroad that helped free more than 300 slaves. A slave herself, Tubman ran away only to return to Delmarva nineteen times to free others. During the Civil War she served in the Union army as a nurse, scout, and spy. A marker denotes the location of the **Brodess Plantation** where Tubman lived with her mother and siblings. Green Briar Road in Bucktown. Call (410) 288–1000.

For more information about Harriet Tubman and the Underground Railroad, stop by the **Underground Railroad: Harriet Tubman Museum.** A grant of $25,000 from the Maryland Commission for Celebration 2000 is allowing archaeologists to "locate structures, graves, and artifacts associated with Tubman's life and better protect and interpret this nationally significant site." There's a gift shop with items from such countries as Kenya and Nigeria, Native American goods, and local products.

There is no admission fee, and the museum, located at 424 Race Street, Cambridge, is open from 10:00 A.M. to 5:00 P.M. Friday and Saturday and by appointment. (410) 228–0401.

Annie Oakley Lived Here

As you're driving through the area, you might stop by 28 Bellevue Avenue on Hambrooks Bay in Cambridge. For about five years, beginning in 1912, this was the home of Wild West sharpshooter Annie Oakley. It was designed and built by Oakley and her husband, Frank Butler, when they retired to Cambridge. The bungalow was typical of the period, except for a few features characteristic of the Butlers' unique lifestyle. You can drive by and see the second floor balcony from which Oakley could shoot ducks on the Bay.

It makes one wonder, why here? According to Thomas A. Flowers, the Old Honker, in his book *Shore Folklore: Growing Up with Ghosts, 'n Legends, 'n Tales, 'n Home Remedies,* Oakley and Butler moved here because in her travels all over the world, she "had never seen a more beautiful spot than Hambrooks Bay." Butler was known to fish for perch in the bay, and Oakley's black-and-white bird dog Dave was known to stand so stock still that Oakley could shoot an apple off his head.

The Bucktown Village Store has other interesting stories and events regarding Tubman and the Underground Railroad. Talk with Jay or Susan Meredith at (410) 901–9255 or (410) 228–7650.

With the construction of the limited access US 50, the quaint town of Vienna was bypassed, so it takes a little bit of going off that beaten path to find its treasures. One of those gems is the *Vienna Heritage Museum,* set in a former gas station, where you can see remembrances of the rural life and industries located in and near the town, including equipment from the Elliott Island Button Factory, the oldest existing and last mother-of-pearl button factory that was in existence in the United States. It ceased operation in 1999, and the equipment was donated by the Martinak family on Elliott Island. Contact Bob Williams, the museum's proprietor, about walking tours through this quaint and historic town. Ask for a copy of a walking tour brochure.

The museum is open on the second and fourth Sunday of the month, from 11:00 A.M. to 5:00 P.M. at 303 Race Street, Vienna. Call (410) 376–3840 or visit www.tourchesapeakecountry.org.

South of Cambridge is the *Blackwater National Wildlife Refuge,* a marvelous sanctuary of more than 28,000 acres. The refuge boasts the largest nesting population of bald eagles in the East, north of Florida. There is a $3.00 charge per car and a $1.00 charge per person on foot or bicycle unless you have a Golden Age, Golden Eagle, Golden Access, or Blackwater National Wildlife Refuge Pass, or a current Federal Duck Stamp. There is no admission fee to visit the new (2006) welcome center and observation deck. Besides the bald eagle and the great blue heron, you will see black ducks, the endangered Delmarva fox squirrel, and countless other animals and birds. Do stop by in November and December when the Canada geese fly overhead. Bring your insect repellent in July and August.

Take State Route 16 west to State Route 335 in Church Creek and turn left onto Key Wallace Drive. Follow the signs to the refuge, located at 2145 Key Wallace Drive, Cambridge. The refuge is open daily, Labor Day through Memorial Day, from dawn to dusk; the visitor center is open daily from 9:00 A.M. to 4:00 P.M. Call (410) 228–2677 for additional information.

Six miles west of Cambridge on State Route 343 is ***Spocott Windmill,*** the only existing post windmill in the state for grinding grain. There used to be eighteen of these windmills, each resting on a single pole at the base, throughout Dorchester. When you stop by, you can also see a tenant farmhouse (circa 1775), a one-room Victorian-era schoolhouse (1870), a country store museum, and a blacksmith shop. The windmill was reconstructed in 1971, based on a windmill built here about 1850 by John H. L. Radcliffe, which was destroyed in the blizzard of 1888. You're invited to tour the windmill, climb its steep steps, and dawdle around for as long as you like. Corn is ground on special occasions. Check with the Spocott Windmill Foundation about special events, such as Spocott Windmill Day. The Spocott Windmill is on State Route 343, 6 miles west of Cambridge.

East New Market, originally Crossroads, could easily be called Churchtown or Churchville, for at each of the four entrances to the town stands a church. On State Route 16 South, it is Trinity United Methodist; State Route 16 North, St. Stephen's Episcopal; State Route 14 West, First Baptist; and State Route 14 East, Salem German Evangelical and Reformed Church. These churches reflect the diverse denominations represented in this area.

Indians dwelled here; the first European mention of the region was in a grant to Henry Sewell dated 1659 in London, England. The first white settler is believed to have been a Quaker, John Edmondson, who came from Virginia in the 1660s to seek religious freedom. Edmondson was followed by the

trivia

James B. Richardson, a master shipwright known along the waterways as "Mr. Jim," built the 1971 reproduction of the Spocott Windmill, likening it to the wooden boats he has built and repaired. The mill has canvas sails with a wingspan of 52 feet. The wide sails turn a wooden shaft and a series of wooden gears that turn the upper millstone, grinding the grain against the bottom millstone. These post windmills appeared in England at the end of the twelfth century. It's estimated that there were about eighteen post windmills in the county.

O'Sullivane family, and this historic district contains almost all of their early residences.

In addition to the churches, the town is known for its historical architecture, and the entire town is designated a historic district. Colonial homes are the core of the town's architecture, but among the almost seventy-five buildings are a number from the eighteenth, nineteenth, and twentieth centuries. Many of the brick walks laid in 1884 still exist.

For additional tourism information write to Dorchester County Tourism, 2 Rose Hill Place, Cambridge 21613, call (410) 228–1000 or (800) 522–TOUR, or visit www.tourdorchester.org.

Wicomico County

For a long time Salisbury was known as the last great gasp going east (or the first coming west) on the way to the beach at Ocean City. Now it's a community in its own right with a world-renowned museum, a zoo that doesn't overwhelm you with its size, and some interesting shopping. You could spend your vacation here and avoid the hot, sweaty, shoulder-to-shoulder, sand- and sunblock-covered visitors catching the rays on the shore.

For an impressive look into the peninsula's past, stop by the ***Edward H. Nabb Research Center for Delmarva History and Culture,*** where you can find some of the nation's oldest artifacts. Genealogists from around the world visit this center situated at Salisbury State University.

The center is named for Cambridge attorney Edward H. Nabb, whose forebears came to the Eastern Shore in the early eighteenth century as an indentured servant. In endowing the center with a $500,000 challenge grant, Nabb said, "Let's face it. This [the Chesapeake Bay region] is where the United States began. There should really be a center somewhere here as a repository for that information."

Because many settlers came up the Chesapeake before moving elsewhere, the Eastern Shore is an important national genealogical source for family history. They even have some records the Salt Lake City–based Church of Jesus Christ of Latter-day Saints genealogical resource center doesn't have. The Nabb Center has copies of the oldest continuous sets of courthouse records in the continental United States, dating from 1632.

Recognizing the center's potential, the late Wilcomb Washburn, head of the American Studies Program at the Smithsonian Institution, donated his personal library of more than 10,000 volumes before his death, and the Donner Foundation of New York has established a $75,000 Washburn memorial at the center.

The center, at 1101 Camden Avenue, is open Monday from 10:00 A.M. to 9:00 P.M., Tuesday through Friday from 9:30 A.M. to 4:00 P.M., and by appointment. It may be closed during school breaks, so for more information call (410) 543–6312, or visit www.nabbhistory.salisbury.edu.

The **Country House** in Salisbury is the largest country store in the East and delights all the senses with sounds of soothing music, the smell of potpourri and candles, and the feel of quality merchandise. You'll discover every colonial home furnishing you could wish to find as well as beautiful decorative accessories and old-time candy. Looking for that perfect something for your kitchen, bedroom, or bathroom? It should be here. You can select from an array of curtains, lighting fixtures, pottery, collectibles, furniture, shelving, rugs, baskets, and dried flowers. There are also some Victorian-style items, and the Christmas section is open year-round.

trivia

The late Edward H. Nabb had a pilot's license and was the only person on Earth to receive all three of the world's top power-boating awards: induction into the Power Boat Racing Hall of Fame and American Power Boat Association Honor Squadron; and the Medal of Honor of the Union of International Motor Boating. He was one of the last people to "read" for the bar in Maryland, attending some classes, but never officially enrolling toward a law degree. For more than forty years he was a member of Maryland's oldest law firm, Harrington, Harrington and Nabb.

Owners Mike and Norma Delano handpick every item in the store, and they love to stop and talk with their customers. The shop is open Monday through Saturday 10:00 A.M. to 5:30 P.M.; on Friday night it's open until 8:00 P.M. From Thanksgiving to Christmas the store stays open until 8:00 P.M. Monday through Friday. You'll find the Country House at 805 East Main Street in Salisbury. Call (410) 749–1959 or (800) 596–4666 or log on to www.thecountryhouse.com.

Salisbury Pewter, formed in 1980, is a company of dedicated workers who believe that although modern technology can be helpful, the most important part of their business is to maintain the heritage of their craft. Many of their methods have been handed down for centuries, and each piece of pewter they create is meticulously handcrafted and contains no lead. They offer a customizing service, and there is one wall with letters of appreciation from elected high officials for a series of pewter pieces created for an appreciation award. On weekdays you can see the crafters working pewter from raw product to a finished piece of art.

The shop is open Monday through Friday from 9:00 A.M. to 5:30 P.M., Saturday from 10:00 A.M. to 5:00 P.M. Call the store for Sunday hours. Salisbury

Pewter is at 2611 North Salisbury Road. The mailing address is P.O. Box 2475, Salisbury 21801; call (410) 546–1188 or (800) 824–4700 (out of state). Or visit www.salisburypewter.com.

If you hate a zoo that rambles forever and ever and tries to be encyclopedic in its collection, you'll love the smallness and intimacy of **Salisbury Zoo and Park.** Founded in 1954 by the city to advance animal conservation and environmental awareness, the zoo has about 400 mammals, birds, and reptiles native to the Americas, with exhibits of spectacled bears, monkeys, jaguars, bison, bald eagles, and a wonderful waterfowl collection.

The snug twelve-acre facility embraces a branch of the Wicomico River and has plenty of shade trees, exotic plants, and wildlife, making for a cool, peaceful setting for family outings. No gift or food concessions are in the zoo, but there are plenty nearby, and picnic tables and toilet facilities are inside the park.

The zoo is located at 750 South Park Drive, Salisbury; admission and parking are free. Pets are not permitted. The zoo is open daily from Memorial Day to Labor Day from 8:00 A.M. to 7:30 P.M. and until 4:30 P.M. the rest of the year. It is closed on Thanksgiving and Christmas. Group guided tours are available by appointment; call (410) 548–3188 or visit www.salisburyzoo.org.

Of major note is the **Ward Museum of Wildfowl Art,** which houses what is perhaps the largest collection of decorative bird carvings in the world, including many antique decoys. The museum is named for internationally renowned waterfowl carvers and painters Lem and Steve Ward of Crisfield, Maryland. During their lifetimes they produced more than 25,000 decoys and decorative birds, which the men called "counterfeits." Their workshop has been re-created, and on display are more than one hundred fine examples of their old classic hunting decoys as well as their decoratives. Lem did most of the painting, while Steve did most of the carving. Steve died in 1976, and Lem died in 1984 at the age of eighty-eight.

The museum has changing exhibits featuring oils of wild animals or the art of the Northwest Indians. You can experience the story of this Native American art form, decoy carving, from its beginning to the present. And if you don't want to venture into the wetlands yourself with the bugs and the mud, in the museum you can experience the sights and sounds of the wetland habitat of native American wildfowl. Even the setting is close to spectacular. The waterfront setting overlooks a bird sanctuary where ducks, geese, herons, ospreys, and songbirds flock, as though to perform for you. An on-site gift shop has a wide selection of wildfowl-related items.

Located at 909 South Shumaker Drive, the museum is open Monday through Saturday from 10:00 A.M. to 5:00 P.M. and Sunday from noon to 5:00

If It Looks like a Duck . . .

The Ward Foundation was established to save the art form of decoy carving, which has grown from the carving of working decoys designed to catch birds to the decorative carving of collector's items. The foundation's annual summer seminars at 909 South Shumaker Drive in Salisbury offer hands-on instruction by some of the most talented artists and teachers in the field, such as Ernie Muehlmatt, Pat Godin, Bill Koelpin, Bob Guge, Larry Bath, and Jim Sprankle. Intensive weeklong sessions cover such topics as anatomy and research, shaping, texturing, burning, priming and painting, and various brush techniques. Room and board are provided on campus. For information about the seminars, contact the Ward Foundation at (410) 742–4988.

P.M. Guided group tours are available. Admission is $7.00 for adults, $5.00 for seniors age sixty and older, $3.00 for college students (with valid ID), and for children age three through twelve. For more information contact the Ward Foundation at (410) 742–4988 or visit the Web site at www.wardmuseum.org.

If you have ever heard the railroad expression about "highballing it down the road" and wondered what it meant, take a visit to Delmar to see the *High Ball.* (Delmar lies in both Delaware and Maryland; State Street straddles the border. There was a time when the two halves—two mayors, two town councils, two school systems—fought over municipal functions, but things have been patched up for some time.)

Along the tracks near State Street you will see a large white ball, which was raised on high to signify that the line was clear, giving rise to the term "highballing." A small museum is housed in the library, on the Delaware side of town, at 101 North Bi-State Boulevard; (302) 846–9894; www.delmarlibrary.org.

Driving along the flat stretch of State Route 54 west of Delmar near Mardela Springs, you will parallel the southern end of the north-south section of the *Mason-Dixon line.* One could even say this is the cornerstone of the Mason-Dixon line. A double crownstone was installed in 1768 by Charles Mason and Jeremiah Dixon to settle the boundary disputes between the Penn and Calvert families, whose coats of arms it bears. There is a small parking lot and a brick and wrought-iron pavilion protecting the stones.

Called the Middle Point monument because it marks the middle of the Delmarva Peninsula, the crownstone also is a triangulation point of the National Geodetic Survey. The stone was broken off at ground level by vandals in 1983, and another stone originally set by colonial surveyors in 1760 was defaced by removal of the Calvert coat of arms. The Maryland Department of Natural

Resources and Delaware's State Boundary Commission jointly replaced the monument on October 24, 1985. Call (410) 548–4914.

Two ferryboats continue service in this part of Maryland, survivors of the many that once linked water-isolated communities on the Wicomico River, between Wicomico and Somerset Counties. Both are small, both are free, and both operate all year, weather conditions and tides permitting.

The **Upper Ferry** crosses between Allen and State Route 349 in Salisbury and takes about three minutes. It is an outboard motor–propelled cable ferryboat with no name. A ferry has been running here since at least 1897; the current one has a capacity of two cars plus six passengers, with a maximum vehicle size of five tons gross weight. Bicycles are permitted.

The Upper Ferry runs Monday through Friday March through September from 7:00 A.M. to 6:00 P.M. and the rest of the year from 7:00 A.M. to 5:30 P.M. Monday through Friday and 7:00 A.M. to 1:00 P.M. on Saturday. Call (410) 548–4873.

The **Whitehaven–Mt. Vernon Cable Ferry,** called the Whitehaven Ferry, is 6 miles downriver from the Upper Ferry and connects Whitehaven to Widgeon; it has been operating since 1690. The modern ferryboat, the *Som-Wico,* takes about five minutes for a crossing and can hold three cars plus ten passengers. Bikes are permitted.

Whitehaven is the oldest incorporated town on the river and once was a vital deepwater port and shipbuilding area. Both ferries are run by the Wicomico County Road Department. Call (410) 548–4873 for more information.

Contact Lewis R. Carman, Tourism Director, at the Convention and Visitor Bureau, P.O. Box 2333, Salisbury 21802-2333, for more details on tourism, or call (410) 548–4914 or (800) 332–8687.

Worcester County

The town of Berlin in eastern Worcester (pronounced like "rooster") County has no connection to the city in Germany; instead, it is a corruption of Burley Inn, the name of the site on which it was constructed. A guided map for a **Berlin walking tour** includes a town park and monument dedicated to Comm. Stephen Decatur, a native of Berlin. The oldest homes were built during the Federal period, later homes adopted the Victorian style, and twentieth-century homes are typified by the "bungalow." The walking tour brochure can be picked up at local Berlin businesses.

Berlin is another designated Maryland Arts and Entertainment District. The town has five working galleries, numerous specialty shops, multiple perfor-

Laying Back in Berlin

"People tell us they've gone to Ocean City for thirty years and never stopped in Berlin," says Debbie Frene, owner of the mainland village's Victorian Charm, a boutique full of scented candles, handbags, and other accessories. Dating to the 1790s, Berlin offers the quintessential day trip for those suffering from sunburn, boredom, or other summer-resort afflictions. Berlin is a little bit of St. Michaels or Chestertown on the far eastern shore, and is just seven miles west of Ocean City.

Runaway Bride, the hit movie with Julia Roberts and Richard Gere, was set here, and scenes from *Tuck Everlasting* were also shot here, albeit after re-creating the look of older days (yes, they dumped tons of dirt on the streets to do so).

You can simply prowl the ultra-quaint streets lined with boutiques like Victorian Charm, the Globe (a fabulous restaurant/art gallery in an old theater), and the cafe and antiques store at An a Fare to Remember.

From Ocean City, follow U.S. Highway 50 west about 7 miles and turn south on State Route 818, which becomes Main Street. For more information call (410) 641–4775 or log on to www.berlin.sailorsite.net or www.berlinmdcc.org.

mance art venues, and annual arts festivals and a fiddlers' convention. The Berlin A&E committee meets the second Friday of each month at 9:00 A.M. in the Berlin Town Hall. You're invited to attend if you're a local artist who would like to be included in the program, or one who's considering moving to the Berlin area. For more information, contact Debbie Frene at (410) 641–2998; www.berlinmdarts.org.

A typical Federal-style post-and-beam house is the **Calvin B. Taylor House Museum.** It was built about 1825 and now is used as the town museum. The gable-front house features a Palladian window with Victorian glass, restored wood graining, and a magnificent front doorway with butterfly medallions, sunbursts, and fluted, engaged columns. The house was supposed to be destroyed and replaced by a new post office and parking lot, but it was saved in 1981 by the Berlin Heritage Foundation. With $100,000 in private donations from the community, the house was restored from its dilapidated condition.

Although Robert J. Henry, who was instrumental in bringing the railroad to Berlin, lived in the house, the most famous occupant was Calvin B. Taylor, the founder of the Calvin B. Taylor Banking Company, which is still in existence. Much of the house and appointments are original to the times that various occupants lived in the house, including C.B. Taylor's bank desk, with its hidden doors on the side and front.

The Taylor House is at 208 North Main Street in Berlin at the intersection with Baker Street, across from the Stevenson Methodist Church. The house is open Monday, Wednesday, Friday, and Saturday, mid-May through the end of October, from 1:00 to 4:00 P.M. and for such special events as concerts. Call (410) 641–1019 or visit http://taylorhousemuseum.org. There is no admission charge, but a $2.00 donation is suggested.

In the middle of the historic district is the ***Atlantic Hotel,*** a faithfully restored 1895 Victorian hostelry that was rescued from the depths of distress to become this showpiece, which was named to the National Register of Historic Places in 1980. Each of the seventeen guest rooms (each with private bath) is beautifully furnished with antiques and is unique in its decor. Rich green and burgundy, delicate rose and aqua, deep mahogany tones, tassels, braid, lace, and crochet help transport you to a gentler time and quieter pace.

A parlor—for reading, letter writing, or conversation—is on the second floor. A continental breakfast is provided.

The Atlantic Hotel and all of Berlin will look familiar to you if you saw the Richard Gere and Julia Roberts movie *Runaway Bride*. The town was called Hale in the movie and all the shops were renamed; only the Atlantic kept its own identity. The Atlantic Hotel Inn and Restaurant is located at 2 North Main Street, Berlin. Call (410) 641–3589 or (800) 814–7672 for information or reservations. The Web site is www.atlantichotel.com.

Seven miles east of Berlin is ***Assateague Island National Seashore*** and the Assateague State Park, reached by State Route 611. Nearly two million peo-

Atlantic Hotel

ple visit this seashore annually. A two-room visitor center is open for interpretive classes and exhibits, which include a small touch tank of marine life. During a visit here you can take a guided walk; view a demonstration on how to catch blue crabs, clams, and ribbed mussels (mighty tasty steamed or sautéed in butter); or join a naturalist at the Old Ferry Landing to explore the width of Assateague Island. You will travel by foot and bike or car from the salt marsh to the pounding surf, discovering relationships between the various barrier island life zones.

The famed **Chincoteague ponies** can be seen on Assateague, for two herds of the wild ponies make their home here. The herds are separated by a fence at the Maryland-Virginia state line. Managed by the National Park Service on the Maryland side, horses are often seen around roads and campgrounds. The horses sold at auction every July are on the Virginia side. No road connects the two states within the park. Supposedly, the horses are descended from domesticated stock that grazed on the island as early as the seventeenth century; Eastern Shore planters put them here to avoid mainland taxes and fencing requirements. Smaller than horses, these shaggy, sturdy ponies are well adapted to their harsh seashore environment. Marsh and dune grasses supply the bulk of their food, and they obtain water from freshwater impoundments or natural ponds.

Although they appear tame, they are unpredictable and can inflict serious wounds by kicking and biting. The Park Service strongly recommends that you do not pet or feed the ponies.

While at the park, you may see great blue herons, snowy egrets, dunlins, American widgeons, black-crowned night herons, peregrine falcons, and numerous other birds on the Maryland side.

Legend has it that Edward Teach (Blackbeard the Pirate) kept one of his fourteen wives, a base of operations, and buried treasure on Assateague.

The Assateague Island National Seashore visitor center is open daily from 9:00 A.M. to 5:00 P.M.; 7206 National Seashore Lane, Berlin. Call (410) 641–1441 or (800) 365–2267 or log on to www.nps.gov/asis. The Assateague State Park, Maryland's only ocean park, is at 7307 Stephen Decatur Highway, Berlin; (410) 641–2120 or (888) 432–2267; www.dnr.state.md.us.

The **Viewtrail 100** signs you will see on secondary state and county roads mark a scenic bicycle trail, which is maintained by the Worcester County Tourism Department. You can join the trail in Berlin as it sweeps down to Pocomoke City, past the access to Furnace Town, Nassawango Creek Cypress Swamp, Milburn Landing on the north bank of the Pocomoke River, and many other interesting attractions.

The **Pocomoke River** is the northernmost swamp river on the East Coast, and along its banks are descendants of cypress trees that were used to make our country's first ships. Here you can view eagles, egrets, hawks, and vultures, as well. For more Maryland bike trail information, call (800) 252–8776.

The *Beach to Bay Indian Trail* is a self-guided driving trail that goes from Smith Island in the Chesapeake Bay in Somerset County up to Princess Anne, Pocomoke City, Snow Hill, Berlin, and Ocean City. It was opened in 1988 and is jointly sponsored by Somerset and Worcester Tourism, Ocean City, the State of Maryland, the Department of Transportation, and the Department of Natural Resources.

A carved-wood relief sculpture in polychrome, called **The Power of Communication,** hangs over the postmaster's door in the Pocomoke City Post Office. Perna Krick of Baltimore executed the commission in 1940. The figure of a Native American with an airplane reflects the history of the area, from early tradition to the development of communication, from primitive methods to present-day service.

Ms. Krick was born in Ohio in 1909 and attended the Dayton Art Institute. She studied under J. Maxwell Miller at the Rinehard School of Sculpture in Baltimore, receiving two European traveling scholarships. By the time she received this commission from the Federal Works Agency, her work had been exhibited at the Baltimore Art Museum, the Pennsylvania Academy of Fine Arts, and the Architectural League in New York.

Ocean City is a family-oriented town on the ocean. It lies 7 miles east of Berlin. Thousands of college kids come here every summer to work and vacation. There is plenty to do, from kite flying (probably my favorite activity), to boating, fishing, golfing, and beach-related activities. As with any resort, there are dozens (if not hundreds) of restaurants, eateries, bars, and food stands along the 3-mile boardwalk, and you have to try some of the famous saltwater taffy and Thrasher's french fries with vinegar. Rather than trying to drive through traffic, which can be terrible in the summer, try the bus. As they say in Ocean City, "Avoid the fuss, take the bus." Ride all day for only $2.00. Call (410) 723–1606 for the schedule. There is also a boardwalk tram that runs 2.5 miles between the Inlet and 27th Street from 10:00 A.M. to midnight daily during the summer. Weekend service is offered in the spring and fall from 10:00 A.M. to 6:00 P.M., weather permitting. Call (410) 723–1606.

One of the traditional sights around Ocean City is the airplanes flying advertising banners about 200 feet above sea level. Robert Bunting of Berlin bought a small crop duster in 1982 and started airplane advertising by flying up and down the beach with banner messages. *Ocean Aerial* is so popular that a half dozen banner-bearing, single-engine aircraft are used for this kind of advertising. Each banner must have forty or fewer letters. Some carry marriage proposals; others tell you about the newest restaurant in town.

If you would like to have one carry your message for the world to see while the plane flies "low and slow," it will cost between $50 and $160 per banner. If you go watch the ground crew rig the planes, you will see them set the banner between two upright poles that are 6 feet apart. (It is said that if the ground crew is feeling prankish, they will close the poles to only 2 feet apart.) Then the plane flies about 85 miles per hour to pick up the banner. Usually the pilot makes it on the first trip, but it has taken as many as six tries to hook a banner. You are looking at some first-class flying.

Between Memorial Day and Labor Day, each pilot logs about 500 hours, flying from 10:00 A.M. to 4:00 P.M. seven days a week, and together the pilots can fly as many as 110 banners in one day, although the average is about 45 to 50. For more information call (410) 641–2484 or visit www.ocean-city.com/aerial.htm.

There may be a gazillion places to stay while in Ocean City, but you'll be hard-pressed to find a place more charming or host and hostess so memorable as Vicky and Charlie Barrett and the ***Inn on the Ocean.*** As the name indicates, the inn is the only one on the ocean. That means you're steps from the beach and boardwalk, but it's set back enough to be quiet and peaceful.

A large wraparound veranda allows for people-watching at your leisure and a setting for the humongous breakfast (during warm weather). A fireplace in the living room warms the soul and the body during the winter. Each of the six guest rooms has a ceiling fan, TV/VCR, and private bath and is decorated with luxury and comfort in mind. Bicycles and beach equipment are complimentary so you don't have to worry about packing all that "stuff."

The bed and breakfast was constructed in 1938 and features Victorian-style architecture.

An active community member, Vicki was cochair of the OC Beach Birds art project in 2003 where some eighty 5-foot fiberglass birds were transformed into unusual works of art by regional artists and displayed throughout the city. This is similar to the Chicago cows, the DC party animals (elephants and donkeys), and panda-mania exhibits. The birds were auctioned after the exhibit with the proceeds going to public art in Ocean City.

The Inn on the Ocean is located at 1001 Atlantic Avenue (Tenth Street and the Boardwalk); call (410) 289–8894 or (888) 226–6223) or visit www.bbon line.com/md/ontheocean.

The Ocean City restaurant that has to be a first on anyone's list is ***Phillips Crab House.*** Eating at this restaurant, which was started by Shirley and Brice Phillips from Hooper's Island on Chesapeake Bay, has been a ritual in Ocean City since 1956. The two of them have become such an institution and such an integral part of their community that they were honored in 1989 by the Ocean City Good Will Ambassadors Grand Ball and again in 2000 by the Maryland

Tourism Council during National Tourism Week, as the most prominent tourism industry family.

Phillips has branched out with several locations, among them in Baltimore's Harborplace, Washington, D.C., and Norfolk. But the Ocean City location is the one to visit. It was a shingle-covered shack in the boonies when it opened. Now it is in the middle of everything that is happening and can seat 1,400 diners at one time. Despite its size, you will have to arrive early or plan to wait a while, because there is always a line for dinner. This is where you come to eat crabs, piled in mounds on broad sheets of paper that cover tables that once held sewing machines.

If steamed crabs, spiced shrimp, and crab cakes don't appeal to you, there is always fried chicken or Virginia baked ham served with corn on the cob, watermelon, and cole slaw. A children's menu is also available.

Phillips Crab House is at Twenty-first Street and Philadelphia Avenue in Ocean City. For information call (410) 289–6821 or visit www.phillipsseafood .com.

Ocean City has been named one of America's greatest golf hometowns by *Golf Digest* magazine, which compared 244 counties based on the number and quality of courses, golf days per year, and course congestion in the golf criteria, and crime rates, airport access, off-course amenities, and cost of living in the non-golf category. With nearly two dozen courses within a thirty-minute drive, it's easy to understand why the area was honored.

The ***Greater Ocean City Golf Association*** helps market combined packages with the courses and accommodations, so you can have your golf and ocean or bay vacation created for you. The association is at 9935 Stephen Decatur Highway, #141; (410) 213–7050.

Those of you who served aboard the ***USS 324,*** a World War II submarine that was built in 1944 and saw battle in the Java and South China Seas, will find her serving a new function as a reef in the Atlantic Ocean about 15 miles off Ocean City. The *Blenny* was scuttled in 1989 also about 15 miles offshore. It acts as a base for algae and soft coral growth, which will attract small fish and then larger fish, fishermen, and divers.

Ocean City is not just for summer fun. It is a year-round community that sponsors a great number of activities during the winter season, including workshops, entertainment, an annual Christmas parade, a traditional lighting and trimming of a 30-foot tree on the beach, and the placement of holiday decorations throughout the town. Call (800) 62–OCEAN or visit www.ococean.com for details about these and numerous other events.

One of the unfortunate duties of Ocean City residents is lifesaving, for some people will do stupid things, and some people will be the victims of circumstances even without being stupid. The **Ocean City Life-Saving Station Museum,** located on the south end of the boardwalk, shows some early life-saving equipment and sands from around the world, shipwreck artifacts, antique bathing suits, models of old Ocean City hotels and businesses, photos of famous storms, and tales (not tails) of mermaids.

It's open all year, with hours of 11:00 A.M. to 10:00 P.M. daily during the summer. Admission is $3.00 for adults and $1.00 for children (twelve and under). Call (410) 289–4991 for off-season hours and information, or log on to www.ocmuseum.org.

A brochure about Christmas in Ocean City (as well as in Berlin, Snow Hill, and Pocomoke) is available from the Ocean City Public Relations Office, P.O. Box 158, Ocean City 21842. You can call the office at (410) 289–2800.

For additional information on Worcester County, contact the Maryland Lower Shore Tourist Information Center, US 13 North, 144 Ocean Highway, Pocomoke City 21851 (410–957–2484), or Worcester County Tourism, P.O. Box 208, Snow Hill 21863 (800–852–0335) or log on to www.visitworcester.org.

Somerset County

Skipjacks can be seen in the watermen's villages of Deal Island, Chance, and Wenona. Over Labor Day weekend this last fleet of working sailboats races in the Tangier Sound off Deal Island in the annual Skipjack Races.

With a little time, you also might want to stop by the **Teackle Mansion** in Princess Anne on Sunday afternoon. This is a very elaborate example of the Federal style of architecture in 1802 and then in 1818 and 1819, erected by Littleton Dennis Teackle (1777–1848), an influential man of the early 1800s. Teackle and his wife Elizabeth Upshur Teackle (1783–1835) moved to this area from Accomack County in Virginia, shortly after they were married in 1800. Teackle was a merchant, statesman, and entrepreneur, owning agriculture and timber lands, and trading with merchants in England and the Caribbean. He established the Bank of Somerset in 1813 and served for many years in the Maryland House of Delegates.

The mansion was sold and eventually became apartments, until Maude Jeffries and her sister Catherine Ricketts founded Olde Princess Anne Days Inc. The funds this organization raised bought and restored the mansion and has supported its continued renovation. An infusion of $25,000 from the Maryland Commission for Celebration 2000 has supported an archaeological survey of the property that will map and retrieve sensitive archaeological resources.

Located at 11736 Mansion Street, Princess Anne, the mansion is open on Wednesday, Saturday, and Sunday from 1:00 to 3:00 P.M. April through mid-

Skipjack

December, and Sunday from 1:00 to 3:00 P.M. December through March. Call (410) 651–2238 or (800) 521–9189 or visit www.teackle.mansion.museum for information.

The Teackle Mansion is also the home of the Somerset County Historical Society (410–651–2238).

The *J. Millard Tawes Historical Museum* in Crisfield exhibits items pertaining to the late Maryland governor J. Millard Tawes, the history and development of the Crisfield seafood industry, local art and folklore, and the anthropological history of the area. For a broader look, check on the guided trolley and walking tours of Crisfield.

The museum, 3 Ninth Street in Crisfield, is open Monday through Saturday during the summer from 9:00 A.M. to 5:00 P.M. Call (410) 968–2501 for more information or log on to www.crisfieldheritagefoundation.org. Admission is $2.50 for adults.

You also might want to try some seafood, for Crisfield is the self-proclaimed Heartland of the Chesapeake Bay, or take a ferry out to Smith or Tangier Island. For these pleasures, you could not come to a more perfect place.

I love finding crafters who not only create wonderful decorative and wearable art, but who will fashion something to your specific request. Jim and Mary Anne Wendell of *Wood and Woolens,* in Crisfield, are such people. Jim's specialty is woodworking. He has a one-man shop, in a 24-by-24-foot frame building that was constructed in 1996.

Jim makes custom furniture and unique woodcrafts (including a child's rocking horse, wooden animal toys, trucks and other vehicles, picture frames, bread slicing box, and an afghan or quilt rack—great for displaying some of his wife's handiwork) and offers them for sale at shows on the Delmarva Peninsula and through the mail or their Web site. I saw his selection of business card holders and requested a special design for my daughter, Jazz (a rhinoceros, but that's another story). He e-mailed a design, I approved it, and almost before I could spell rhinoceros, it was in my mailbox. What a wonderful surprise gift for my daughter! And, very reasonably priced.

Mary Anne, on the other hand, works with woolens. She features patterns for unique cable sweaters, in the Trot Line Collection (celebrating the watermen of the Chesapeake Bay), and offers handmade cloth dolls and cuddly bears, using handspun yarn and other natural fibers. Periodically, she'll even sell her patterns if you'd like to try your hand at crafting such items. Their studio at 5 Minden Avenue, is open by chance or by appointment. Call (410) 968–3548 or visit http://hometown.aol.com/wood2knits/.

Knut Aspenberg is another spectacular crafter in the Crisfield area. His love is making models of working and pleasure boats, using basswood, mahogany, oak, poplar, and pine. He loves working with old and abandoned furniture in which the wood has been seasoned. With a series of saw cuts, a 2-inch board in real size becomes a $\frac{1}{16}$-inch replica on a $\frac{3}{8}$-inch-to-a-foot scale. His work is available at the Annapolis Marine Art Gallery in Annapolis. Or, you can commission him to re-create your boat. Send photos or take a visit so he can take the measure of your boat and note any special details. It may take six months or so, but you will treasure the miniature as much (or more) as you do the full-sized version. Visit Knut at 10577 Harrison Point Road, Chance; (410) 784–2130.

Two of Maryland's ten ferries—the Whitehaven and Upper Ferries—operate between Somerset and Wicomico Counties. Check the Wicomico County section for additional details.

For additional tourism information write to Somerset County Tourism, P.O. Box 243, Princess Anne 21853. Call (410) 651–2968 or (800) 521–9189, or log on to www.visitsomerset.com.

Places to Eat on the Eastern Shore

BERLIN

Atlantic Hotel Inn and Restaurant,
2 North Main Street,
(410) 641–3589,
(800) 641–3589,
www.atlantichotel.com

CAMBRIDGE

Port Side Seafood Company,
201 Trenton Street,
(410) 228–9007

CRISFIELD

Cove Restaurant,
718 Broadway Street,
(410) 968–9532,
www.coverestaurant.net

Mi Pueblito Grill,
333 Main Street,
 (410) 968–9984,
www.mipueblitogrill.com

Side Street Seafood Restaurant,
204 South Tenth Street,
(410) 968–2442,
www.crisfield.com/sidestreet

Watermen's Inn,
901 West Main Street,
(410) 968–2119,
http://crisfield.com/
watermens

DELMAR

Linda's Railroad Cafe,
18 North Pennsylvania Avenue,
(302) 846–3687

EASTON

Chez Lafitte,
13 South Washington Street,
(410) 770–8868

General Tanuki,
25 Goldsborough Street,
(410) 819–0707

Inn at Easton,
28 South Harrison Street,
(410) 822–4910

Legal Spirits,
42 East Dover Street,
(410) 822–0765

Mason's,
22 South Harrison Street,
(410) 822–3204

Out of the Fire,
22 Goldsborough Street,
(410) 770–4777

Portofino,
4 West Dover Street,
(410) 770–9200

Restaurant Columbia,
28 South Washington Street,
(410) 770–5172,
www.restaurantcolumbia
.com

Restaurant Local,
Tidewater Inn,
101 East Dover Street,
(410) 822–1300,
www.restaurantlocal.com

Scossa,
8 North Washington Street,
(410) 822–2202

FRUITLAND

Restaurant 213,
213 North Fruitland Boulevard,
(410) 677–4880,
www.restaurant213.com

GRASONVILLE

Fisherman's Inn and Crab Deck,
3116 Main Street,
(410) 827–6666,
www.crabdeck.com

Harris' Crab House,
433 Kent Narrows Way North,
(410) 827–9500,
www.harriscrabhouse.com

Holly's,
108 Jackson Creek Road,
(410) 827–8711,
www.hollysrest.com

GREENSBORO

Harry's at the Goldsborough House,
116 West Sunset Avenue,
(410) 482–6758,
www.anywheregourmet.com/
Harrys/index.htm

KENNEDYVILLE

Kennedyville Inn,
11986 Augustine Herman Highway,
 (410) 348–2400,
www.kennedyvilleinn.com

OCEAN CITY

Embers,
Twenty-fourth and Coastal Highway,
(410) 289–3322

Fager's Island,
Fifty-ninth Street, In-the-Bay,
(410) 524–5500

Jules,
11805 Coastal Highway,
Suite N,
(410) 524–3396,
www.julesoc.com

Marlin Moon Grille,
12806 Ocean Gateway,
(410) 213–1618,
www.marlinmoongrille.com

Nebula,
9211 Coastal Highway,
(410) 524–8090,
www.ocnebula.com

**Wharf Restaurant and
Lounge,**
12801 Coastal Highway,
(410) 250–1001

OXFORD

Latitude 38 Bistro & Spirits,
26342 Oxford Road,
(410) 226–5303,
www.latitude38.org

Robert Morris Inn,
North Morris Street,
(410) 226–5111

ROCK HALL

Inn At Osprey Point,
20786 Rock Hall Avenue,
(410) 639–2154

ST. MICHAELS

Bistro St. Michaels,
403 South Talbot Street,
(410) 745–9111

Inn at Perry Cabin,
308 Watkins Lane,
(410) 745–5178

Michael Rork's Town Dock,
125 Mulberry Street,
(410) 745–5577,
(800) 884–0103,
www.town-dock.com

208 Talbot,
208 Talbot Street,
(410) 745–3838,
www.208talbot.com

STEVENSVILLE

Hemingway's Restaurant,
(Exit 37S) off Route 50,
357 Pier 1,
(410) 643–CRAB

Places to Stay on the Eastern Shore

BERLIN

**Atlantic Hotel Inn and
Restaurant,**
2 North Main Street,
(410) 641–3589,
www.atlantichotel.com

BOZMAN

**Harris Cove Cottages Bed
'N Boat,**
8080 Bozman-Neavitt Road,
(410) 745–9701,
www.bednboat.com

CHESAPEAKE CITY

Inn at the Canal,
104 Bohemia Avenue,
(410) 885–5995,
www.innatthecanal.com

CHESTERTOWN

**Hill's Inn Bed and
Breakfast,**
114 Washington Avenue,
(410) 778–1926,
www.chestertown.com

CLAIBORNE

**Claiborne Cottage By the
Bay,**
10449 Claiborne Road,
(410) 745–6987

Maple Hall,
23253 Maple Hall Road,
(410) 745–2673,
www.maplehall.com

CORDOVA

**Peaches and Dreams Bed
and Breakfast,**
12824 Peach Lane,
(410) 820–5644,
(202) 762–3553

CRISFIELD

**My Fair Lady Bed and
Breakfast,**
38 West Main Street,
(410) 968–0352,
www.myfairladybandb.com

EASTON

**Bishop's House Bed and
Breakfast,**
214 Goldsborough Street,
(410) 820–7290,
(800) 223–7290,
www.bishopshouse.com

Inn at 202 Dover,
202 Dover Street,
(866) 450–7600,
www.theinnat202dover.com

**McDaniel House Bed and
Breakfast,**
14 North Aurora Street,
(410) 822–3704,
(877) 822–5702,
www.bnblist.com

NEAVITT

Grandview,
6601 Broad Creek Road,
(410) 745–5069,
(717) 392–4876,
www.grandviewatpleasure
point.com

OCEAN CITY

There are dozens, if not hundreds, of hotels, motels, boardinghouses, apartments, bed-and-breakfasts, and condo units for rent in Ocean City. They are bayside or oceanside, seasonal and year-round. They are available on a weekly basis (Saturday to Saturday, Sunday to Sunday), a full weekend only, or by the night. For your first visit, you might want to contact the Chamber of Commerce (410–213–0552) or one of about a dozen vacation rental establishments and ask for information about this resort area.

Fenwick Inn,
13801 Coastal Highway,
(410) 250–1100,
(800) 492–1873,
www.fenwickinn.com

Inn on the Ocean,
1001 Atlantic Avenue,
(410) 289–8894,
(877) INN–ON–OC,
www.bbonline.com/md/ontheocean

OXFORD

Combsberry,
4837 Evergreen Road,
(410) 226–5353,
www.combsberry.net

Robert Morris Inn,
314 North Morris Street,
(410) 226–5111,
www.robertmorrisinn.com

POCOMOKE CITY

Littleton's Bed and Breakfast,
407 Second Street,
(410) 957–1645,
www.littletonsbandb.com

PRINCESS ANNE

Hayman House Bed and Breakfast,
30491 Prince William Street,
(410) 651–1107,
www.haymanhouse.com

ROCK HALL

Inn at Osprey Point,
20786 Rock Hall Avenue,
(410) 639–2194,
www.ospreypoint.com

Tallulah's on Main,
5750 Main Street,
(410) 639–2596,
www.tallulahsonmain.com

ROYAL OAK

The Oaks,
25876 Royal Oak Road,
(410) 745–5053,
www.the-oaks.com

Royal Oak House B&B,
PO Box 296,
(410) 745–3025

SMITH ISLAND

Ewell Tide Inn,
4063 Tyler Road,
(410) 425–2141,
www.smithisland.net

ST. MICHAELS

Adams Water Chestnut Cottage,
417 Water Street,
(410) 745–6770,
www.waterchestnut.com

Bay Cottage Bed and Breakfast,
24640 Yacht Club Road,
(410) 745–9369,
(888) 558–8008,
www.baycottage.com

Butterfly Point Waterfront House,
24642 Yacht Club Road,
(410) 745–9022,
www.butterflypoint.com

Dr. Dodson House Bed and Breakfast,
200 Cherry Street,
(410) 745–3691,
www.drdodsonhouse.com

Five Gables Inn & Spa,
209 North Talbot Street,
(410) 745–0100,
(877) 466–0100,
www.fivegables.com

Inn at Perry Cabin,
308 Watkins Lane,
(410) 745–2200,
(800) 722–2949,
www.perrycabin.com

STEVENSVILLE

Kent Manor Inn,
500 Kent Manor Drive,
(410) 643–5757,
(800) 820–4511,
www.kentmanor.com

TILGHMAN ISLAND

Black Walnut Point Inn,
Black Walnut Road,
(410) 886–2452,
www.tilghmanisland.com/blackwalnut

TYLERTON

Inn of Silent Music,
(410) 425–3541,
www.innofsilentmusic.com

VIENNA

Nanticoke Manor,
Church Street at Water Street,
(410) 376–3432

WITTMAN

Watermark Bed and Breakfast,
8956 Tilghman Island Road,
(800) 314–7734,
www.watermarkinn.com

OTHER ATTRACTIONS WORTH SEEING ON THE EASTERN SHORE

Academy Art Museum,
Easton,
(410) 822–2787,
www.art-academy.org

Avalon Theatre,
Easton,
(410) 822–0345,
www.avalontheatre.com

Chesapeake Bay Maritime Museum,
St. Michaels,
(410) 745–2916,
www.cbmm.org

Delmarva Shorebirds,
Salisbury,
(410) 219–3112,
(888) BIRDS–96,
www.theshorebirds.com

Eastern Neck National Wildlife Refuge,
Rock Hall,
(410) 639–7056,
http://easternneck.fws.gov

Furnace Town Historic Site,
Snow Hill,
(410) 632–2032,
www.dol.net/~ebola.ftown.htm

Janes Island State Park,
Crisfield,
(410) 968–1565,
(888) 432–CAMP,
www.dnr.state.md.us

Julia A. Purnell Museum,
Snow Hill,
(410) 632–0515

Nathan of Dorchester,
Cambridge,
(410) 228–7141,
www.skipjack.nathan.org

Pocomoke State Forest,
Snow Hill,
(410) 632–2566,
www.dnr.state.md.us

(James B.) Richardson Maritime Museum,
Cambridge,
(410) 221–1871,
(800) 522–TOUR

Smith Island Museum and Cultural Center,
Ewell,
(410) 425–3351,
www.smithisland.org

Washington College,
Chestertown,
(410) 778–8500,
(800) 422–1782,
www.washcoll.edu

Waterman's Museum,
Rock Hall,
(410) 778–6697,
(800) 506–6697,
www.havenharbour.com

Delaware

The **Delmarva Peninsula** has always been DelMarVa to me, for DELaware, MARyland and VirginiA. It would never have occurred to me to question whether it should have or at some other time might have been VaMarDel or MarVaDel or some other variation of the three states. Wade B. Fleetwood, who wrote a column about the people and places of the Eastern Shore, did question it, and now so have I. We have drawn no conclusion. It could be from north to south, or alphabetical, or political. I don't know. The only positive thing my research has given me is that it was referred to as DelMarVa as early as 1870 when the fourteen counties of the Eastern Shore (three in Delaware, nine in Maryland, and two in Virginia) were discussing separate statehood. Why fight tradition?

So, if the Delaware of Delmarva comes first, why does this book list Maryland first? Because. *Maryland Off the Beaten Path* was here first, and it wasn't until the third edition that it expanded its scope.

Poor Delaware is just too tiny to claim its own volume. I know, someone out there is bound to say, "Well, all of Delaware is off the beaten path," and to a great extent that is very deliciously true. Nancy Sawin, a famed Delaware illustrator, has

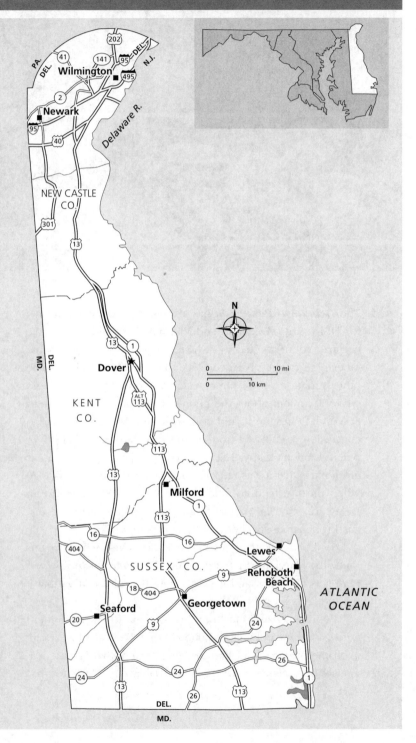

DELAWARE

PA.
DEL.
202
41
141
95
DEL.
N.J.
Wilmington
495
2
Newark
95
40
Delaware R.

NEW CASTLE CO.

301

13

MD.
DEL.

13
1

Dover

ALT
113

KENT CO.

113

13

Milford
113
1

16
16

404
16

Lewes

SUSSEX CO.

9

Rehoboth Beach

18
404
Georgetown

20
Seaford

9
24

ATLANTIC OCEAN

24
24

26

13

26
113
1

DEL.
MD.

N

0   10 mi
0   10 km

caught the state and the peninsula in many of her books. Her books can be difficult to find, but they're a treasure of information about everything from outhouses to swamps to lighthouses. By the way, she's the same Nancy Sawin who was named to the USA Field Hockey Hall of Fame in 1988.

Despite Delaware's diminutive size, the Delaware Estuary is the major staging area for 80 percent of the snow geese in the Atlantic flyway. Delaware also is known as the state without sales tax, and there are a number of outlet stores and malls, particularly at Rehoboth Beach (what else are you to do besides shop on a rainy day during your vacation?). For outlet information call (888) SHOP–333 or visit www.shoprehoboth.com.

trivia

British captain Samuel Argall landed in a sheltered bay off the Atlantic Ocean during a ferocious storm in 1610. He named the bay De La Warr, after Thomas West, the third Baron of De La Warr and the governor of Virginia, a man who never did and never would step foot in the state. The name was shortened to Delaware and applied to the river that feeds the bay and to the Native Americans who lived there.

Everywhere you turn in Delaware there's a delightful treasure, whether it's watching children getting on a school bus, eyes and bodies filled with excitement and anticipation, or the changing song patterns of rain falling pitter patter on the car roof, interrupted by the overhanging trees dropping huge glops of water. The scenic ponds created to supply energy to the dozens of grist- and lumber mills are too perfect to be cap-

trivia

Delaware is the second smallest state in the nation (Rhode Island is the smallest). It is about half the size of Los Angeles County in California.

tured by mere artists or mere words. They have to be experienced firsthand. And the friendliness of everyone you meet is too precious to appreciate in one visit. You may have to move to Delaware and spend a lifetime in this Small Wonder and the First State (to ratify the Constitution).

JUDY'S FAVORITE ATTRACTIONS IN DELAWARE

Delaware Agricultural Museum and Village

Dover Air Force Base

Trap Pond State Park

Zwaanendael Museum

New Castle County

Starting from the north of Delaware, we begin in Wilmington, the largest city in the state, and branch out and then south. Wilmington was laid out in 1731 by Quakers and was an important shipping center. Early in the 1800s, Eleuthère Irenée du Pont and his two sons moved into the area and, seeing the abundant waterpower potential, started their gunpowder business. Their influence on the development of the city and surrounding area cannot be overstated. Eventually the du Ponts would be responsible for building public schools and creating some of the most incredible museums and museum settings.

trivia

Delaware is also known as the Diamond State, because it was considered a "jewel" among states due to its strategic location.

Draped on either side of the Brandywine Creek that runs from the heart of Wilmington are Brandywine, Alapocas, and Rockford Parks. ***Brandywine Park*** was designed by Frederick Law Olmsted, creator of New York City's Central Park and the National Zoo in Washington, D.C. There's a playground here, a zoo, and the Josephine Garden, with its Japanese cherry trees. The park is open daily from dawn to dusk, with the zoo open from 10:00 A.M. to 4:00 P.M. Admission to the park is $3.00 a day per car for Delaware-registered vehicles and $6.00 a day for out-of-state registered vehicles from May 1 through October 31. The park is located at 1001 North Park Drive; (302) 739–9191; www.destateparks.com.

The admission for the zoo, which is wheelchair accessible, is $5.00 for adults, $3.00 for children three to eleven, and $4.00 for senior citizens, from June through September. It's $4.00, $2.00, and $2.00 from October through May. (302) 571–7788, ext. 200; www.brandywinezoo.org.

A little farther north is the ***Delaware Art Museum,*** with one of the country's most important assemblages of English pre-Raphaelite paintings in the

A Whale of a Mural

Downtown Wilmington, near the Amtrak station, is the site of a Wyland mural. Wyland was born in 1956 in Detroit, Michigan, and saw his first grey whales migrating off the California coast when he was fourteen. He started painting whales and dolphins when he was sixteen. By 1974 he had painted his first mural, an Alps mountain scene in Royal Oak, Michigan. The Wilmington painting, called *Whaling Wall XLIV, Marine Mammals,* was done in 1993. It's located between Shipley and Market Streets on Martin Luther King Boulevard.

Bancroft collection. American artists also are represented, and a hands-on section is great for children to learn about art.

Located at 2301 Kentmere Parkway in Wilmington, the museum is open Tuesday through Saturday 10:00 A.M. to 4:00 P.M., until 8:00 P.M. on Wednesday, Sunday noon to 4:00 P.M. The museum is closed on New Year's Day, Thanksgiving, and Christmas. The admission for adults is $10.00; seniors over sixty, $8.00; and students with identification, $5.00. There's no admission fee on Sunday. Call (302) 571–9590 or visit www.delart.org.

There are other special places to visit, and the **Hagley Museum** is one of them. Set on 240 landscaped acres at the original DuPont mills on State Route 141 North, there are numerous exhibits showing the maturation of this country's economic growth.

trivia

Wilmington was a major iron- and steel-working center where the entire suspended superstructure of the Brooklyn Bridge was manufactured.

When you consider how explosive gunpowder is, you can look at the architecture and design of the mills with great appreciation. The three side walls farthest from the water were made of heavy stone. The side wall along the creek was made of wood. When the inevitable explosion took place, it would blow out the less-sturdy wooden wall into the creek. This prevented the force of the explosion from blowing out walls that would have otherwise damaged nearby buildings.

The Hagley is open daily 9:30 A.M. to 4:30 P.M. from mid-March to December 30, and weekends 9:30 A.M. to 4:30 P.M. the rest of the year. The Hagley is closed Thanksgiving, Christmas, and New Year's Eve. Admission is $11.00 for adults, $9.00 for seniors and students, and $4.00 for children. Call (302) 658–2400 or log on to www.hagley.lib.de.us.

trivia

Old Swedes Church in Wilmington, built in 1698, is the oldest Protestant church still in use in the United States. The pipe organ was built by the Austin Company of Hartford, Connecticut, and has sixteen stops and sixteen ranks of pipe, for a total of 913 pipes.

Next to the Hagley is the **Delaware Toy and Miniature Museum,** with more than one hundred dollhouses and rooms, antiques, and newly crafted miniatures, which document European and American history from the eighteenth century forward. Within the collection are dolls, toys, trains, boats, and planes. Among the features are toys by Bliss, Hubley, Ives, A.C. Gilbert, Schoenhut, and McLoughlin. A permanent Victorian Christmas parlor is a particularly nostalgic scene, even if you never experienced one. There's no better way to connect the

TOP ANNUAL EVENTS IN DELAWARE

FEBRUARY

Cultural Exhibit,
Rehoboth Beach,
(302) 227–8408

Delaware Antiquarian Book Show/Sale,
Wilmington,
(302) 655–3055

MARCH

St. Patrick's Day Parade,
Dover,
(302) 678–9112

APRIL

Great Delaware Kite Festival,
Lewes, (Good Friday)
(302) 645–8073

MAY

Blessing of the Fleet,
Lewes,
(302) 645–5297

Delmarva Hot Air Balloon Festival,
Milton,
(302) 684–8404

JUNE

Best of the Beach Beebe Art Auction,
Rehoboth Beach,
(302) 227–8408

Delmarva Chicken Festival,
Dover,
(800) 878–2449

JULY

Cottage Tour,
Rehoboth Beach,
(302) 227–8408

Delaware Seashore Sandcastle Contest,
Rehoboth Beach,
(302) 227–2800

State Fair,
Dover,
(302) 398–3269

AUGUST

Delaware State Fair,
Harrington,
(302) 398–3269

Delaware State News Sandcastle Contest,
Rehoboth Beach,
(800) 282–8586

generations than by discussing the reminiscences of earlier times as prompted by the Nuremberg kitchens, the dollhouses, and period toys. If you like art in miniature, this is the place to visit.

A reference library and, of course, a museum sales shop are available for the incurable (myself included).

The Toy and Miniature Museum is located on Route 141. Admission is $6.00 for adults, $5.00 for students and those who are sixty-two and older, and $3.00 for those younger than thirteen. Children under two are admitted free. A Triple A discount is available for adults and seniors. Reservations are required

Outdoor Fine Art & Fine Craft Exhibit,
Rehoboth Beach,
(302) 227–8408

SEPTEMBER

Craft Festival at Winterthur,
Wilmington,
(302) 888–4600,
(800) 448–3883

Towne and Country Fair,
Seaford,
(302) 629–9690

OCTOBER

Celebrity Chefs Beach Brunch,
Bay Center, Ruddertowne,
(302) 65–MEALS,
(800) 62–MEALS,
www.mealsonwheelsde.org

Sea Witch Halloween Festival and
Fiddlers' Convention,
Rehoboth Beach,
(800) 441–1329

NOVEMBER

Nemours Mansion and
Gardens Tours,
Wilmington,
(302) 651–6912

Rehoboth Beach Independent
Film Festival,
Rehoboth Beach,
(302) 645–9095

World Championship Punkin
Chunkin Festival,
Millsboro,
(302) 945–9062

DECEMBER

First Night Dover,
Dover,
(302) 734–8228
www2.newszap.com/firstnight

First Night Wilmington,
Wilmington,
(302) 573–5506

for a guided tour. The museum is open Tuesday through Saturday from 10:00 A.M. to 4:00 P.M. and Sunday from noon to 4:00 P.M. It is closed on Monday. Call (302) 427–TOYS (8697) or log on to www.thomes.net/toys.

Hockessin is a delightful little town just outside of Wilmington. As noted earlier, one of the pleasures of the Delmarva is the chance to pick up a Nancy Sawin book; she's done at least eleven, including *Delaware Sketchbook, Back-roading Through Cecil* (MD) *County, Between the Bays* (Delaware and Chesapeake), and even one on outhouses entitled *Privy to the Council Seats of Yore,* with sketches of a variety of "necessary" buildings, from lean-tos and Alpine chalets to one that was fenced and shingled and one that had four columns on its porch.

One of my great delights is driving through the state and trying to spot the objects Ms. Sawin has drawn. Sawin was born in Wilmington in 1917, and when she retired in 1974 from a life in education, she started writing and illustrating books on local history. Her home is adjacent to Sandford School, where she had been teacher, coach, and headmistress. She refers to her home as a "semimuseum of early Americana," and some of the items therein are for sale.

Visitors are welcome, but please contact her first. Write Nancy C. Sawin, 147 Sawin Lane, Hockessin 19707; or call (302) 239–2416.

As you're driving around this area you may want to try the **Back Burner** restaurant. They have delicious seafood and meat entrees and friendly and attentive service. It's a small space, and people from Wilmington make a special drive "to the country" for the food. The Back Burner is at 425 Old Lancaster Pike in Hockessin; call (302) 239–2314; or log on to www.backburner.com.

A little north of Wilmington is the anomaly of modern government known as **Arden.** It was one of three towns (along with Ardentown and Ardencroft, which would come later) created under the principles conceived by Philadelphia-born economist Henry George and his Theory of Single Tax. Born in 1839, George proposed that land only should be taxed, thereby creating the concept of the "single tax." Thus, in 1895 a group of single taxers from Philadelphia invaded Delaware with their political evangelism. Frank Stephens, a Philadelphia sculptor, with the help of architect Will Price and soap manufacturer Joseph Fels, acquired a Brandywine farm of 160 acres and started the village of Arden. It continues to this day as a single-tax entity.

Utopian in nature, the community also incorporated the artistic ideas of William Morris and the Arts and Crafts Movement, the Garden Cities planning ideas of Ebenezer Howard, and some social theories of Petr Alekseevich Kropotkin (1842–1921). Many of the homes are tiny, for they were summer places, but there definitely is a mix of new and old, fancy and ramshackle, set on lots of various sizes.

The three villages are surrounded by woodlands, including the Naaman's Creek natural area, designated as one of Delaware's Outstanding Natural Areas. There are two things that drive the residents of Arden: the Arden Club and the Arden Community Recreation Association. Music, dance, theater, visual arts, and such crafts as pottery and ironwork are still highly valued in the three Ardens. Because there isn't a permanent physical display place for all the local artists, they've created a virtual one that features painters, sculptors, photographers, knitters, leather workers, and performing artists. Check it out at www.ardenartists.com.

There is not much for the tourist to "see" in the way of historic buildings or museums, so you have to look at their activities calendar, scheduling your visit for the contra dancing/square dancing every month, the Arden Fair (the Saturday before Labor Day), the Shakespearean productions (*Merchant of Venice* and *Comedy of Errors* were presented recently) in the little (130-seat) outdoor theater on the Arden Green, and the Candlelight Music Dinner Theater in Ardentown that has shows throughout the year. Call (302) 475–2313 for information.

Old New Castle, a section of New Castle, is filled with colonial-era homes and buildings that the Rockefeller Foundation initially wanted to restore as a living museum of colonial America. However, the locals raised such a fuss that the Rockefellers went to Williamsburg, Virginia, instead. Rather than reconstructing the history represented at Williamsburg, New Castle exudes the past from every brick and slather of mortar. It was here that William Penn set foot in North America for the first time. From those Quaker beginnings, the town became a trade center through shipping. A disastrous fire leveled the business area in 1824, but the town was restored when the railroad came through less than a decade later. The railroad was later rerouted into Wilmington, and the town has sat there ever since.

trivia

The only Revolutionary War battle fought in Delaware was the Battle of Cooch's Bridge (east of Newark), on September 3, 1777. It's said the new thirteen-star flag was first unfurled during this battle, a delaying action to slow the British advance toward Philadelphia. The area in which the Battle of Cooch's Bridge took place can be seen from a 90-foot observation tower in Iron Hill Park, west of State Route 896 via Welsh Tract Road or Old Baltimore Pike in Newark.

Among the houses that are open for your inspection and journey into the past are the Amstel House, the Dutch House, and the George Read II House and garden. You can also tour the restored Court House, or just spend a lazy afternoon on the green.

The *Amstel House* dates from the 1730s and was the home of colonial governor Nicholas Van Dyke. The furnishings show how life was during the colonial period and include a complete colonial kitchen. Yeah, we know George Washington was everywhere, and that includes attending a wedding here. Amstel House is at Fourth and Delaware Streets, and it's closed in January and February. Phone (302) 322–2794; the Web site is www.newcastlehistory.org.

In the *Dutch House* you are touring what is thought to be the oldest brick house in Delaware. Constructed in the late seventeenth century, it has been restored and contains wonderful decorative arts and historical items. It's located

trivia

Iron Hill, just south of Newark, is the home of one of the highest hills in the state (which isn't saying much). On a clear day, from the top of the Iron Hill Tower, you can see four states: New Jersey, Pennsylvania, Maryland, and, of course, Delaware.

at 32 East Third Street in New Castle; call (302) 322–2794.

Both the Amstel and Dutch Houses are open March through December, Tuesday through Saturday 11:00 A.M. to 4:00 P.M. and Sunday 1:00 to 4:00 P.M. They're open on weekends the rest of the year but closed on holidays. Admission to each is $4.00 for adults, or you can get a combination ticket for $7.00 for adults. Tickets for children are $1.50 for one house and $2.50 for a combination ticket.

George Read was one of the signers of the Declaration of Independence and the U.S. Constitution, and his son's home, called the **George Read II House,** was built over a seven-year period starting in 1797. It's a superb illustration of Federal-style architecture. Note the carved woodwork, fanlights, silver door hardware, and period furnishings as you tour through the twelve rooms (three of which are in the Colonial Revival style). A Philadelphia-style adaptation of a Victorian garden, designed in 1847, decorates the side and back yards. You have a choice of touring this home on your own or calling for an appointment for a guided tour. If you have the time, I recommend the latter.

The George Read II House, at 42 The Strand, is open Sunday and Tuesday through Friday from 11:00 A.M. to 4:00 P.M. and Saturday from 10:00 A.M. to 4:00 P.M. from spring through fall. It's open on weekends in the winter but closed on holidays. The admission is $5.00 for adults, $4.00 for seniors and youngsters thirteen to twenty-one, and $2.00 for children six through twelve. Call (302) 322–8411 or log on to www.hsd.org/read.htm.

trivia

New Castle was the original state capital of Delaware. In 1777 Dover was named the new capital. Delaware is one of four states in the country in which the initial letter of the capital is the same as the initial letter of the state. The others are Honolulu, Hawaii; Indianapolis, Indiana; and Oklahoma City, Oklahoma.

Surely you've noted that the top of the Delaware border, where it meets Pennsylvania, is the arc of a circle. The spire at the top of the **New Castle Court House** is the center point of the 12-mile radius that marks that arc. Although New Castle was the colonial capital of Delaware from 1732 to 1777, the courthouse is now restored to its 1804 appearance. Flags of the Netherlands, Sweden, Great Britain, and the United States represent the various governments that have had jurisdiction over New Castle.

Located at 211 Delaware Street, between Market and Third Streets, the New Castle Court House is open Tuesday through Friday 10:00 A.M. to 3:30 P.M., Saturday 10:00 A.M. to 4:30 P.M., and Sunday 1:30 to 4:30 P.M.; closed on state holidays. There is no admission charge. Call (302) 323–4453 or (800) 441–8846 or visit http://history.delaware.gov/museums/ncch/ncch_main.shtml.

trivia

The Delaware State Seal was adopted on January 17, 1777, and contains the coat of arms. It also shows a farmer, corn, and a wheat sheaf (signifying the agricultural vitality of the state), a ship (symbolizing New Castle County's ship-building industry), a militiaman with his musket (honoring the role of the citizen-soldier in the maintenance of American liberties), an ox (representing animal husbandry), and water (for the Delaware River).

If there's time, stop by the hexagon-shaped **Old Library Museum** (40 East Third Street; 302–322–2794), the Old Presbyterian Church, and the Original Ticket Office. Then reward yourself with a picnic stop at the green. Located on Delaware Street, between Third and Market Streets, it was laid out by Peter Stuyvesant in 1655.

For additional information write to the Wilmington Convention and Visitors Bureau, 1300 Market Street, Suite 504, Wilmington 19801, or call (302) 652–4088. You can also contact the New Castle Visitors Bureau, Box 465, New Castle 19720; (302) 322–8411 or (800) 748–1550; www.newcastlecity.net/visitors.

On your way south on U.S. Highway 1, you'll cross the Chesapeake and Delaware Canal at St. Georges on a bridge opened on December 23, 1995. Called the "relief route," the new US 1 will extend from Tybouts Corner on the northern end to the Frederica/Felton area south of Dover. The bridge is a six-

Pass the Peas, Please

Fort Delaware, outside of Delaware City, has a calendar full of activities and tours of the site, now a state park, where Confederate soldiers where kept during the Civil War. There's said to be a ghostly sighting every once in a while. The fort is on Pea Patch Island, surely as strange a name as you might find anywhere. Legend has it that the captain of a ship plying the Delaware River didn't realize how shallow the sandbar was in the middle. His ship ran aground and sank. The freight it was carrying was peas—all sizes. They sprouted and thrived and caught silt coming down the river. It started piling up and the peas kept growing. It's now nearly two acres of land.

trivia

Welton Academy, the 1950s school that was the setting for the 1989 Oscar-winning film *Dead Poets Society*, starring Robin Williams, was actually filmed at St. Andrew's School, 350 Noxontown Road, Middletown. Other locations for the film are in New Castle and Rockland.

lane cable-stayed design. Lead engineer W. Denney Pate's previous cable-stayed bridges include the Sunshine Skyway in Tampa, Florida; Varina Enon bridge near Richmond, Virginia; Cochrane Bridge in Mobile, Alabama; and the Neches River bridge near Port Arthur, Texas.

The *Courtyard Newark University of Delaware,* in Newark, operates as a Marriott franchise, and students from the university's department of hotel, restaurant, and institutional management staff the hotel. Even though the hotel has all the bells and whistles, one of the 126 guest rooms will be used to test new concepts, from enhanced Internet access to energy conservation. Public space reflects the latest demands from business and leisure travelers with a business library featuring individual workstations with high-speed dataports and ergonomic chairs; a pantry-style, twenty-four-hour "grab and go" food and beverage area; and a lounge area where guests can work, meet, and dine in a relaxing setting. The hotel is at 400 Pencader Way; (302) 737–0900; www.courtyard.com.

Kent County

Kent, the middle of the three Delaware counties, has Dover as its focus. This is the home of the Dover Air Force Base and some Amish families (with their attendant farmers' markets and horse-drawn buggies); it is also the county seat. It's a hubbub of activity and constant change. Here you'll also find such unusually named places as Slaughter Beach, Seven Hickories, Dutch Neck Crossroads, and Little Heaven and an abundance of protected open spaces where you can explore what nature has left for you and the people of Delaware have protected for you.

Some of the information presented here is thumbnail in nature because it's easy to find your way around such places as Dover; other areas are a little more difficult to uncover and receive a bit more attention.

The town of *Smyrna,* just off U.S. Highway 13 at State Route 6, is pretty small, but it is growing. At the moment there's no department store, and a few other "big town" conveniences are missing. But the town's charm more than makes up for what it lacks. Actually, Smyrna is a historic town that straddles the two counties of New Castle and Kent. The line of demarcation is Duck Creek, located on the north side of the town.

On the south side of Smyrna, **Lake Como** (with a freshwater beach) is a beautiful, small lake surrounded by houses with well-manicured yards and the Delaware Home and Hospital. As one local said, "If I focus [into the past], I can see children playing with buckets and shovels in the sand, moms and dads and older kids in striped woolen swimwear walking on the beach, swimming in the cool waters, and diving off the end of the pier."

East of Smyrna, is an area that grew from the fur trapping and shipping trades of the early nineteenth century. You'll enjoy a visit here if you stop by the nearly 16,000-acre **Bombay Hook National Wildlife Refuge,** where you're sure to spot plenty of ducks, geese, and shorebirds during migrating season (more than 1.5 million shorebirds traverse Delaware in the annual migration in late May and early June) and other wildlife year-round. More than 256 species of birds, 33 species of animals, and 37 species of reptiles and amphibians inhabit the refuge.

You can drive along the 12-mile loop or hike on the nature trails and climb the observation towers for a panoramic view. The refuge is open daily from dawn to dusk, and a visitor center is open daily during summer and on weekdays during winter. Admission to the refuge is $4.00 per private vehicle or $2.00 if you're on foot or coming in by bike. Those with a Golden Age Passport enter for free. The refuge is at 2591 Whitehall Neck Road, Smyrna; (302) 653–6872; http://bombayhook.fws.gov.

The **State House** in Dover is the second-oldest continuously used statehouse (the one in Annapolis, Maryland, is first). This restored 1792 structure has period furnishings and an exhibit of artifacts and historical items. Included in

trivia

"Woodburn," the official home of Delaware's governors, was built in 1790–1791 by Charles Hillyard and is considered one of the finest Middle Period Georgian homes in the state. Prior to being purchased by the state in 1965, the home was owned by an abolitionist, two U.S. Senators, three doctors, and a judge. It is located at 151 Kings Highway in Dover; (302) 739–5656.

trivia

The Blue Hen chicken was adopted as Delaware's state bird on April 14, 1939, but its history as a symbol of the state dates from Revolutionary War days. The men of Capt. Jonathan Caldwell's company, recruited from Kent County, brought their fighting game chickens with them, and when the men weren't fighting the enemy they amused themselves with cockfights. The reputation for the tenacity of the cocks in their fights spread throughout the army, and the men of Delaware, equally tenacious, were compared to the fighting Blue Hens.

the tour is information about legislative and judicial activities and how these actions affected the population, including slaves and free blacks. Guided thirty-minute tours upon demand are available between 10:00 A.M. and 4:30 P.M. Tuesday through Saturday and 1:30 to 4:30 P.M. on Sunday. The State House is located at South State Street, on the east side of the green. The entrance is at 406 Federal Street. There is no admission charge; call (302) 739–4266; or visit www.destatemuseums.org.

Free guided tours start from the Delaware Visitor Center and the private, nonprofit **Sewell C. Biggs Museum of American Art,** which is located behind the statehouse. Biggs, a native of Middletown who died in 2003, collected art from the eighteenth century to modern times and founded this museum in 1993. This building is made of brick and cast iron and was one of the first fireproof buildings in the state.

The Biggs Museum, 406 Federal Street, is open Wednesday through Saturday from 10:00 A.M. to 4:00 P.M. and Sunday from 1:30 to 4:30 P.M. Call (302) 674–2111; or visit www.biggsmuseum.org.

If you're at the State House, then you're in the **Capital Green,** which was laid out in 1722. It is lined with historic buildings and is the very ground upon which the U.S. Constitution received its first signature in 1787. From here, Delaware's Continental Regiment mustered for the Revolutionary War, and from here they marched to join Washington's army. Political rallies still are held here, and in May there's Old Dover Days, with many private homes and buildings open to the public. If you're taking a guided tour, be sure to ask your leader about the woman who sent poisoned candy to her lover's family, resulting in the death of at least one person. This isn't a modern revenge happening; it took place in the 1890s.

At the **Hall of Records,** near Legislative Hall, is the public archive for the state. This is where you can find the original 1682 charter of King Charles II and William Penn's order for the platting of Dover.

The Hall of Records is at Legislative Avenue and Duke of York Street; no charge. It's open Monday through Friday from 8:30 A.M. to 4:15 P.M. Closed on holidays. Call (302) 739–5314.

While in Dover, a must stop—if you're a fan of the TV show *Homicide* or other police-based shows, or your reading preferences tend toward procedurals—is the **Delaware State Police Museum.** This state-of-the-art educational facility provides an opportunity to learn the history of the Delaware State Police law enforcement methods, a look at a 911 command-and-control console, and a display of uniforms and weapons. There are exhibits about substance abuse, highway safety efforts, and a variety of other important topics, with talks presented by specially trained troopers and volunteers. You can also catch a close-up view of patrol cars and motorcycles.

Located at the State Police Headquarters Complex, 1425 North DuPont Highway, the museum is open Monday through Friday (except state holidays) from 9:00 A.M. to 3:00 P.M. and the third Saturday of each month from 11:00 A.M. to 3:00 P.M. There is no admission charge. Phone (302) 739–7700; or visit www .delawaretrooper.com/museum/index.html.

So, your life is filled with CDs—for music, for computer programs, and who knows what else? Your children have never even known an eight-track, much less heard of a Victrola. Now's the time to correct that. Stop by the *Johnson Victrola Museum* in Dover to see this tribute to Eldridge Reeves Johnson (a Delaware native who was an inventor, businessman, and philanthropist), the inventor and founder of the Victor Talking Machine Company (1901). Designed to look like a 1920s store, the museum has an extensive collection of phonographs, records, and memorabilia related to the company, including an original oil painting of Nipper, the dog who listened to "His Master's Voice."

The museum is open Tuesday through Friday from 10:00 A.M. to 3:30 P.M. and Saturday from 9:00 A.M. to 5:00 P.M. There's no admission charge (donations are accepted) to the museum, located at 406 Federal Street (at Bank Lane and New Street); phone (302) 739–4266 or log on to www.destatemuseums.org.

Go north of Dover about 2 miles and you'll see the *Delaware Agricultural Museum and Village,* covering 200 years of the agrarian heritage of Delaware, with dairy and poultry farming objects, horse-drawn equipment, and tractors from 1670 through the 1950s. There's a barbershop, farmhouse, general store, one-room schoolhouse, sawmill, train station, and blacksmith and wheelwright shops, all representing structures from the Civil War to the turn of the twentieth century.

Some of the programs that have been featured are A More Abundant Life: Rural Delaware and Culture in New Deal Art, The Ten Ton Tomato Club and Other Tales, and Christmas on the Farm. Special events include Fall Harvest Festival and A Farmer's Christmas.

The museum and village are located at 866 North DuPont Highway, Dover. They're open Tuesday through Saturday 10:00 A.M. to 4:00 P.M. and Sunday 1:00 to 4:00 P.M. from April through December; closed on Sunday January through March. Closed on holidays. Admission fees are $5.00 for adults, $3.00 for seniors sixty and older and for children from six to seventeen. Call (302) 734–1618; or visit www.agriculturalmuseum.org.

Head south of Dover about 4 miles if aviation is your passion. One of the more exciting places to visit is the *Dover Air Force Base.*

I know you've seen a lot of historic buildings around here, but this may be the first time you've seen a World War II hangar that's listed on the National Register of Historic Places. It was the site of the Army Air Force's rocket test center and is now the home of the *Air Mobility Command Museum.* On display at the museum is a collection of vintage planes from 1941, including a C-47 Gooney Bird and a B-17G. Other World War II artifacts also are on display. For those who've always wanted to take flight in one of these magnificent birds, there's now a flight simulator open to those who are ten and older. An experienced pilot guides you through take-off, flying, and landing. The simulator is open on Wednesday and Saturday from 10:00 A.M. to 2:00 P.M. and other times by appointment, depending on volunteer availability. Call (302) 677–5938, Option 2, to request a day and time.

trivia

Each C5A or C-5 Galaxy, the largest cargo airplane in the world, at Dover Air Force Base is big enough to hold several football fields.

The museum is open Tuesday through Sunday 9:00 A.M. to 4:00 P.M. and is closed on federal holidays. There is no admission charge. Dover Air Force Base is on U.S. Highway 113, and the museum is at 1301 Heritage Road, Dover. Enter through the State Route 9 entrance. Call (302) 677–5938 or visit www.amcmuseum.org.

Come summertime and people of a certain age think of drive-in movie theaters. Take heart, they're not all gone. The *Diamond State Drive-in Theater* has preserved, in Felton, the tradition on weekend nights in the summer. The history of the theater started in 1940s, went downhill in the early 80s when it was showing "adult" movies, then closed in the mid-80s. A decade later and the theater is back in business. They show family and first-run movies, and there's a snack bar to fill your appetite. One change, though, is the lack of speakerphones. In these modern days, you listen to the audio on your radio. The theater is at 9720 South Dupont Highway; (302) 284–8307; www.dsdit.com.

South of the Air Force base is the *John Dickinson Plantation,* the boyhood home of John Dickinson, who in 1778 drafted the Articles of Confederation, for which he was known as the "Penman of the Revolution." His 1740s brick home and the reconstructed outbuildings are typical of eighteenth-century

Horseshoe Crabs

While found along the western shores of the Atlantic Ocean, from Maine to the Yucatan, the Delaware Bay area is home to the largest population of **horseshoe crabs** (*Limulus polyphemus*), which date back 250 million years ago. One reason for the horseshoe crab's longevity might be because it can go for a year without eating and can endure extreme temperatures. They are more closely related to scorpions, ticks, and land spiders than crabs, although they are not dangerous to humans. They grow when they molt (usually sixteen times over nine to twelve years until they become full-size adults), increasing in size by about one-fourth each time and living for about thirty years. During the high tides of the new and full moon in May and June, thousands of horseshoe crabs descend on the Delaware Bay shoreline to spawn (laying as many as 20,000 tiny eggs). You can view this spectacle at night from an elevated spot using binoculars or field glasses.

plantation architecture and lifestyle, with the added benefit that the home is furnished with family pieces and period antiques.

The Plantation is open Tuesday through Saturday 10:00 A.M. to 3:30 P.M. and Sunday 1:30 to 4:30 P.M.; free tours are available during those hours. It is closed on Monday and holidays and on Sunday in January and February. There is no admission charge. The John Dickinson Plantation is at 340 Kitts Hammock Road, Dover. Call (302) 739–3277; or log on to www.destatemuseums.org/jdp.

Just southeast of Dover on Alt. 113, in **Magnolia,** is the "town sign" that states: THIS IS MAGNOLIA, THE CENTER OF THE UNIVERSE, AROUND WHICH THE WORLD REVOLVES. Magnolia is noted as being one of those little peninsula towns that has not lost its personality in this modern age.

The house you'll be looking at when you see this sign is the John B. Lindale House, a Victorian with really neat twin towers. It is a private residence, but you can still admire it.

A tribute to agriculture can be found in Harrington at the **Messick Agricultural Museum,** with its extensive display of farm implements of the early twentieth century. You'll see automobiles, a covered wagon, various engines, horse-drawn plows and vehicles, tools, tractors, and trucks. There's also an early-twentieth-century kitchen and smokehouse.

trivia

Swedish immigrants built the first log cabins in America in Delaware, in 1638.

The museum, located at 325 Walt Messick Road, Harrington (off US 13 West of Milford), is open Monday through Friday from 7:30 A.M. to 4:30 P.M. and by appointment on weekends and holidays. There is no admission fee. Call (302) 398–3729.

There are a number of annual events in Harrington, including the Crab Feast in late August, Heritage Day in late September, and the Delaware State Fair in late July. This is a real old-fashioned state fair that still has strong agricultural roots and has not been "citified."

For additional information contact the Kent County Tourism Convention and Visitors Bureau, 9 East Lockerman Street, Suite 203, Dover 19901, (302) 734–1736, (800) 233–KENT, www.visitdover.com, or the Delaware Tourism Office, 99 Kings Highway, Box 1401, Dover 19901, (302) 739–4271, www.visit delaware.com.

Sussex County

Even if you've never heard of Sussex County, you've most likely heard of Rehoboth Beach and possibly even Bethany Beach, although both are billed as "quiet resorts." They are primarily residential and have been promoted as great family vacation and residential areas.

The 84-foot-tall white brick *Fenwick Island Lighthouse,* with a Third Order Fresnel lens projecting light 15 miles into the ocean, was commissioned on August 1, 1859, to protect ships from venturing onto the treacherous shoals extending 5 to 6 miles out from the Delaware coastline. It was automated in 1940, then decommissioned in 1978. A public outcry brought about the reinstallation of the original light, weighing about 1,500 pounds, and it has been in service since then. It's at the eastern terminus of the Mason-Dixon line at the Delaware-Maryland border. There's a cluster of buildings here, the lighthouse, two keepers' dwellings (now in private ownership), storage sheds, and the tower. The light is listed on the National Register of Historic Buildings. The Coast Guard deactivated it in 1978, but the Friends of the Fenwick Island Lighthouse has maintained it.

The lighthouse, between Delaware Route 521 and 146th Street, is open to the public most days, but you are not allowed to climb the

trivia

The entrance to Bethany Beach, just south of the Delaware Seashore State Park, is marked by a 26-foot Native American totem pole. This greeting to Bethany Beach was sculpted by Dennis D. Beach and installed in the spring of 1994. It replaced a carving by Peter Toth, who donated his totem in 1976. Unfortunately, Toth's totem fell victim to termites and nasty storms. Chief Little Owl, named for a chief of the Nanticoke tribe, represents an eagle protecting an Indian by clutching him to its breast.

lighthouse. There's no admission charge, but donations are accepted. For more information call (302) 539–4115.

On the south side of the Fenwick Island Lighthouse is one of the original **Transpeninsular Line Markers,** which was erected on April 26, 1751. This stone marked the east end of the 70-mile-long line that connected the Atlantic Ocean to the Chesapeake Bay, denoting what was then the southern border of Pennsylvania. Those three lower counties are now Delaware. A little more than a decade later, Mason and Dixon used the midpoint of the line when they surveyed the border between Pennsylvania and Maryland. The marker is 1 block south of Delaware State Routes 1 and 54, South Fenwick Island. Call the Bethany–Fenwick Island Chamber of Commerce, (302) 539–8129.

trivia

The first beauty contest was held in Rehoboth Beach in 1880, and Miss United States was selected, with Thomas Edison as one of the judges.

DiscoverSea is the place to visit to view hundreds of artifacts recovered from shipwrecks along the Delmarva coastline, dating from colonial days. Dedicated to preserving our maritime heritage, the museum opened in July 1995 after more than seventeen years of research and hard work. Stop by for a visit, a lecture, or a beach tour and travel to the past via this hands-on experience.

Open daily Memorial Day through Labor Day from 11:00 A.M. to 8:00 P.M. and on weekends from 11:00 A.M. to 3:30 P.M. the rest of the year. There is no admission fee to DiscoverSea, which is located at 708 Ocean Highway, Fenwick Island. Call (302) 539–9366 or (888) 743–5524 for additional information or log on to www.discoversea.com.

A Cool Fund-raiser

In 1997 the Bethany-Fenwick Area Chamber of Commerce started a January 1 **Exercise Like the Eskimos** to raise funds for scholarships for area high school seniors. By 2002 they were awarding $6,000, double what was given in the past. What's involved? It's some 250 people running into the Atlantic Ocean—which is about forty degrees! This polar bear stuff has always sounded to me like a cardiologist's heaven, but that's another story. Teams and individuals are invited to participate, with entry fees of $25 for adults and $15 for students. Everyone registered gets a free hat. The team with the most participants receives a trophy. Hot chocolate and T-shirts are sold. Mangos' Oceanfront Restaurant serves a New Year's buffet, and part of that charge benefits the scholarship. If freezing your buns off sounds like a lot of fun, call the chamber of commerce at (302) 539–2100; or visit www.thequietresort.com.

If you'd like to try your hand at *treasure hunting* using a metal detector, the local beaches offer a potential bonanza, or at least a short entertainment. Your find may be change, jewelry, or an ancient relic, and you're particularly likely to find something after a crowded day on the beach or after a good Nor'easter. You can rent or buy a metal detector from Sea Shell City, with rentals going for about $25 for a half day and $40 for an entire day. When searching for treasure, remember, don't trespass, cover your holes, don't go across the sand dunes, don't litter, and stay out of legally protected historic or archaeological sites. If you're really considerate and others haven't been, you'll take whatever litter you may find and dispose of it. Sea Shell City is located at 708 Ocean Highway in Ocean View. Call (302) 539–9366 or (888) 743–5524; or visit www.seashellcity.com.

Think Wyoming and you're thinking the Wild West. This Wyoming is in Delaware, south of Dover and north of Felton. And the Wild West is the *Wicked R. Western Productions, Inc.* Randy and Jennifer Ridgely have sixty acres of countryside and they teach more than three dozen lessons a week and hold four to six birthday and other celebratory parties every weekend in the summer. Regardless of your age or gender, they have something that could be of interest to you. Try an overnight women's ranch retreat, cowboy 101, kids dude ranch camp, spring horse sale, and bull riding clinic. Come fall, there's a corn maze, burlap maze, corn play bin, a straw playground, and more. Wicked R. Western is at 2621 Sandy Bend Road; (302) 492–3327; www.wickedr.com.

As one might expect, the southwest Delaware town of *Laurel* (originally Laureltown) was so named because of the abundance of laurel bushes growing along Broad Creek. Settled in 1802, the town was the largest in Sussex County by 1859 and was once a thriving shipping center and port town. With more than 800 buildings on the National Register of Historic Places, it is the largest designated historic district in the state of Delaware. Many properties were destroyed in the Great Fire of 1899, but others survived. Pick up a *Walk-*

Here's Grist for Your Mill

The *U.N.O.I. Grain Mill* in Seaford is the last operating mill in the state. It was built in 1885 and purchased by the United Nation of Islam (not related to the Nation of Islam) a few years ago to make flour from the grain they grow on the Eastern Shore.

They're in the process of restoring the mill, hoping to put the old water wheel back in running order. For more information about the former Hearns and Rawlins Mill, White Dove flour, and other products, and the possibility of a tour, call (302) 629–4455.

ing Tour of Historic Laurel brochure from the historical society to see some of the fascinating moments from the past.

As small as Bethel and the area around it are, there are enough people to see and talk to—and even things to do and learn—that you might find ways to spend an entire day there—even a lifetime. Start with the **Laurel-Woodland Ferry,** more commonly called the Woodland Ferry, that crosses the Nanticoke River just as boats have done since 1793. The cable-operated ferry is the last free river ferry in Delaware. Operated from sunup to sundown, the ferry may make up to 300 trips on a busy day, saving its passengers a road trip of nearly 20 miles.

Signs on State Route 78 in Laurel and Reliance, State Route 490 south of Blades, and State Route 80 at Seaford indicate if the ferry is running. Call the Seaford Chamber of Commerce at (302) 629–9690 for additional information.

On the western side of the Nanticoke is the town of **Woodland,** with a population of about one hundred people. As the Nanticoke is known for its shad and Woodland is known for its hospitality, you might want to schedule your visit for the annual spring shad supper held by the women of the Woodland Methodist Church.

While in Bethel you'll want to stop by **Jeff Hastings' farm market** (302–875–3420) to buy some fresh produce. He has been known to have some spectacular seedless watermelon. And just past his place is the **Bethel Market** on Main Street (302–875–2318), which has soft ice cream that's made with real milk, not the skimpy, thin, fat-free stuff. You have to time your tastes to the days of the week. According to Mark Shaver (who has been connected with this family store for

summertimetreat

The farmers of Delaware produced more than 78 million pounds of watermelon in 2003, making the state eleventh in production in the country.

twenty-five years), they used to have only vanilla. Then some customers started requesting chocolate, so he did that one day a week. Then they started clamoring for more. So then it was chocolate three days a week, on Monday, Wednesday, and Friday. Now you can have your choice of vanilla, chocolate, or twist.

Across Main Street is the post office, where Bettie Stoakley was the postmaster from 1980 to early 2007, serving 120 families. Yes, it's an old house, and as you go in you'll notice the bottom tread and riser of some stairs that used to go up to a second floor. Stoakley says it's been that way since before she arrived. It's located at 7746 Main Street in Bethel.

In Laurel, Milton, Ridgeville, Milford, and other places, you'll see **murals by Jack Lewis** (www.reubachergallery.com), a graduate of Rutgers with a mas-

trivia

ter's degree in education. You'll find them on exterior walls, in banks, in the family court in Georgetown, and even in a prison. Lewis taught art in the state for thirty years, and he participated in a Fulbright Scholarship exchange program. Lewis says he's basically a watercolorist, and murals are not his chief interest. Fortunately, he has dabbled in the area of murals, for our enjoyment.

Lewis and **Howard Schroeder** (1910–1995), a nearly life-long friend of Lewis', were fundamental in starting the Rehoboth Art League, the premier art and cultural institution of area. Schroeder (http://howardschroederart.com) came to the area as a military artist during World War II. Look for Schroeder's paintings at the University of Delaware and the Peninsula Gallery in Lewes. He was featured on the CBS *Sunday Morning* show in 1987. Lewis and Schroeder were included in the Artists Biographies program (www.teleduction.com) that also featured artists Mary Page Evans, Helen Farr Sloan, Edward L. Loper, and Charles Parks.

The Laurel area is noted for at least one other bit of historical trivia. On June 21, 1904, some signals were crossed and the schooner *Golden Gate,* traveling down the nearby Broad Creek, was struck by a mail train. Luckily the train engine automatically uncoupled, so the rest of the train didn't fall into the creek. This may be the only occurrence of a train and sailing ship colliding.

trivia

The **Spring Garden Bed and Breakfast,** with Gwen (or Gwenie) North as your hostess, is an excellent place to use as a base for your local explorations. Her half Victorian and half colonial home has been lovingly restored and is among the buildings on the National Register of Historic Places. North's family has been in this area since the seventeenth century, and Gwen has her finger on about as much history as you'll want. She was the first winner of the Governor's State Tourism Award. There are two bedrooms downstairs and four upstairs. The gardens are particularly inviting, and Gwen grows enough herbs to offer some to her guests so they'll remember her even when they return home.

Call Spring Garden, Delaware Avenue Extension in Laurel, at (302) 875–7015. Talk to Gwen about the ***sweet potato houses,*** and if you're really interested, she'll tell you where to see some, or she'll call Kendall Jones for you, and he'll take you on a tour.

In a nutshell, or in a potato skin if you will, the life of a sweet potato is not easy. The seeds first must be started indoors in February. Then they must be transplanted to warm beds, then to the outdoors, and then harvested and dried. Sweet potatoes apparently are horrible if eaten when freshly harvested. They'll keep all winter if they're stored at a constant fifty-degree temperature. These buildings were constructed to hold the very productive sweet potato cash crop.

The buildings are usually two to three stories tall and are long and relatively narrow. The outer walls are made of three or more layers of wood siding. On the exterior is a horizontal layer, followed by a diagonal layer in the center, and a vertical layer on the inside. All this helped to insulate the building, and sometimes a form of tar paper or sawdust was used between the layers to further insulate it. Inside is a series of bins, about 3 feet by 9 feet, where the potatoes were stored. Sometimes access to the bins was from a central aisle, sometimes from a perimeter walkway. A stove at one end had to be tended morning and night once the first frost had set in. The second and third floors did not butt against the walls; this helped ventilation and ensured an even distribution of the heat to the upper and lower floors.

Sweet potato house

trivia

Emily P. Bissell (1861–1948) created the first Christmas seals when she drew pictures on stamps in 1907. She sold the stamps to raise funds to aid tubercular children. Emily lived in Delaware and was a cousin of a doctor at a tuberculosis sanitorium in Delaware along the Brandywine River.

A blight hit the extremely labor-intensive crop in the 1940s and destroyed the industry. Now, some of the sweet potato or potato houses have been converted into office or living space. If you'd like to just drive by one, there's an excellent example across from the old Christ Church on State Route 24, about a mile east of US 13 just south of the intersection with State Route 9. It's slightly different from most sweet potato houses because of the number of windows it has, but you'll get the idea.

Gwen's Spring Garden B&B is one of three (soon to be more) on a ***Bike and Bed program.*** This four-day/three-night inn-to-inn bike touring experience averages 30 to 45 miles of back-roads pedaling. You'll go through small towns and past so many antiques stores that you wish you were in a car so you could cart home some of those treasures, or be glad you're on a bike and can't buy anything. You'll also go past a bison farm. The package includes three nights' accommodation, hotel tax, luggage transportation from inn to inn, three breakfasts and three dinners, snacks at each inn on arrival, detailed maps with points of interest, and secure bike storage.

Eli's Country Inn near Greenwood also participates in the program. This is a painstakingly renovated farmhouse in the country, where you literally can hear the quiet.

Two rooms downstairs are accessible, and there is plenty of room on the porches and decks for sitting around in the afternoon if you don't want to go do something. With seventy-eight-plus acres planted with soybeans, fresh fruits, and vegetables, you can also do some gardening if you want. The organ is original, and the home has a vacuum cleaner motor powering it.

Eli's Country Inn is on State Route 36 in Greenwood. Call (302) 349–4265.

There's no telling where you might think you are when you go through ***Trap Pond State Park.*** This 2,000-plus acre park was once part of the large freshwater swampland of southwestern Sussex County. The pond was created in the early 1800s for a sawmill that processed the bald cypress trees from the area. The park has the northernmost publicly owned stand of bald cypress in the country.

In the 1930s the federal government purchased the area, and the Civilian Conservation Corps developed the recreation site. Within the park are bald cypress trees, wetlands, wildflowers, wildlife, a nature preserve, a picnic area,

The Oklahoma Connection

When you try to trace Native American bloodlines from the original residents of Delaware, you have to go to Bartlesville, Oklahoma. Yes, that's where you'll locate the headquarters of the Delaware Indians. The Delaware or Lenni Lenape (first people) were a friendly tribe who gradually gave up their lands to the new settlers. They moved westward into Pennsylvania, then Ohio, then Indiana. Some even went to Canada, where they still occupy two small reserves in Ontario province. By 1820 they had crossed the Mississippi River into Missouri, then Kansas, and finally moved into Indian Territory in 1866. An 1867 agreement with the Cherokees allowed them to purchase land where they now reside. The Delawares comprise approximately 10,000 people today.

a playground, a primitive camping area for youngsters, more than 7 miles of hiking trails, a canoe trail (perhaps the only marked canoe trail on the Eastern Shore), camping, and a rent-a-camp program that lets you rent equipment to see if you like the experience before investing in all the gear.

Birders can spy on great blue herons, owls, hummingbirds, robins, mockingbirds, cardinals, finches, warblers, bald eagles, and pileated woodpeckers. Pets are permitted in some areas of the park, but they must be kept on a leash and attended to at all times. Bicycles and horses are permitted on designated trails.

Motorboats (electric only) are permitted in some areas of the pond and are limited to a no-wake speed of 5 miles per hour. Rowboats, pedal boats, and canoes may be rented in the summer. The park is part of a trash-free program, which means you carry out everything you carry in.

The entrance fee is $3.00 per Delaware-registered vehicle and $6.00 for out-of-state vehicles. The park is on County Road 449, 33587 Baldcypress Lane, near Laurel. Call (302) 875–5153 or (302) 875–2392 (campground) or log on to www.de stateparks.com/tpsp/tpsp.htm.

At *Lewes* (pronounced Lou-iss, not lose) you'll find the Delaware side of the Lewes–Cape May, New Jersey, ferry. The hour-plus ride is a

trivia

Lewes, known as the "first town in the first state," has had another distinction bestowed upon it: The National Trust for Historic Preservation has named it a Distinctive Destination. Honored in 2006, it joined Prescott, AZ; Monterey and Palm Springs, CA; Waimea, HI; Bowling Green, KY; Arrow Rock, MO; Philipsburg, MT; Saranac Lake, NY; Bartlesville, OK; West Chester, PA; and Milwaukee, WI. It was selected for its parks, historic district, museums, antiques shops, galleries, fine restaurants, and more.

From POWs to Pickles

The Kendzierski family apparently owns the only known privately owned fort in the United States. Fort Saulsbury is 6 miles east of Milford, near the town of Slaughter Beach, in the northeast corner of Sussex County. The fort was constructed in 1917 and 1918 in a location that would serve to protect the mouth of the Delaware Bay and River during World War I. The fort was named for Delaware's U.S. Senator (1859–71) and attorney general (1850–55) Willard Saulsbury Sr. The casements were 14 feet thick, steel-reinforced concrete, with 6 feet of earth on top for camouflage. Since completion came so close to the November 1918 armistice, the fort wasn't fully staffed as a defensive facility until World War II, and then only until Fort Miles at Cape Henlopen was completed in 1942. The fort then became a POW camp for German and Italian soldiers. The fort was deactivated on January 11, 1946, sold to the Kendzierski family, then served as a pickle processing and storage operation for the Liebowitz Pickle Company. It later was a storage spot for the Milford Salvage Company. It's unused today, but thought to be the only surviving World War I–era fort that is essentially unchanged.

great way to avoid driving up the New Jersey Turnpike and then down to the beach towns of southern New Jersey or Atlantic City. The fare is $29.00 per car April through October and $23.00 the rest of the year, plus a passenger fee (from $3.50 to $7.50, depending on age and time of the year). It's located at 43 Henlopen Drive in Lewes. Call (302) 644–6030 or (800) 64–FERRY or log on to www.capemaylewesferry.com.

If you drive the 20 miles along the beach from the Maryland border to Lewes, you may notice seven **concrete towers** rising up about 80 feet. They've been there since the days when German U-boats were a threat to our shores. There have been days when people were ready to tear them down. After all, they weren't being used. But there was never enough money, so they still stood. Now, people (perhaps the same ones) have decided the towers are historic.

That means you may climb the 115 steps of the **Cape Henlopen State Park tower** to the top for a lovely view that stretches from the Rehoboth boardwalk to Gordons Pond, taking in the Atlantic Ocean, Delaware Bay, and the outlying salt marsh. It's open seven days a week in good weather. Park admission during the season is $4.00 for Delaware-registerd vehicles and $8.00 for out-of-state vehicles. Tower admission is free with park admission. Call (302) 645–8983 or visit www.destateparks.com/chsp/chsp.htm.

But there are other reasons to come to Lewes, which is the northernmost of the coastal towns and is actually on the Delaware Bay rather than on the

Atlantic Ocean. You can't miss the **Zwaanendael Museum** (Valley of the Swans), a Dutch Renaissance building that is an adaptation of the town hall at Hoorn in the Netherlands. No, it wasn't brought over stone by stone, and it wasn't built three centuries ago. Instead, it was built in 1931 (the tercentenary of the founding of Lewes). Inside are exhibits of historic military and maritime artifacts from 1631 to the War of 1812 and about the HMB *DeBraak*, a British brig that sank near Lewes in 1798.

Zwaanendael Museum

The Zwaanendael Museum, 102 King's Highway in Lewes, is open Tuesday through Saturday from 10:00 A.M. to 4:30 P.M. and Sunday from 1:30 to 4:30 P.M. It is closed on Monday and holidays. There is no admission charge. Call (302) 645–1148; or visit www.destatemuseums.org/zwa.

Also recommended for those interested in nature are the **Prime Hook National Wildlife Refuge** in Milton (302–684–8419, http://northeast.fws.gov/de/pmh.htm), and the **Seaside Nature Center,** at Cape Henlopen State Park, (302) 684–8983; www.destateparks.com/chsp/chsp.htm.

The Zwaanendael Merman

It's said the first "mermen" (no, not the surfing music group) to reach American shores came from the Japanese in 1822 and that by 1842 P.T. Barnum displayed his first merman as the "Feejee Mermaid." Many fine museums own a merman specimen, but few choose to exhibit it. Therefore, because you get so few opportunities, one of the things you're sure to want to see at the Zwaanendael Museum is the merman. This one is about a foot long, and in 1941 it was loaned to the museum by a prominent local family who received it from a sea captain. The last family member died in 1985, and the museum collected $250 in donations to buy the merman from the estate. Although the museum has tried to provide the best exhibits on maritime history, the public won't allow the removal of the merman from display.

At the *Lewes Historical Society Complex* is a furnished country store from the early years of this century, the 1798 Burton-Ingram House with period Chippendale and Empire antiques, and other historic buildings that were moved to Lewes. They include the blacksmith shop (now an extension to the gift shop), the Hiram Burton House, a doctor's office, an early plank house (early Swedish-style construction), the Ellegood House (the gift shop), and the Rabbit's Ferry House. Walking tours begin at the Thompson Country Store, which was operated by the Thompson family from 1888 to 1962, at Shipcarpenter and West Third Street. Reservations are required for groups. The complex is open Monday through Saturday from 11:00 A.M. to 4:00 P.M. and Sunday from 1:00 to 4:00 P.M., mid-June until Labor Day; tours are available by appointment. Tours are $5.00 for adults; children under twelve are free. It's located at 110 Shipcarpenter Street. For additional information, call the Lewes Historical Society at (302) 645–7670; www.historiclewes.org.

For curiosity's sake, stop by the *Cannonball House* at 118 Front Street in Lewes to see a cannonball in the foundation of the building, a souvenir of the War of 1812.

If you're in the area on the first weekend of November, you should stop by the Eagle Crest Aerodrome to witness the *Punkin Chunkin contest.* It's

Chad Moore, Owner and General Manager

Just two blocks from the beach, restaurants, galleries, antiques shops, boutiques, and all that is Rehoboth Beach, the *Bellmoor Inn, Spa and Executive Retreat,* with 78 rooms and suites is a marvelous place for a family getaway, ladies (or men's) weekend, executive retreat, or a nice romantic escape. As a member of Select Registry, Distinguished Inns of North America, the inn, owned and managed by Chad Moore, ranks up there as a delightful place to spend some beach time.

The Jefferson Library is a 500-square-foot snuggle-up place with a wood-burning fireplace and game tables or you can enjoy the Garden Courtyard or even a quiet stay by the adults-only pool. Although equipped with the modern high-tech conveniences of a huge hotel, the Bellmoor feels much more like a bed-and-breakfast.

The Bellmoor Club Floor is an adult-only, all-suite floor with another library, king-sized beds, fireplaces, hydrotherapy tubs, and balconies. A complimentary hearty country breakfast and afternoon refreshments are provided, and the day spa offers a variety of relaxing and rejuvenating spa treatments, massages, facials, manicures and pedicures, and a fitness center. It is located at 6 Christian Street; (302) 227–5800 or (800) 425–2355; www.thebellmoor.com.

just what it sounds like, a contest to see who can hurl pumpkins the farthest distance by the use of catapults and other odd contraptions. Located at the corner of County Roads 305 and 306 in Long Neck. Admission to the event is $7.00 per day, plus $2.00 parking fee. No pets allowed.

trivia

The sand dunes at Cape Henlopen can reach 80 feet, and the Great Dune is the highest sand dune between North Carolina's Cape Hatteras and Cape Cod in Massachusetts.

For information contact the Lewes Chamber of Commerce and Visitor's Bureau at 120 Kings Highway, Lewes 19958; (302) 645–8073, www.punkinchunkin.com.

While meandering along west of Cape Henlopen on Route 36, if you get a yen for a little fishing, stop by *Abbott's Mill Nature Center,* at 15411 Abbott's Pond Road in Milford. It's one of a number of lakes and ponds in the area, but the nature center also has a historic gristmill, trails meandering through pine woods and along a stream, and canoeing and fishing. An Autumn at Abbott's Mill Festival is held the third Saturday in October. Year-round family programs, particularly for children from three to eighteen, but also for adults and families, are highlighted. For information call (302) 422–0847 or log on to www.delawarenaturesociety.org.

Places to Eat in Delaware

BETHANY BEACH

Patsy's Gourmet,
121 Campbell Place,
(302) 537–2433,
www.patsygourmet.com

DEWEY BEACH

Mama Maria Italian,
1608 Highway One,
(302) 422–2661,
www.mamamaria.com

DOVER

Polisenos Pizza,
761 Main Street,
(302) 734–8838

FENWICK ISLAND

Fenwick Crab House,
Coastal Highway,
(302) 539–2500

LEWES

King's Homemade Ice Cream Shop,
201 Second Street,
(302) 645–9425

Lighthouse Restaurant,
Fisherman's Wharf,
(302) 645–6271

NEWARK

Deer Park Tavern,
108 West Main Street,
(302) 369–9414

McGlynns Pub and Restaurant,
108 Peoples Plaza,
(302) 834–6661

NEW CASTLE

Arsenal on the Green,
30 Market Street,
(302) 328–1290

Casablanca Restaurant,
4010 North Dupont Highway,
(302) 652–5344,
www.thecasablanca restaurant.com

REHOBOTH BEACH

Back Porch Cafe,
59 Rehoboth Avenue,
(302) 227–3674

Library Square Cafe,
227 North Rehoboth
Boulevard,
(302) 424–0515

SELBYVILLE

Mr. Bill's Terrace Inn Crab House,
37314 Lighthouse Road,
(302) 436–7500

SMYRNA

Thomas England House,
1165 South DuPont
Highway,
(302) 653–1420

WILMINGTON

Brandywine Room,
11th and Market Streets,
(302) 594–3156

Places to Stay in Delaware

There are dozens of hotels, condominiums, motels, apartments, houseboats, and other accommodations along the beaches of Dewey, Fenwick, Bethany, and Rehoboth. Some offer week-long (Saturday to Saturday or Sunday to Sunday) rentals, weekends, or one-night options. Some are open only

OTHER ATTRACTIONS WORTH SEEING IN DELAWARE

Abbott's Mill Nature Center,
Milford,
(302) 422–0847

Brandywine Park Zoo,
Wilmington,
(302) 571–7747

Cape Henlopen State Park,
Lewes,
(302) 645–8983

Delaware Center for the Contemporary Arts,
Wilmington,
(302) 656–6466

Fisher-Martin House,
Lewes,
(302) 645–8073

Fort DuPont State Park,
Delaware City,
(302) 834–7941

Nemours Mansion and Gardens,
Wilmington,
(302) 651–6912

Trees of the States Arboretum,
Georgetown,
(302) 856–5400

Wilmington Blue Rocks,
Wilmington,
(302) 888–2015,
www.bluerocks.com

Winterthur Museum, Garden, and Library,
Winterthur,
(302) 888–4600,
(800) 448–3883

seasonally. Some are on the ocean, some are several blocks away. Note that accommodations statewide usually are full the first weekend after Memorial Day and the third weekend after Labor Day, due to the NASCAR races at Dover Downs.

CLAYMONT

Wilmington Hilton,
Interstate 95 and Namen's Road,
(302) 792–2700

DELAWARE CITY

Olde Canal Inn,
30 Clinton Street,
(302) 832–5100

DEWEY BEACH

Atlantic Oceanside Motel,
1700 Highway 1,
(302) 227–8811

Chesapeake Landing,
101 Chesapeake Street,
(302) 227–2973

DOVER

Dover Inn,
428 North DuPont Highway,
(302) 674–4011

Little Creek Inn,
2623 North Little Creek Road,
(302) 730–1300,
(888) 804–1300,
www.littlecreekinn.com

Sheraton-Dover,
1570 North DuPont Highway,
(302) 678–8500,
www.sheraton.com

LEWES

1897 House Bed and Breakfast,
801 Savannah Road,
(888) 227–1897

Inn at Canal Square,
122 Market Street,
(302) 644–3377,
(888) 644–1911

MILTON

Captain William Russell House Bed and Breakfast,
320 Union Street,
(302) 684–2504

MONTCHANIN

Inn At Montchanin Village,
Route 100 and Kirk Road,
(302) 888–2133

NEW CASTLE

Armitage Inn,
Delaware Street and The Strand,
(302) 328–6618,
www.armitageinn.com

OCEAN VIEW

Cedar Breeze Bed and Breakfast,
30680 Cedar Neck Road,
(302) 537–7015,
www.cedarbreeze.com

REHOBOTH BEACH

Abbey Inn,
31 Maryland Avenue,
(302) 227–7023,
(302) 923–1176

Beach House Bed and Breakfast,
15 Hickman Street,
(800) 283–INNS

Henlopen Hotel,
511 North Boardwalk,
(800) 441–8450

WILMINGTON

DoubleTree Hotel,
700 King Street,
(302) 655–0400,
www.doubletree.com

Hotel DuPont,
100 West Eleventh Street,
(302) 594–3100

Indexes

Entries for Bed-and-Breakfasts, Museums, and Restaurants also appear on pages 216-17.

GENERAL INDEX

BED-AND-BREAKFASTS

MUSEUMS

RESTAURANTS

About the Author

Judy Colbert is a longtime resident of Maryland. An award-winning freelance writer and photographer, Judy's more than 600 articles and photographs have appeared in such publications as *Washingtonian, Maryland, AAA World, Home & Away, Frequent Flyer, McCall's, Lodging,* and *Washington Flyer.* She has appeared on television and radio programs, including *Good Morning America* and *Arthur Frommer's Almanac of Travel.*

Other titles that Judy has authored include *Virginia Off the Beaten Path,* published by The Globe Pequot Press; *Country Towns of Maryland and Delaware,* published by Country Roads Press; and *Fun Places to Go with Children in Washington, D.C.,* published by Chronicle Books.